Praxis of Collective Building

jovis *research 6*

Andjelka Badnjar Gojnić

Praxis of Collective Building

Narratives of Philosophy and Construction

jovis *research 6*

Content

Introduction: Towards Mutual Highlight of Praxis Philosophy   6
and Construction

Montage   8
The Social and Its Relevance   10
The Case and Its Relevance   12
Praxis   18
Action   19
Imagination   20
Lebenswelt   21
Theory   22

Praxis and Action: Towards Building as a Collective Practice   28

The New City and the New Production Challenge   30
The Role of Objects as Mediators   36
The Aesthetics of Group Production   45
Conclusion   55

Praxis and Imagination: Towards Participation in Prefabrication   58

New Voices in the Philosophy of Praxis   59
The Imagination of the Work Cooperative   64
Imagining a Modern Kind of Housing   71
Praxis on the Construction Site: Can Prefabrication Be a Craft?   75
Imagination as Part of Material Culture   79
The Question of Autonomy   86
Conclusion   94

Praxis and *Lebenswelt*: The Construction Site as Lifeworld   98

A Critique: What is Praxis about in Scientific Civilization?   99
Construction Site and *Lebenswelt*   112
From Construction Site to Social Contract   131
Action and System, Yes or No?   137
Conclusion   141

Conclusion: Praxis and Theory   146

Literature Review   158
Endnotes   170
Bibliography   185
Acknowledgements   196

Introduction:
Towards Mutual Highlight of Praxis Philosophy and Construction

This book deals with interactions between the philosophy of praxis and construction site histories. Using philosophy as a companion, it seeks to contribute to the study of architecture from a social perspective. It does so by considering historical cases in which architecture was responsive to philosophical ideas about production that were present in societies and picked up by citizens, triggering their involvement in construction as a collective endeavour. The focus of this work, therefore, is on the practices of collective production of architecture that involve makers in the building process. The overarching question asks how a collective comes into being through the praxis of making. It is a relevant one because it contains aspects of both architectural production (making) and of theoretical reflection (praxis philosophy). The question heralds an exchange between the social aspirations of architecture and arguments by which operative philosophy can contribute to them. While there is a lot written about the former, architectural studies still lag behind when it comes to active exchange with social theories. In what sense can dialogue between disciplines be established without distorting the arguments of each? How can theories be more spatial and architectures more social? Can the building process contribute to a better understanding of social theories by offering a canvas for one of their possible interpretations? From another side, can reflecting on theories while performing building work assist in the emergence of socially informed spaces? In order to unpack these concerns, the study explores housing construction during social modernization in the second half of the twentieth century in largely peripheral geographies. It explores the stories of anonymous protagonists who were able to build with public prospects, and for whom participation was linked to the process of making.

The method of microhistory promises to be relevant and helpful in reflecting the abstract concerns of praxis philosophy onto the documentary analysis of construction projects. Charles Joyner's characterised this method as addressing the general by observing the small.[1] The concept was afterwards developed and further established by Italian historians, gaining international acclaim through Carlo Ginzburg's *The Cheese and the Worms: The Cosmos of a Sixteenth-Century Miller* (1976, in English 1980). In this work, deviant characters including an Italian peasant and a declared heretic were used to give voices to people who had hitherto been silent.[2] However, merely promoting the agency of their subjects was far from the overall aim of such microhistories. In addition to doing so, they opposed the establishment of general patterns and instead were eager to test and refine standing generalisations. As Giovanni Levi, another of its proponents, maintains, this approach believes »that microscopic observation will reveal factors previously unobserved«, and that »by altering the scale of observation new meanings« will emerge. Only after this treatment will it be possible »to draw far wider generalizations although the initial observations were made within relatively narrow dimensions and as experiments«.[3] It is as though historical episodes contain social and cultural DNA that, when tested, inform the understanding of the overall design of past society and culture.[4] Ginzburg also gave credit to the use of testing in historical analysis when he recalled praxis philosopher Antonio Labriola's argument that history, as a process, implies discovery through experimentation; but that historical knowledge implies experiment as well.[5] Relying on experimentation, the power of microhistory lies in reconstructing past events by connecting a wide range of data to create a three-dimensional analytic narrative in which people and abstract forces shape events. As such, it can serve to illuminate events in political, social and cultural history for which definitive truths cannot be produced, only empirical research into past episodes carried out in order to make the overall argument more persuasive.[6]

The method of microhistory appears to be compatible with the efforts of praxis philosophy. We can even say that praxis philosophy can only become complete by being accompanied by microhistories of making. This work, therefore, suggests that praxis philosophy is extended by means of a praxis of construction, and that we must consider both building and social theories in order to understand the social capacity of architecture. For this, the intention is to establish their montage by highlighting the connected philosophy and in-depth histories of particular construction sites. Bearing in mind the importance of this method, it makes sense to introduce it before the historical cases.

Montage

The question of how a collective comes into being through the praxis of making is developed through three narratives, each consisting of two parallel stories. One of these stories refers to developments in the philosophy of praxis in Yugoslavia and internationally in the second half of the twentieth century. The other covers construction episodes starting in Yugoslavia and eventually reaching the Global South. These two threads are used to narrate one alongside the other historically and theoretically. Only with the employment of narrative as a method can gaps and connections between different fields be shown. In this sense, there is an artificial attempt to reconstruct parts of narratives by which an exchange can be established and new learnings emerge. The hypothesis to prove is that construction was able to mediate collective production because it was based on praxis. This means that mediation was possible while construction and philosophical discussion existed in intensive proximity to the point of their being able to influence each other historically. Working from this historical condition, I further reinforced the theoretical links to additionally establish the existence of mediation. To explore this premise, the narratives adopt a questioning approach: a dialogue between philosophy and architecture. On one side are the voices of praxis philosophers who offer a different view of praxis and its relation to materiality. On the other is the history of construction, traced through documentary material such as newspapers, photographs, contracts, records, oral histories and books. These two sides are assembled in such a way that there is always a degree of approximation. Documentary material is a source that can be asked questions about the means of collective production and the possibility of praxis as a basis for it. This overlap allows us to better understand the legacies of societal modernization in making modern architecture, with the Yugoslavian case being one of many. A few general insights can be expected from our existing understanding of this particular case: how collectives came into being by making architecture; how political context and the social contract can be used for trials of alternative construction methods; which channels might establish the operative function of philosophy towards material culture. In this sense, the microhistories to be studied are just some of the possible relevant examples offering the opportunity to work on the interplay between large and small, between theory and documents, finally producing a kind of docu-fiction. This interplay applies to the whole thesis, and if I were to propose a fictional character to populate the narratives that follow, it would be a philosopher walking through a construction site.

The answers reached through this exchange are not always positive; friction is also a part of argument. A perfect match between the disciplines is never achieved, as the aim is not to identify philosophy with practice but to narrate each other mutually in order to gain a better understanding of particular histories while simultaneously testing existing theories. A fitting personification of this process may be found in Roland Barthes' description of structural man in his seminal essay »The Structuralist Activity«, presented as an assembler working with fragments of knowledge. About his activity, Barthes writes:

> »We can in fact presume that there exist certain writers, painters, musicians in whose eyes a certain exercise of structure represents a distinctive experience, and that both analysts and creators must be placed under the common sign of what we might call structural man, defined not by his ideas or his languages, but by his imagination, in other words, by the way in which he mentally experiences structure. [...] Structural man takes the real, decomposes it, then recomposes it; this appears to be little enough (which makes some say that the structuralist enterprise is ›meaningless‹, ›uninteresting‹, ›useless‹, etc.). Yet from another point of view, this ›little enough‹ is decisive: for between the two objects, or the two tenses, of structuralist activity, there occurs something new, and what is new is nothing less than the generally intelligible: the simulacrum is intellect added to object, and this addition has an anthropological value.«[7]

In the proposed narratives, I will adopt these terms in the sense intended by Barthes: that of decomposing and recomposing the real. Here, imagination is meant not to distort facts or to blur accuracy, but to articulate historical readings captured from a particular perspective. As perspectives are rarely neutral, the best we can hope for is transparency in the exercise and relevancy of the readings taken as initial sources. Imagination provides a tool for articulating these historical sources, and history is enormously helpful in discovering connections. Accumulated life events and data about meetings between groups and individuals, decisive moments in personal biographies and words and ideas that travel through the blueprint of the press all serve to establish narratives as simulacra of micro-histories threaded together by a theoretical approach. Often, we find what we are looking for; aiming, in this particular case, to overcome the opposition between reason and imagination. Even less recent studies on rethinking imagination through culture and creativity see this opposition as a long-lasting product of cultural modernity; one that is, however, not without alternatives in new cultural forces. In these new practices, reason and imagination appear in antithetic unity, seeking to overcome the well-known distinction between reason and the human passions and senses. In the light of culture-creation practices, *phantasia*—for Aristotle, the intermediary between perceiving and thinking—acquires the capacity to supplement reason.[8] Accordingly, tension and opposition between reason and imagination also become part of the argument. Moreover, this distance becomes a tool for investigating culture. Finally, rethinking imagination represents a potential for contemporary philosophy and its ability to raise issues—this time not on transcendental grounds, but with regard to its reciprocal interference in other disciplines.[9]

The Social and Its Relevance

As already stated, the motivation for this arrangement of theory and practice is found in architecture that is seen as a social endeavour—a fundamental architectural principle with a long tradition, of which this work is part. As Adrian Forty points out, the word »social« brought with it a lot of baggage, though far less was achieved than had initially been asserted to be possible. Forty argues that architectural modernism struggled to deliver on its promises to improve mankind's social existence due to the poverty of the language used to articulate the relations between distant positions such as social practice and physical space. Where the results were more explicit was in the perception of the collective as a means of production, rather than as a way of using objects. Forty goes on to say that, to date, architects and critics have not succeeded in articulating the social in terms other than the expression of productive labour. Here, the nineteenth-century tradition that includes John Ruskin and William Morris, the emergence of the New Objectivity in the early 1920s, the rise of the Bauhaus and later twentieth century practices like Walter Segal's managed to formulate a means of production seen as a collective process.[10]

The case of Yugoslavia's building history is not too far removed from this first line of thinking (which Forty would call conventional), as collective engagement is addressed in the process of making. However, when considered from the perspective of disciplines other than architecture history, the bond between architecture and the social is not associated with distinctions such as those of production and use, and is instead understood as activity. In the work of German social scientist Heike Delitz, the sociology of architecture is a means to address the discipline's growing interest in social activity, aiming to show how deeply architecture is involved in social life.[11] In her work, she studies cross-cultural cases of architectural forms of collective existence and argues that there are ways in which buildings are actively involved in making and unmaking societies. In these studies, architecture is seen not as secondary to social practices, but as a constitutive element of the transformation of societies, as a medium of the social. Further on, Delitz refers to political theorists, pointing out how space operates through the social. Ernesto Laclau and Chantal Mouffe, for example, hold that the social exists at least as an effort to construct the impossible object.[12]

Cornelius Castoriadis explains that the social-historical is the flux of self-alteration that can only exist in the form of the figures by which it makes itself visible.[13] From a theoretical perspective, architecture makes a difference to the social because it makes visible and transforms the collective, just as the maker transforms the building. This mutual influence, where form is seen as a process of transformation that ultimately affects the protagonist, offers a slightly more optimistic view of the relevance of the social than is present in Forty's argument. At the same time, this pleads for the use of shared methods between disciplines to further study this relation. This means that when wanting to talk about social in architecture today, we might need more than manifestos. From the architectural production side, we need documentary knowledge of particularities contained in the concept of micro-history; from the social theory side, we need to exploit the operative capacities of ones such as praxis philosophy.

Although the social practice in architecture seems to have had a high risk of failure, attempts should not necessarily be ruled out in contemporary society. As Jeremy Till points out in the Foreword to *The Routledge Companion to Architecture and Social Engagement*, the prerequisite for establishing social practice is to have the hope, often hard to find, that such practices are possible. Optimism currently seems to be a necessary pragmatic tool rather than a point of view. »The luck of ability and opportunity to think outside of the pervasive economic system limits considerations of social alternatives, and, with it, spatial alternatives.«[14] In this spirit, the proposed narratives seek to offer a constructive view toward collective engagement in making as a social endeavour. The capacity of imagination to voice questions and play a role in establishing the distance and reciprocity between philosophy and building is taken here as a helping method. It is a means for creating a storyboard where segments of philosophy interact with ones of construction. The degree of naiveté present represents not the absence of critical thinking, but the conviction that an excess of critique in the case of the already-fragile attempt to bind together architecture and social production undermines the possible benefits. As Peter Sloterdijk wrote in his *Kritik der zynischen Vernunft* in the already-distant 1980s:

»The discontent in our culture has assumed a new quality: it appears as a universal, diffuse cynicism. The traditional critique of ideology stands at a loss before this cynicism. It does not know what button to push in this cynically keen consciousness to get enlightenment going. Modern cynicism presents itself as that state of consciousness that follows after naïve ideologies [...].«[15]

Although not distorted for the same purpose, the stories are selected to offer hopeful scenarios. At the same time, the aim is to avoid too much fetishism for a protagonist of the collective building. This is not always a dissident who at once reflects and challenges the governing system. Protagonists are seen as a part of society that is not divided binarily into dissidents and bureaucracy. Here, Castoriadis's critique of Marxism is highly relevant, as it opposes this simplified but very illustrative division into superstructure and infrastructure, into us and them: »These superstructures are no more than a fabric of social relations, neither more nor less ›real‹, neither more nor less ›inert‹ than the others, and just as ›conditioned‹ by the infrastructures as the infrastructures are by them.«[16] Conversely, he explains, what does exist is social production, which is made by all of us as conscious individuals. When this social production is successful, it relates directly with negotiation, materials and sites, as well as with a process of making and a sense of being part of a certain entity. That this sense-making further appears to fall within the scope of technological advancement corresponds to what a long line of philosophers have argued in their various readings of praxis. This work relies on their findings in order to promote emancipatory ideas about production, and the possibility of direct engagement between material and citizens willing to take part in collective effort and public prospects.

The Case and Its Relevance

The initial story is set in the post-war Yugoslavia that was experimenting with self-managed production, something that had consequences for emerging urbanism and architecture in the country. At the same time, the philosophy of praxis was developing in the country as a means to address these efforts. The country's state of experimentation on matters of the economy, material culture and philosophy make it relevant to the study of collective building from the perspective of praxis philosophy. Construction in post-war Yugoslavia was a material undertaking at a time when Marxism was being questioned, both within the country and internationally. In keeping with the country's well-known special place between East and West, there was a parallel development of the philosophy of praxis and an attempt to establish various forms of collective building practices in the decades following World War II. This heritage of Yugoslavia as a laboratory of politics, economics and culture has been covered extensively, particularly coming to greater international attention in recent times. In terms of architecture, the work of Vladimir Kulić and Maroje Mrduljaš was significant in reaching a wider audience, beginning with the curatorship of the exhibition *Unfinished Modernizations—Between Utopia and Pragmatism* (Zagreb: Udruženje hrvatskih arhitekata, 2012). Dating from the same period is *Modernism In-between. The Mediatory Architectures of Socialist Yugoslavia* (ed. Vladimir Kulić, Maroje Mrduljaš and Wolfgang Thaler, jovis, 2012), which offered a comprehensive, well-documented analysis of architecture within the context of the politics and culture created. Their work laid the basis for more fragmented and detailed studies at both local and international levels, such as Dubravka Sekulić's work on the export practices of a Yugoslav building enterprise, Energoprojekt (*Constructing Non-Alignment: The Case of Energoprojekt*, Volume 3 of *Non-aligned Modernisms*, Museum of Contemporary Art, 2014–2017). Prior to these publications, Ljiljana Blagojević had carried out a thorough synthesis of the history of modernism and planning in Belgrade. Her book *Modernism in Serbia: The Elusive Margins of Belgrade Architecture* (MIT Press, 2003) highlighted the origins of the idea of modernism and was followed by *Novi Beograd: Osporeni modernizam* (Zavod za udžbenike, 2007). For many researchers in the field, the latter became a vital reference for the city's planning history, summarizing the involvement of architects in crucial projects and at the same time offering a thesis on the unfinished city. Interest in Yugoslavia culminated in the 2019 MOMA exhibition that brought together much of the developed research and established Yugoslav modernism as a distinct case (*Toward a Concrete Utopia: Architecture in Yugoslavia 1948–1980*, ed. Martino Stierli and Vladimir Kulić, The Museum of Modern Art, 2018). With their well-developed arguments and extensive research scope, these publications promoted the argument for modernism and non-aligned architectures long after it was first announced in other cultural spheres.[17]

Decades previously, in the context of the *Praxis* journal, the international philosophical discourse in Yugoslavia also actively promoted the country as a meeting point for East and West. The EXAT 51 group and the New Tendencies movement did the same for art, as explained in *Impossible Histories* (MIT Press, 2006, ed. Dubravka Djurić and Miško Šuvaković), the recent catalogue of the exhibition *EXAT 51: Synthesis of the Arts in Post-War Yugoslavia* (curated by Katia Baudin, Tihomir Milovac, Kunstmuseen Krefeld, 2017) and Armin Medosch's book, *New Tendencies. Art at the Threshold of the Information Revolution 1961–1978* (MIT Press, 2016). The heritage of the land at this intersection was the subject of many works of literature, most notably those by Ivo Andrić about the bridge that connects the two sides (*Na Drini ćuprija, Travnička hronika*, both 1945). At home, Predrag J. Marković wrote a well-known book describing how the culture of Belgrade was historically situated between East and West (*Beograd izmedju istoka i zapada 1948–1965*, Službeni list Beograd, 1996).

The theme of the Yugoslavian case as a search for common ground between East and West also appeared in works dealing with the heritage of socialist humanism, like the one by Ákos Moravánszky, Torsten Lange, Judith Hopfengärther and Karl R. Kegler, *East West Central. Re-Building Europe 1950–1990* (Birkhäuser, 2016, 2017). This three-volume collection presents many cases, including Yugoslavia's, in which the idea of a central intermediary and dialogue was often promoted using the heritage of social humanism. Another example dealing with this exchange and the new ground it brought was the book *Team 10 East: Revisionist Architecture in Real Existing Modernism* (Museum of Modern Art Warsaw, 2013/2014), edited by Łukasz Stanek. As the title indicates, it aims to capture the resonance of Team 10 practices in the East. The articles by Aleksandar Kušić (»New Belgrade Block No. 22: Order and Freedom«) and Jelica Jovanović (»Alexis Josic between Yugoslavia and France: Housing the Greatest Number«) address the application of modernism to housing production in Yugoslavia. Stanek later published an extensive study of socialist architecture worldwide, presenting the diversity of work practices that existed in its production (*Architecture in Global Socialism: Eastern Europe, West Africa, and the Middle East in the Cold War*, Princeton University Press, 2020). In exploring largely overlooked archives, the author highlighted the place of the Global South in relation to socialist production.

The growing interest in the Yugoslavian case and its condition as a laboratory has, of course, been studied across a broader scope than just in books dealing predominantly with architecture. Contemporary museums in Zagreb, Belgrade and Ljubljana addressed the same phenomenon in the art, consumer culture, and ethnographic and anthropological scenes (e.g. *Yugoslavia 1918–1991*, ed. Ana Panić, Jovo Bakić, Srđan Cvetković, Ivana Dobrivojević, Hrvoje Klasić, Vladimir Petrović, Museum of Yugoslavia, 2014). A significant example was the exhibition about nonaligned constellations in Ljubljana, curated by Bojana Piškur, which brought a contemporary freshness to the heritage in question (*Southern Constellations. The Poetics of Non-Aligned*, curated by Bojana Piškur, Moderna galerija, 2019). Searching for positive threads in existing histories, the collection offered a contemporary reading of the participatory processes that existed. Along the same lines, the recent book by Bojana Videkanić, *Nonaligned Modernism: Socialist Postcolonial Aesthetics in Yugoslavia* (McGill-Queen's University Press, 2020), makes bold connections in interpreting histories from the perspective of an individual who experienced the context first-hand.

This book adds to this string of research by using the condition of the laboratory in production to emphasize the process of making. It focuses on the pragmatism of building on construction sites by a variety of agents ranging from volunteers and self-governed enterprises to microbrigades. These histories of construction sites are found to be an original and often overlooked resource of the overall Yugoslavian experiment representing the responsiveness of people to the construction of socialism. Their micro-stories reveal bottom-up processes in everyday life that managed to create pop-up realities not strictly aligned with and absorbed by mainstream political scopes.

Seen as a laboratory creating a sort of microcosmos, Yugoslavia's existence could in many ways be described as »under construction«. To summarise briefly, the country emerged from World War II with the heritage of a resistance movement and the desire to create a socialist society. The first version followed Eastern bloc communism and did not last beyond 1948. After this year of conflict with Stalin, a new attempt at socialism emerged, known as self-governance or self-management. It was built around the idea of bottom-up unions and cooperatives eventually creating a governing system. These efforts produced a reality that lasted for forty years—with frequent changes in legislation.[18] The novelty here was the attempt to find a means of achieving socialism other than through dogmatic interpretations of Marxism. Accordingly, the economy established in 1950 became known as the third way, with the ambitious goal of being neither capital- nor state-oriented. Following this attempt, the country adopted a position of neutrality in the Cold War in 1961 and led the Non-Aligned Movement that brought together former colonial states and created a market for itself.

A great deal has been said about these rather exceptional moments in Yugoslav history:[19] that it was made possible by its position between the blocs divided by the Iron Curtain and so was, in a way, a result of the conflict; that it was supported by the US with the aim of proposing a different kind of socialist constitution to that of the USSR; that it was ideologically implemented and, as such, did not have the chance to develop further; that the region did not have the tradition of self-governed movements needed for this development; that existing class divisions and segregations did not correspond to the level of emancipation required to breathe life into the experiment. Finally, it was said that a one-man show could not function in the world economy. As such, the experiment was doomed to failure when it encountered flows of capital directed either by states or by a free market. All of these statements contain some truth. All shed light on the events and are presumptions that are taken into account here; this article is not about supporting a single political system. Nevertheless, it is also true that the Yugoslavian attempt was long-lasting and that its condition of ongoing societal construction coloured everyday life. It made the country a living laboratory in which many new realities emerged. These realities were microcosmoses of their own, with stories that have no straightforward conclusions. In a context in which the new political system was being trialled in a number of different ways, it can hardly be said that this attempt at participation was not taken seriously by citizens, or that they were without critical thought; that there was no legislation or constitution, or that there were no explicit regulations granting the right to a new kind of self-governing citizenship. Citizens received flats, education and health care for free, and even summer holidays and daily meals in milk restaurants.[20] The offer was not conditional on other circumstances and did not exclude exchange with the rest of the world. Borders were crossed physically and culturally, both to the east and the west.[21] This meant that this laboratory state gained confidence early on and encouraged citizens' practical attempts to realise the vision of a society that worked. This became even more explicit when societal construction was followed by intensive material rebuilding, due first to war damage and then to the need for new housing and work.

An attempt to promote participation was accompanied by a lively philosophical debate on praxis that brought together philosophers worldwide. Initially, this drew heavily on new readings of Marx that opposed dogmatic interpretations. Philosophers who joined the new movement came from universities in Zagreb and Belgrade, and eventually set up a philosophical journal called *Praxis*.[22] The initially quite small group consisted of Branko Bošnjak, Danko Grlić, Milan Kangrga, Ivan Kuvačić, Gajo Petrović, Rudi Supek and Predrag Vranicki. Their interpretation of the means of participatory democracy drew on Marx's early writings about humans as beings of praxis. No specific philosophical tradition was followed for this course of thinking. What was unique about the praxis movement in Yugoslavia was that it had no single discourse on praxis, instead representing the meeting of plural voices. It seemed that the initial aim was largely to use different praxis theories as pragmatic tools to resolve existing societal issues related to the theme of production.

The purpose of philosophy as activism was clearly promoted in the first issue of *Praxis*, titled »A quoi bon Praxis?« In writing on the topic, the editor Gajo Petrović recalls that Greek letters are used for the word praxis on the cover not solely to refer to its ancient meaning, but to combat a purely instrumental view of practice, and also to point out that when the journal, like the Ancient Greeks, discussed the everyday it is acknowledging it as a source for philosophy.[23] There was an enthusiasm in the treatment of praxis as a tool for active citizenship and the everyday life of society. This contributed to wider publicity of the attempt, attracting an audience far beyond disciplinary boundaries. This was, above all, a result of the way knowledge was gathered by means of the summer school for philosophy held on the picturesque Adriatic island of Korčula. The School lasted for ten days in the summer in the years from 1963 to 1974. Due to its position between East and West, it was a place many were allowed to travel to. It served as a meeting point and a kind of East-West forum for philosophers and students. Among many international press reports about the School's mediatory work, the German magazine *Spiegel* offered the following lines:

»For years, philosophers had been working from Zagreb around a small journal (also published in German) called *Praxis* to ensure that the philosophical ties between East and West were not completely severed. From 1963 onwards, the *Praxis* circle even organized annual East-West meetings of thinkers on the Adriatic island of Korčula. Friends of Heidegger, such as the Freiburg philosophy professor Eugen Fink, met there with Eastern philosophers, such as rebellious communist Leszek Kołakowski, or the German-American student idol Herbert Marcuse. In particular, the ideas of humanitarian-communist thinkers like Sartre, Bloch and Marcuse seeped from Korčula into the slogans of students in Prague, Warsaw and Bucharest [...].

The summer school on Korčula also took place this year – on the threshold of the Vienna Congress of Philosophers and with a suggestive theme: ›Marx and the Revolution.‹ Of course, at first it looked as if the 150 ›new leftists‹ from Yugoslavia, the Federal Republic of Germany, Czechoslovakia, America, France and Scandinavia were preparing for an attack in Vienna against Western bourgeois society. Amid the thunder of the passing night storm and in the light of a paraffin lamp lit because of a power failure, Ernst Bloch, the grandfather of humanitarian communists, proclaimed: ›There is no doubt, the future belongs to socialism.‹ Afterwards, Marcuse paid homage to the student rebels of Europe; Frankfurt professor Jürgen Habermas tried to develop strategic concepts for the overthrow of ›late capitalism‹.«[24]

An impressive list of names headed the school's curriculum, starting with Zygmunt Bauman, Umberto Cerroni, Erich Fromm, Agnes Heller and Henri Lefebvre. Lucien Goldmann, György Lukács, Howard L. Parsons and Kostas Axelos were also present. From Germany, philosophers such as Ernst Bloch, Herbert Marcuse, Jürgen Habermas, Hans-Georg Gadamer and Eugen Fink took part in discussions. Many of them were regular participants and worked on the editorial board and considered the major themes addressed by the School, including:

1963:	Progress and Culture / *Fortschritt und Kultur*
1964:	Meaning and Perspectives of Socialism 1964 / *Sinn und Perspektiven des Sozialismus*
1965:	What is History? / *Was ist Geschichte?*
1966:	The School was cancelled due to pressure from the League of Communists of Croatia
1967:	Creativity and Creation / *Schaffen und Verdinglichung*
1968:	Marx and Revolution / *Marx und die Revolution*
1969:	Power and Humanity / *Macht und Menschlichkeit*
1970:	Hegel and Our Time / *Hegel und unsere Zeit—Lenin und die Neue Linke*
1971:	Utopia and Reality / *Utopie und Realität*
1972:	Freedom and Equality / *Freiheit und Einigkeit*
1973:	The Essence and Limits of Civil Society / *Die bürgerliche Welt und der Sozialismus*
1974:	Art in a Technologized World / *Kunst in der modernen Gesellschaft*.[25]

The themes discussed at the summer school were representative of the journal, and its lectures and debates were published in *Praxis* in Serbo-Croatian, English, French and German (fig. 1). Alongside the content it drew from these gatherings, *Praxis* published thematic issues on well-known praxis philosophers such as Antonio Gramsci, György Lukács, Lucien Goldmann and Martin Heidegger. Marx was, of course, unavoidable, and was addressed in a number of dedicated issues including *Die Aktualität der Gedanken von Karl Marx* (1967), *Marx and Revolution* (1969) and *Marx, Marxisme,*

Marxologie (1970). Finally, *Praxis* covered many themes relating to the everyday life of Yugoslavian society, such as in the issue titled »One moment in Yugoslavian socialism« (»Un moment du socialisme Yougoslave«, 1971). Here, Yugoslavian philosopher Rudi Supek outlined comparisons between Proudhon's concept of the unit of the producer and the Yugoslav example of self-governance, presenting extensive critical arguments about contradictions in the Yugoslavian case.

    With its activism and debates, *Praxis* served as both a promoter and a critic of the Yugoslav attempt while also addressing the progress and failures of society. At the same time, the construction of socialism was very much identified with changes in materiality. The philosophical and political reconstruction of Marxism in Yugoslavia went hand in hand with the country's physical reconstruction. This concept found its most explicit embodiment in the construction of a new city. New Belgrade was intended to be the capital of a new society, reflecting the country's development. However, not only the city itself but also a great deal of broader material culture was at stake. Rather than representing an imagined community, anthropological research showed that the federation was seen as a very real fabric of ideas for all of those who, over a forty-five-year period, tried to achieve it.[26] In this sense, processes of material building on the one hand and societal and philosophical discussions on the other were two sides of the same coin. This is what makes the Yugoslav case relevant in exploring the relation between intensive material production and philosophical debate, or between practice and theory.

    The plurality of voices arising from the philosophy of praxis can be seen as a series of concepts or a pool of ideas that resonate with and question material culture. In this sense, praxis takes the role of a fictive character directing a critical lens and asking questions about how the extended idea of praxis was mirrored in material practice. How did construction respond to ideas from around the world that informed the Yugoslavian field of culture? How were Marxist ideas about production interwoven with the process of construction? Was it possible to say that material practice somehow mirrored philosophical thinking? And, if so, in what way was praxis the basis for the collective production of architecture? The range of questions that a fictional character could ask is wide, as there was no single definition of practice but rather a series of different philosophical interpretations of what practice should represent. Which of the different positions presented on the front covers of the journal could be relevant to material culture? Furthermore, what was material culture about? These questions inform the thread of the three narratives that make up the structure of this thesis. Each addresses the meaning of praxis from a different philosophical viewpoint and pairs it with histories of construction. In this way, each chapter offers a particular link between the theory of praxis and the practice of construction. This is explicit in their titles, which present keywords that frame the relevant viewpoint. These words refer both to the type of praxis as a basis for theoretical reflection and to the events in construction.

Praxis

Praxis is the key concept connecting the chapters, each of which focuses on a particular philosophical interpretation of praxis relevant in our reflections on construction. These interpretations help to explain the main preoccupations around production that emerged as a result of geopolitics and international philosophical debate drawing from Marxian insights. The relevance of praxis philosophy to the historical moment in question, both in Yugoslavia and internationally, was written about by Yugoslav philosopher Gajo Petrović. Petrović, one of the most well-known contributors to the *Praxis* journal and its lifelong editor, became known for his book *Marx in the Mid-Twentieth Century* and for his summary of the development of praxis philosophy in *A Dictionary of Marxist Thought*. Here, he supported the argument that Marx directed the meaning of praxis toward social aspirations. »In Marx the concept of praxis became a central concept of a new philosophy which does not want to remain philosophy, but to transcend itself [...] in the revolutionary transformation of the world.«[27] This argument had its origin in *Economic and Philosophical Manuscripts* and *Theses on Feuerbach*, in which Marx reintroduced the terminology of praxis as a specific form of human practice that is above all sensory and social, leading to the production of objects. In supporting this view, Marx writes: »The chief defect of all previous existing materialism [including Feuerbach's] is that the object, actuality, sensuousness is conceived only in the form of the *object or perception [Anschauung]*, but not as *sensuous human activity, practice [Praxis]*, nor subjectively.«[28]

Marx influenced the shift in the way the material world was understood, opposing the predominance of the practical between subject and object as resulting purely from perception. Conversely, he saw the object as engaging the physical and emotional senses of producers and becoming a social thing.[29] Since Marx, there has been a renaissance in the philosophy of praxis. German philosopher Jürgen Habermas pointed this out when he wrote that Marx's perspective on human emancipation determines modern interpretations of the philosophy of praxis. These stances are summed up as follows by Marx:

»Human emancipation will only be complete when the individual man has absorbed into himself the abstract citizen, when [...] he has recognized and organized his own powers as social powers [...].«[30]

By understanding praxis as a social action first, Antonio Labriola interpreted Marxism as a philosophy of praxis and influenced Antonio Gramsci's reading of praxis as the collective will of citizenship (*Lettere dal Carcere*, written 1929–1935, published 1947). Later, György Lukács spoke of praxis in relation to the political constitution and utopianism of the communist left (*Geschichte und Klassenbewußtsein: Studien über marxistische Dialektik*, 1923). At around the same time, Herbert Marcuse identified praxis with the concept of radical action and doing (*Tun*) and studied the interrelation of labour and praxis (*Beiträge zu einer Phänomenologie des Historischen Materialismus*, 1928; *Über die philosophischen Grundlagen des wirtschaftswissenschaftlichen Arbeitsbegriffs*, 1933).[31]

All of these emergent positions on Marxian heritage were discussed in Yugoslavia. They were crucial because praxis in the mid-twentieth century became a concept used to fight dogmatic interpretations of Marxism led by bureaucratic state politics. As Yugoslavia took a side opposing that of the Eastern bloc, its philosophers supported the existing shift toward the individual. On the international scene, this shift was explicit in works such as those by Henri Lefebvre, who focused on the relation between praxis and everyday life in his books *Métaphilosophie* (1965) and *Sociologie de Marx* (1966). Maurice Merleau-Ponty and Jean-Paul Sartre brought an existential view to praxis, casting it as a means of introspection into the individual's inner world. Ernst Bloch and Cornelius Castoriadis related praxis with imagination in quite distinct ways. Jürgen Habermas extended the philosophy of praxis into one of action with a focus on communication and participation. The *Praxis* philosophical circle referenced the work of the aforementioned philosophers to offer indications of how production relates to space in a non-alienated manner. In many cases, it also considered production as a collective endeavour: as part of a common social vision with prospects for individuals in their roles of citizens. In the articles discussed in the following chapters, therefore, these philosophers address material culture in their arguments. The production of space and life in cities in general is often bound up with descriptions of how praxis is relevant to an active individual. The search for associations between these descriptions on the abstract level and their interpretation in the local construction context offers a path for the development of narratives.

Action

The first chapter, then, is titled »Praxis and Action«, and refers to the early post-war period when the huge destruction to be addressed called for huge construction. This was the time of migration to the cities, of fast decisions and active labour behind the scenes to get everyday life going again. This reaction, born of austerity and no little post-war enthusiasm, came from the youth work movement that handled the post-war reconstruction almost entirely. The scale significantly overcame the immediate response needed for a recovery of life. Voluntary youth actions became an ongoing phenomenon in the construction of socialism, with around two million people taking part over forty years. Although the way actions developed changed significantly over the decades, the basic scenario remained the same: young people responded to the calls organized by the Socialist Youth of Yugoslavia and spent a couple of months on construction sites. During this time, they worked and lived in a commune. Actions involved constructing everything from a single building to roads, railway and cities like New Belgrade. The organization of these actions aimed to represent a participative society with a brigade that functioned according to shared goals and responsibilities.

The creation of a temporary society of producers who exchanged labour for something intangible, such as experience or gratification, was regarded as very Marxian. It was publicly promoted as such: an experimental action representing society at the small scale, based on shared life and production.[32] But in addition to this official vision, the parallel with Marxist praxis is relevant as a comparison to the perspective of volunteers. This aspect is what the first chapter explores, creating a link between actions in building and Marxist readings of praxis as active labour. The narrative offers notes on how Marxian praxis was interpreted, to what extent it was discussed in Yugoslavia, how this debate is intertwined with the engagement of labour from a historical viewpoint and to what extent Marxian praxis can be likened to the endeavours of the volunteers. Some sources for this chapter can be found in the 1965 and 1967 editions of *Praxis* journal titled *Sinn und Perspektiven des Sozialismus* and *Die Aktualität der Gedanken von Karl Marx*. These were based not solely on Marx's writings but also on new interpretations. Yugoslavian philosopher Gajo Petrović was a life-long researcher of the notion of praxis in Marx. On the international scene, the most explicit in this respect were contributions by Henri Lefebvre, who extensively analysed Marxian praxis while setting it in the context of everyday life. Readings of how praxis works in Marx are also found in the book with the same title as the first chapter, *Praxis and Action* (1971), written by American philosopher Richard J. Bernstein, himself part of the praxis debate in Yugoslavia.

Imagination

The second chapter, »Praxis and Imagination«, follows the further development of building practices. The intensive voluntary labour was decreased as early industry joined the construction effort, relying largely on unspecialized work. This industry had a two-fold dream. The first was to create cooperatives shared by all enterprises. The second was to ensure housing for all—which was, by constitution, granted as a natural right of citizens—to be built by emerging construction firms. For anonymous citizens, whether residents or members of an enterprise, these two dreams sparked the imagination with regard to what this housing and work would look like. This had the effect of reinforcing citizens' responses to construction. The industry relied on the use of concrete, and Yugoslavia was no different to the rest of the world in that migration to the cities was accompanied by the development of various methods for the reinforcement of this building material.[33] Prefabrication was seen as a means of meeting the demand for housing, and what emerged was a kind of collective effort in establishing this building practice. Explaining how building and imagining overlapped provides the answer to the main question of the second chapter: How was prefabrication bound up with the collective imagination? How did prefabrication become participative? These questions were explored by one of the early building companies, known as the Institute for Materials Testing, which blazed an original trail in establishing prefabrication as an open system. Where history and theory overlapped, philosophical voices appeared to question this new building practice. Ernst Bloch and Cornelius Castoriadis cast light on the link between imagination and material culture. Both were also engaged with philosophical discussions in Yugoslavia. Their positions raised questions that served to describe how the birth of prefabrication was bound up with social imagination. Themes like the importance of hands-on experience and the ability to create a social contract suggest that participation played a part in modernizing society. The underlying intention of my argument is also to posit the overlap between architecture, industrial production and societal modernization as one of learning, despite often being regarded with critical eyes due to the legacies of sprawl and mono-functional large-scale settlements.[34]

Lebenswelt

Once the open system was developed and social labour came into being, Yugoslavia's Institute for Materials Testing started to export the practice worldwide. In the mid-1960s, one of the new destinations was Cuba, just a few years out of its revolution and starting to address housing reform. The third chapter, then, deals with how this transfer to Cuba contributed to the prospect of further modernization. Here, the main inquiry concerns whether modernization was able to preserve the visibility and place of the maker in construction processes. Another consideration is how participation evolved in different political and historical contexts. To this end, the Cuban post-war context is briefly reviewed through notes on housing reform and the decision to test prefabrication. This is followed by a comment on the microbrigade movement, in which work groups built housing for themselves and for the association they worked for. The narrative explains how housing reform was undertaken by unskilled people, and how this was the main reason why Cubans found the Yugoslavian open system applicable. This chapter also focuses on the history of small experimental dwellings built in Havana using Yugoslav technology with the aim of learning to work with prefabrication and modern techniques. It shows how construction involved local people, how contracts were drawn up, how the idea of the construction site travelled overseas, and what happened to the idea of user engagement through prefabrication.

These concerns bring us to the next crucial word and the next important praxis philosopher needed to understand the position of participants, especially in modern technological societies. The word is *Lebenswelt*, and the philosopher is Jürgen Habermas. In his first appearance at the summer school and in the *Praxis* circle, Habermas wrote an article on the topic of technical progress and the world of social life, titled »Technischer Fortschritt und soziale Lebenswelt« (*Praxis* no. 1/2: »Qu'est que l'histoire«, 1966). His critique addressed the position of citizens with regard to technological advancement. Put simply, Habermas posited that the place of the user is lost in modern means of production, and explored how to restore it. To do so, he developed his theory of communication as a new version of praxis philosophy.[35] Closely considering the participant, Habermas builds his theory on the notion of *Lebenswelt*, or lifeworld, as a setting for communication. He describes it as a transcendental site where speaker and hearer meet and reciprocally make statements that reflect the world. In this space, they can criticize and confirm claims of validity, settle disagreements and reach agreements.[36] Drawing on Habermas's critique, the third chapter is titled »Praxis and *Lebenswelt*«. The proposed analogy presents the construction site as a place that engages the lifeworld of its makers. This comparison offers answers to the question of how far a lifeworld was reproduced in the transfer of the building system to Cuba. What was the history of the construction site there? How much participation was there in this meeting of peoples and cultures through prefabrication? What did they communicate about? In this light, the chapter explores whether collective building was possible at all in the context of modernization and industry, as well as considering its failures and achievements.

Theory

The final keyword, which is reserved for the conclusion of this narrative, is theory. In his book *Keywords. A Vocabulary of Culture and Society*, Raymond Williams includes the notion of praxis under the definition of theory. He explains their unity as a development in Marxist thought, whereby praxis means practice informed by theory, as well as theory informed by practice. In this sense, praxis is a tool that aims to unite theory with the strongest sense of the practical, neither as a routinized nor purely instrumental process, but as an activity: the practice of action. The distinction or opposition between theory and practice can then be surpassed.[37] This meaning of theory, with its alter ego of praxis, is relevant to the final questions here. How helpful, in this particular case, was the overlap of philosophy and building in understanding history and reinforcing findings for the sake of architectural theory? What are the limitations of the method, and how successful was the montage of these two fields in creating a coherent argument? Did the argument benefit from the distance between the fields? Can narratives, seen in themselves as testing grounds, prove that the application of theory to architectural practice may be valid as a method?

►1   Selection of front covers of *Praxis* journal with the first international issue titled »A quoi bon Praxis?«
© Korčula City Library Ivan Vidali.

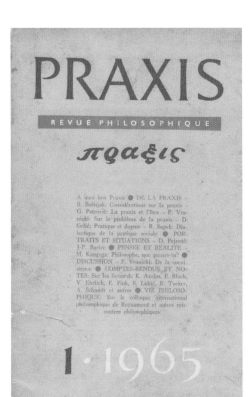

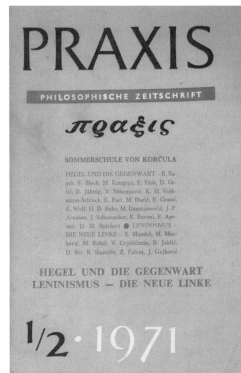

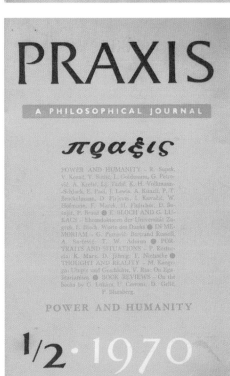

PRAXIS

FILOZOFSKI DVOMJESEČNIK

πραξις

KORČULANSKA LJETNA ŠKOLA

UTOPIJA I REALNOST — R. Supek. OD UTOPIJE DO IDEOLOGIJE — pišu: M. Kangrga, M. Đurić, K. H. Volkmann -Schluck, R. Berlinger, R. Muminović, D. Jähnig. P. Piccone, D. Stojanović, H. Bur- ger ▲ ANARHIJA, BUDUĆNOST, REVO- LUCIJA — pišu: T. Inđić, D. Gudrin, E. Paci, I. Kuvačić, R. Jungk, H.-D. Bahr, V. L. Allen, I. Maksimović, H. Fleischer, Ž. D. Denić, R. Kragalott, S. Shibata ▲ KULTURA, ETIKA, DEMOKRACIJA — pišu: Z. Pešić-Golubović, B. Gojković, O. Chetan, Z. Puhovski, Z. Falout, M. Jilek. N. Bellu, V. Mađarević ▲ IZJAVA RE- DAKCIJE ČASOPISA »PRAXIS«

UTOPIJA I REALNOST

1-2 ∘ 1972

PRAXIS

FILOZOFSKI DVOMJESEČNIK

πραξις

MARTIN HEIDEGGER — pišu: I. Ur- bančič o biti nihilizma, Z. Ponavec o kra- ju filozofije u djelu M. Heideggera i B. Despot: Što jest pitanje ▲ KORČULAN- SKA LJETNA ŠKOLA — pišu H. D. Bahr, D. Rel, P. Quarello, D. M. Borchet, Z. Levy, D. H. De Grood ▲ DISKUSIJA — A. Diemer o pozitivizmu, marksizmu i fenomenologiji ▲ PRIKAZI i BILJEŠKE — pišu: Bl. Despot, T. Meyer, V. Simeu- nović, R. Supek, P. Vranicki, o knjigama: A. Gorza, G. Rohrmosera, G. K. Kalten- brunnera, G. Friedmanna, M. Horkhei- mera, T. W. Adorna, i E. Fischera ▲ OD- JECI — S. Zuravicki o Stvaralačkom marksizmu ili ljevičarskom »radikalizmu«

MARTIN HEIDEGGER
KORČULANSKA LJETNA ŠKOLA

1 ∙ 1971

PRAXIS

REVUE PHILOSOPHIQUE

πραξις

EGALITE ET LIBERTÉ — M. Marković, Z. Golubović, Ž. Puhovski, Lj. Tadić, J-M. Palmier, I. Kuvačić, H. Gyzicki, Dž. Soko- lović, S. Vrcan ● PORTRAITS ET SI- TUATIONS — M. Kangrga, Vom Begriff des Mangels bei Hegel; N. Čačinović-Pu- hovski, Die Dialektik der Aufklärung ● PENSEE ET REALITE — D. Grlić, L'Organisation sociale et le théâtre ● DISCUSSION — G. Skirbekk, Ecology and Marxism; D. Dimitrov, Marxismus und Literatur ● DOCUMENTS — G. Lu- kács, Die Budapester Schule ● IN MEMO- RIAM — Serge Mallet

EGALITE ET
LIBERTE

2-3 ∘ 1973

PRAXIS

A PHILOSOPHICAL JOURNAL

πραξις

BUREAUCRACY, TECHNOCRACY AND FREEDOM - by R. Supek, S. Stojanović, A. Kresić, V. Rus and M. Greiffenhagen ● THE TOPICALITY OF MARX'S THOU- GHT - by M. Prucha, P. Vranicki, A. Hel- ler, M. Životić and H. L. Parsons ● DIS- CUSSION - on Bureaucracy: by J. Marin- ković and Lj. Tadić ● REVIEWS AND NOTES - Books by D. Leković, B. Bošnjak and M. Kangrga ● PHILOSOPHICAL LIFE - Philosophical Meetings in Zagreb, Copenhagen, Heidelberg and Budapest ● DOCUMENTS - At the Beginning of Another Year ● CHRONICLE - Yugoslav Philosophy Today - by G. Petrović

2 ∙ 1967

PRAXIS

FILOZOFSKI DVOMJESEČNIK

πραξις

LUCIEN GOLDMANN — pišu: R. Supek o L. Goldmannu kao čovjeku, misliocu i borcu, P. Vranicki o ličnosti L. Goldmanna, E. Prohić o estetici L. Goldmanna, L. Goldmann — Posljednji referat na Korčulanskoj ljetnoj školi: 1970. i Bibliografija njegovih radova ▲ PORTRETI I SITUACIJE — pišu: K. A. Megil o G. Lukácsu, E. Pajnić o S. de Beauvoir, E. Paci o Fenomenologiji i političkoj ekonomiji ▲ DISKUSIJA — pišu: E. Heintel o dijalektici metajezika i Th. Meyer o J. Habermasu ▲ PRIKAZI I BILJEŠKE — o knjigama E. Tugendhata, L. Goldmanna i E. Finka pišu: M. Damnjanović, V. Potkovac i N. Miščević ● OBAVIJESTI — Informacija o ciljevima i radu Korčulanske ljetne škole

LUCIEN GOLDMANN

2 · 1971

PRAXIS

PHILOSOPHISCHE ZEITSCHRIFT

πραξις

ANARCHIE, ZUKUNFT, REVOLUTION — T. Indić, D. Guérin, E. Paci, I. Kuvačić, R. Jungk, H-D. Bahr, R. Quarelio, V. L. Allen, I. Maksimović, H. Fleischer, Ž. Denić, O. Chetan, V. Madarević, N. Bellu, R. Kragalott, Sh. Shibata, S. Mallet, M. Jilek ● GEDANKE UND WIRKLICHKEIT — K. Axelos, P. Vranicki ● DISKUSSION — I. Kuvačić

ANARCHIE, ZUKUNFT, REVOLUTION

3-4 ° 1972

PRAXIS

FILOZOFSKI DVOMJESEČNIK

πραξις

MISAO GYÖRGYA LUKÁCSA — pišu V. Korać, A. Heller, M. Prucha, N. J. Xenos, L. Goldmann IZ NOVIJE LITERATURE O LUKACSU — pišu V. Mikecin, Lj. Đokić, Ž. Puhovski, G. Svob, G. Flego TRI TEKSTA G. LUKÁCSA — O biti i formi eseja, Organizacijska pitanja treće internacionale, Marxovi osnovni ontološki principi ▲ IZ INDIJSKE FILOZOFIJE — pišu G. Flego, R. Ch. Pandeya, R. Iveković, C. Veljačić ▲ DISKUSIJA — pišu D. Grlić i J. Adler ▲ PRIKAZI I BILJEŠKE, KRONIKA — B. Bošnjak: Tko se protstavlja radnike i filozofe ● PISMA, OBAVIJESTI — DESETO ZASJEDANJE KORČULANSKE LIETNE ŠKOLE

MISAO GYÖRGYA LUKÁCSA

3-4 ° 1973

PRAXIS

A PHILOSOPHICAL JOURNAL

πραξις

NATIONAL, INTERNATIONAL, UNIVERSAL — P. Vranicki, M. Kangrga, R. Supek, V. Cvjetičanin, U. Cerroni, H. L. Pacsows, A. Künzli, I. Tadić, D. Grlić KARL MARX — G. Petrović, J. P. Nettl, D. C. Hodges, G. A. Cohen, M. Marković ● PORTRAITS AND SITUATIONS — K. H. Wolff; G. Simmel; K. Axelos: From «Revolutionary Intellectuals» to «Arguments» ● THOUGHT AND REALITY — I. Kuvačić, M. Damnjanović ● REVIEWS AND NOTES ● PHILOSOPHICAL LIFE ● SPECIAL SUPPLEMENT: IN DEFENCE OF CREATIVE MARXISM AND HUMANIST SOCIALISM — POLAND, CZECHOSLOVAKIA, YUGOSLAVIA — E. Bloch, E. Fromm, H. Lefebvre, G. Lukacs, M. Marcuse, D. Riesman, T. Kotarbiński and others ● APPENDIX: Index of the authors, Praxis 1965

3/4 · 1968

PRAXIS

REVUE PHILOSOPHIQUE

πραξις

UN MOMENT DU SOCIALISME YOU-GOSLAVE – P. Vranicki, N. Popov, R. Su-pek, Z. Pešić-Golubović, I. Kuvačić, B. Jak-šić, M. Kangrga, A. Žvan, G. Petrović, D. Grlić, V. Cvjetičanin, Ž. Puhovski, E. Hor-vat ● PUBLICATION PRELIMINAIRE – E. Bloch ● PORTRAITS ET SITUA-TIONS – J. M. Palmier: Goldmann vivant ● DISCUSSION – V. Milić: Method of Cri-tical Theory ● VIE PHILOSOPHIQUE

UN MOMENT
DU SOCIALISME YOUGOSLAVE

3/4 · 1971

PRAXIS

A PHILOSOPHICAL JOURNAL

πραξις

ANTONIO GRAMSCI – by P. Vranicki, K. Kosik, M. Marković and L. Sober ● PHENOMENOLOGY AND MARXISM – by V. Filipović, K. Axelos and L. Landgrebe ● PORTRAITS AND SITUATIONS – The Preparations of the Sociology of Know-ledge, by K. H. Wolff, The Philosophical Substructure of Lukacs's Theory of Partisans, by P. Ludz ● THOUGHT AND REALITY – Power Politics and Social Criticism, by Lj. Tadić, The Meaning of Engagement in Philosophy by D. Grlić ● DISCUSSION – An Outline of the Community and the Social Situation of Our Times, by M. Damnjanović, The Meaning of Marx's Philosophy, by M. Kangrga ● REVIEWS AND NOTES – Books by H. Lefebvre and D. Grlić ● PHILOSOPHICAL LIFE – International Symposium on Gramsci

3 · 1967

PRAXIS

A PHILOSOPHICAL JOURNAL

πραξις

ART IN A WORLD OF TECHNOLOGY – D. Grlić: Why Art? I. Focht: Art in a World of Technology, D. Pejović: Art and Aesthetics, M. Kangrga: Philosophy and Art ● Portraits and Situations – G. Petrović, Dialectical Materialism and the Philosophy of Karl Marx, D. Grlić: F. Nietzsche's Anti-aestheticism ● THOUGHT AND REALITY – M. Marković: Man and Technology ● DISCUSSION – Z. Pešić-Golubović: What is the Meaning of Alie-nation? ● REVIEWS AND NOTES – Lj. Stfür and B. Supek offering the works of L. Goldmann and A. Gorz ● PHILOSO-PHICAL LIFE – Yugoslav philosophers visit Hungary, Rumania and the U.S.S.R.

3 · 1966

PRAXIS

PHILOSOPHISCHE ZEITSCHRIFT

πραξις

FREIHEIT – G. Petrović, P. Vranicki, D. Grlić, Lj. Tadić und M. Kangrga ● POR-TRÄTS UND SITUATIONEN – D. Pe-jović: Rudolf Carnap, V. Mikecin: Tiefe Wurzeln des Dogmatismus ● GEDANKE UND WIRKLICHKEIT – Z. Pešić-Golu-bović: Sozialismus und Humanismus, V. Milić: Zur Theorie des sozialen Konflikts ● DISKUSSION – M. Čaldarović: Disolu-zionsprozesse im System der Selbstverwal-tung ● BUCHBESPRECHUNGEN UND NOTIZEN – Über die Werke von H. Mar-cuse und S. Mallet ● PHILOSOPHISCHES LEBEN

4 · 1965·

1965

▶2   Summer School of Philosophy in Korčula, 1965–1974 © Korčula City Library Ivan Vidali.

▶3   Herbert Marcuse after the lecture at Korčula Summer School of Philosophy © Praxis Digital Archive, praxis.memoryoftheworld.org.

Praxis and Action: Towards Building as a Collective Practice[1]

»Wealth at once graspable and inexhaustible, the practical-sensuous shows us what praxis is. It is one continuous revelation, a disclosure so unmistakable that we need only open our eyes to perceive the enormous scope of praxis in this human creation which encompasses landscapes, cities, objects of common use, and rare objects. The unity of the sensuous and the intellectual, of nature and culture, confronts us everywhere. Our senses become our theoreticians, as Marx put it, and the immediate discloses the mediations it involves. The sensuous leads us to the concept of praxis, and this concept unfolds the richness of the sensuous. We thus discover that all praxis rests on a twofold foundation: the sensuous on the one hand, creative activity stimulated by a need it transforms on the other. This total phenomenon (need, work, sensuous enjoyment of the sensory object) is found at every level. Work is productive—of objects and of tools for more work. But it is also productive of new needs—production needs and needs for production... Study of praxis, including poiesis, leads to a sociology of forms.«[2]

In 1967, Yugoslavian philosopher Gajo Petrović published *Marx in the mid-twentieth century*. In what would become an internationally recognized book, Petrovic surveyed debates between »creative« and »dogmatic« Marxism. Opposing accretions of Marxian historiography he labeled dogmatic, Petrović called for a creative approach to Marxist thought that could contribute to global production challenges. In doing so, Petrović foregrounded the category of »praxis«.[3] This privilege of praxis was hardly unique among leftist philosophers of the mid-1960s engaged with the politics of the Eastern bloc. Petrović summed up these different positions. Accordingly, relations between praxis and everyday life figured in contemporaneous works of Henri Lefebvre including *Métaphilosophie* (1965) and *Sociologie de Marx* (1966). Existential approaches to praxis appeared in the work of Maurice Merleau-Ponty and Jean-Paul Sartre; Ernst Bloch and Cornelius Castoriadis related praxis to the imagination; Jürgen Habermas made the philosophy of praxis as action central to his work on communication and individual participation.[4]

Significant as these international philosophical currents are, it is also worth stressing the local context. Petrović's book had its origin in political and philosophical debate in Yugoslavia starting in the post-war period and resulting in the establishment of the *Praxis* circle of philosophy. Its particularity was in gathering many international positions on praxis under the umbrella of *Praxis* journal.[5] Explaining the presence of praxis philosophy in Yugoslavia, American philosopher Richard Bernstein, himself a later participant of the circle, observed:

»The group consists of philosophers and social scientists, some of whom were partisans and leaders of the Yugoslavian revolution. They opposed Stalinist tendencies in Eastern Europe [and were] advocates of the principle of self-management and participatory democracies on all levels of society (...). Bloch, Marcuse and Habermas actively participated in the discussions in Korčula, and published in *Praxis*.«[6]

The aim of gathered voices of domestic and international left was to generate discussions on Marx as a way of operatively helping to introduce participation in society. At the same time, their theories were also affected by production trials existing in the country. This was possible because the philosophical reconstruction of Marxism in Yugoslavia was paralleled by the country's physical construction. Last comprised different kinds of experimental building practices, ranging from voluntary youth work to the introduction of participative prefabrication by self-governed enterprises. Existence of experiments in construction in the time when Marxism was questioned in the country and internationally offers the ground to study relation between philosophical and architectural production. This chapter explores the link between the experiment of collective building based on youth voluntarily work actions and Marxian interpretations of praxis as socially active labour.

In the narrow historical sense, the presence of Marxian thought in the country, influenced youth actions directly. In public records, actions aimed to represent society at a small scale, based on participation and non-monetary exchange.[7] In a broader sense, the proximity of theoretical debate and building trials created a particular microcosmos where influences went in both directions from philosophy to construction and vice versa. The argument here tries to reinforce this mutual proximity towards a historic and theoretical montage of construction and philosophy. Marxian literatures produced in the country and wider international readings help to create a theoretical basis to narrate Marxian praxis in analogy with the history of youth actions.

The New City and the New Production Challenge

In order to pin the historic moment, the story starts with a photo collage from 1947, the first depicting a group talking and the second digging at the New Belgrade construction site (►FIG. 1). The photographs convey an impression of the roughness of the beginnings, on flat land in an abstract context, with basic tools. This is even more explicit since we know that the aim of the participants was to start the construction of the entire new city rather than partial building or missing infrastructure. The smallness of the group was due to the fact that this meeting was for preparation only. Its aim was to lay the bases for a major youth work action that was to be conducted the following year. Accordingly, it was in April 1948 that work brigades made up of young people began building the new capital of Yugoslavia. Why did they do this? What was their vision for the new city?

New Belgrade represented a fiction of the socialist city. Its construction was driven by the desire for new beginnings after World War II: a shift in both the political constitution and the means of production followed by edification of cities to accommodate migration from rural areas. Ruined by the war and on the verge of breaking away from the USSR, Yugoslavia was poorly situated in the world economy. It was characterized by sharp divisions between its low-tech agricultural heritage and the civic culture of its major cities. In this context of austerity, work actions emerged

▶1 The first participants in youth work action at the New Belgrade construction site, 1947 © Historical Archives of Belgrade, Nemanja Budisavljević personal fonds.

as an attempt to repair war damage and speed up the path of modernization as the way to achieve autonomy for the country. The basic pattern was that young people answered the call of an organization known as the Socialist Youth of Yugoslavia and spent a month at a particular construction site. Once on site, they lived, worked and learned together. Following the post-war reconstruction process, the actions became an institutionalized practice lasting almost half a century. Their organization was far from homogeneous, as they varied extensively in size and regulation over the years, offering different scenarios of collective work and life.[8]

The New Belgrade work action was among the first and corresponded to the moment of political turn as the country navigated a course between communism and capitalism. This search was both the source and the consequence of Yugoslavia's conflict with Stalin that resulted in the country's expulsion from the Eastern bloc in 1948.[9] As Bernstein describes, Yugoslavia's revival of interest in Marxism had a political significance of resistance. He writes:

»In countries such as Poland, Czechoslovakia, and Yugoslavia, the rediscovery of ›authentic‹ Marxism has been the primary intellectual weapon for the criticism of the totalitarian and bureaucratic tendencies of existing Communist regimes.«[10]

For this, a new generation of philosophers acquired teaching positions at universities in Belgrade and Zagreb, appearing on the scene during Yugoslavia's resistance to Stalin. The *Praxis* school of philosophy had not yet been established, but there was a great deal of discussion as to how to implement Marxian production. Marx's early works (*Rani radovi: Marx i Engels*) were edited in 1953 by future *Praxis* philosophers Branko Bošnjak and Predrag Vranicki. Philosophic societies started to appear at republic and federal levels in 1951. While promoting the exchange of ideas, they also issued publications and interacted with faculties of philosophy. Translations of Marxian literature apart from those with Soviet origins started to appear, acquiring the prefix »classic«, used to describe a book that was widely distributed and promoted. Names such as Lucien Goldmann, Henri Lefebvre, Antonio Gramsci, György Lukács and Ernst Bloch appeared in bookshops. Translations were accompanied by new domestic writings in the form of books, journals and newspaper articles.[11] Among other journals, *Pogledi* (published monthly as of 1952 and dealing with the theory of humanities and natural sciences) played an important part in spreading a non-dogmatic view of Marxism. It was edited by another *Praxis* philosopher, Rudi Supek, who had just returned from Paris, where he had been active on the French leftist scene and resistant movement. As early as in its second issue, the journal featured an extensive text about Charles Fourier's idea of the association of producers. This was followed by contributions by a key figure for the future *Praxis*, Gajo Petrović, who was critical of interpretations of Marx in the USSR. These theoretical discussions reflected the friction that existed in society, in philosophy as well as in politics and other cultural domains: between dialectic materialism under the influence of Stalinism, and the concept of creative Marxism. The conflict was finally resolved at the 1960 philosophical gathering in Bled, Slovenia, with the victory of the wing calling for a revision of Marxian thought and *Praxis* journal stepped on the public scene.[12]

Parallel with philosophy, during the fifties profound changes were affecting legislation and construction. First started with the law on the self-governance of

production (1950), which eventually became the state constitution in 1953. The law ensured the independence of all economic cooperatives and the shift of property from ownership of the state to being owned by enterprises, and labelled as common.[13] The idea of building a socialist city was developed at this time, and migration from rural areas followed. In the period from 1946 to 1950 alone, 1 200 000 people migrated from the countryside to cities, where over 90% found employment. City population grew from 16.6% to 46.5%, making the level of industrial growth in the early sixties one of the highest in the world.[14] Same as preference towards creative Marxism over dialectical materialism, industry was preferred over agrarianism. Coming up with urban plan was means of resistance and affection towards modern architecture came as a consequence of participatory strivings. This was elaborated in a chain of recent literature describing how Yugoslavian in-between status affected the architectural discourse.[15] In this rapidly changing context, building by actions stood at the beginning of process and faced two tasks: as well as responding to austerity, it was also to be first attempt at small-scale self-governed production. This brought volunteers to the fore as the main protagonists of the envisioned process of participation and level of autonomy.[16] Who were they and how did they work? If interpreting Marx was part of the search for a new form of production, to what extent was this both influenced and reflected by the reality of building?

The protagonists joining the actions came predominantly from the countryside.[17] They were laypeople with few expectations of comfort, young, male and female, rather naïve and with a strong desire to be someone. Those not arriving from the countryside joined as workers, apprentices or students, though in significantly lower numbers (▶FIG. 2).[18] The action to build New Belgrade lasted from April to December (1948–1950) and attracted around 141 000 participants in total. Volunteers formed basic units known as work brigades, whose members lived and worked together for a month. Their motivations for taking action varied. Some came with friends, others heard about it at the local culture centre or saw a poster.[19] Yet others wanted to see the city, or just felt proud to take part. Some joined because they wanted to work in construction, take courses for semi-specialization, or learn to read and write. The site where volunteers arrived was historically very much between two worlds. A simple pre-war map (▶FIG. 3)

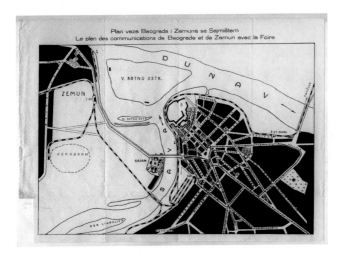

▶3
Plan of connections between Belgrade and Zemun, around 1938, 36.5 × 27cm © Belgrade City Museum.

shows its basic division: historical Belgrade to the east, the small city of Zemun as the last part of the Austro-Hungarian territory to the west, and a blank space between. Nearby there are two big rivers, the Sava and the Danube, and the artificial footprints of the railway, the airport, tramlines and Belgrade Fair.[20] The site was flooded due to the turbulent confluence of the rivers, which was the main geographical reason for its blank status and the main challenge for construction. In mimetic terms, it might be said that the site mirrored Yugoslavia's geopolitical position and its economy.[21]

The young people who were about to start building had little idea of how to do it, but no one expected them to; rather they were encouraged to learn as they built. This was possible because education was part of the programme of actions, organized as emancipation push through practice in the field. Once at the construction site, participants' daily routine combined learning and building. Thanks to their newly acquired learning, volunteers rarely returned to the countryside, instead becoming new citizens. The production of the city was, thus, presented as a personal prospect, an activity that could lead to change in the everyday lives and futures of the protagonists. Being above all a voluntary act of gratification, it corresponded to the present discourse of the Marxian ideal of production as a freely chosen activity which determinates a person fundamentally. Gajo Petrović writes that in Yugoslavia there was a transformation in the understanding of creative Marxism, and that:

»man is neither a ›rational animal‹ nor a ›toolmaking animal‹, he is praxis (…) who by his free creative action molds and changes his world and himself. (…) Could it not be said that the essence of Marx's philosophy is that it is a ›philosophy of action‹, ›philosophy of deed‹ or ›philosophy of praxis‹, that is a theory that does not remain just theory but also demands the act of changing the world and at the same time participates in this act?«[22]

By choosing to produce the city, the volunteers were saying something about themselves. The importance assigned to production as a way of expressing life resonated with the significance it held for volunteers: as part of their adventure, personal experience and the decision to help to build. But as well as their personal prospects, production also represented the utopia of the future city seen as a collective *Umwelt*.

▶4
Work on the banks of the Danube on the New Belgrade construction site © Historical Archives of Belgrade.

Here, too, it responded to Marx's readings; although Marx placed production in a very down-to-earth historic context of everyday life and a given society as a non-imposed phenomenon,[23] he did not exclude the realm of new possibilities. Referring to Marx as »a thinker of the possible«, French philosopher Henri Lefebvre, active in the *Praxis* circle, writes that production in Marx always maintains an aura of both the everyday and the utopian: the transformation of the everyday into utopia. Rather than as an imaginary or a dream, utopia appears here as a dimension of human reality contained in the possibility of transforming the existing by producing anew.[24] This dualistic view of production as both everyday concern and distant goal was at stake in the construction of the new city. Those who engaged in action were average, anonymous citizens engaged in a daily routine. Nevertheless, they were also driven by the idea of a utopia of a future society that felt like an ongoing process of transformation.

For those on the construction site, this transformation took the form of work in brigades in a rather rough set-up with no clear organization of work. The process was one of trial and error. Mechanization was lacking, as were specialized knowledge and qualified people. Larger building companies organized ongoing workshops at construction sites to remount machines that had been destroyed or damaged during the war.[25] Here, the volunteers encountered technology and developed a special relationship between almost precarious pieces of mechanical equipment and their non-specialized manual work. The striking proximity of the two can be seen in a photograph depicting casually dressed women digging the ground next to a rare crane (▶FIG. 4). In a context of high expectations of building and the lack of technological means to carry it out, volunteers introduced collective methods of manual production in an attempt to craft technology. Their work was very much based on trial and error, and their labour was set in the broadest context: investing physical and mental effort in rather particular social circumstances.

The Role of Objects as Mediators

Participants' invested labour acquired ultimate significance in the production of architecture. Its cruciality makes the theme another relevant point for comparison with Marxian discussion in terms of what kind of labour was this. The debate in Yugoslavia inclined towards the Marxian view on labour seen in a holistic sense, as something that engages the whole person. This was mainly influenced by the school of social humanism promoted by Erich Fromm as the active participant of the circle.[26] In arguing for creative Marxism, Petrović frequently referred to Fromm in order to point impossibility to categorize and evaluate different kinds of labour. Fromm asserted that, according to Marx, a person's energy appears in a social process partly as simple physical energy, such as tilling the soil or building roads, and partly in specific forms of mental energy. This means that not just consciousness or physical force is reinforced, but both. In applying philosophy and economy *ad hominem*,[27] labour is not excluded as a lower category of pure reproduction (as in Hannah Arendt, for example); it is one by which actors can gain knowledge. In this Marx's interpretation, labour is not strictly identified with hard effort or repetitive activity related to household and biological issues, and work instead with fine manual and intellectual engagement. Conversely, everything is included under heading of labour, with no difference in appreciation. The only important aspect is whether it is a joyful, creative activity or a kind of exploitation. Petrović further quotes Fromm in arguing for relation between labour and object:

»The objects of labour is, therefore, the *objectification of man's species life*; he no longer reproduces himself merely intellectually, as in consciousness, but actively and in real sense, and he sees his own reflection in a world that he has constructed.«[28]

Such reading of labour appears as highly egalitarian, as reproduction is actually not shifted anywhere. But this also means that the space for expertise—and the expert—is reduced. This statement is taken to an extreme towards Marx's famous quote that human being can be one thing today, and another tomorrow.[29] This was particularly relevant in the case of the actions, due to their unselective engagement of different kinds of protagonists and, at the same time, of labour, avoiding specialization. In architectural production of this kind, a person offered whatever they had, making this the rather original moment when construction could become anyone's business.

By means of labour, holistically understood, a person would produce objects. In the course of discussions about alienated means of production *Praxis* circle in Yugoslavia drew from early Marx's view on material production as *Entäußerung*—the process of natural alienation of the producer's internal power in the process of making an object (objectification). During production, the producer creates the conditions of their life, but they also create themself.[30] In this sense, rather than referring to the defamiliarization caused by carrying out individual tasks in a factory, *Entäußerung* represents a self-interested act from which the product emerges as a natural consequence.

The object in view—a city, in this case—would be result of *Vergegenständlichung* (objectification), seen as the productive and creative process of volunteers, intended as a gift, offered to others. Was this the case on site, and in what sense was the hands-on process of the brigades in building New Belgrade in line with the concept of *Entäußerung*?

In order to answer this question, it is necessary first to explain the role of objects in the production process, and how they were seen by brigade members. In the first instance, before building started, objects offered collective hope to those on the construction site. Their designs were prospects for new politics, new communal forms of housing, free and promoted education and new links to the world. The initiation of these prospects was represented by work camps for the first buildings. The politic was portrayed by the construction of the Federal Executive Council building—that was to lead the project of self-governance in coming decades. Hotel Yugoslavia received international visits during the establishment of the Non-Aligned Movement. The Student City was to host the flow of migration from the countryside striving to gain an education. Inspired by the CIAM, housing was envisioned as a public open block set amid greenery, built following the policy to ensure an apartment for every citizen (▶FIG. 5).

The buildings around which actions were organized formed part of the 1947 Five Year Plan for the Development of New Belgrade into a capital city with 250,000 inhabitants.[31] The plan was very general, and the work on designing buildings was undertaken by emerging planning institutions. The Urban Institute produced the very first drawing for the city as a part of documentation for a competition calling for a vision for the city and the design of public buildings. It was a large-scale contest, open to all citizens, and attracted significant public attention. Following public discussions, the winning entries were incorporated into the first sketch for the city in 1948.[32] Although the plan was substituted by a sequence of others, its relevance for participants in the action was that it offered an image to identify with when starting work. The visions volunteers had in mind once at the site were the winning competition entries and, most especially, a huge physical model of the new city (▶FIG. 6).

The image of the model circulated publicly due to the extensive promotion of the winning designs in press reports. Often the plan was combined with calls for actions that were seen as the way to start construction. On the front page of *Politika*, the leading daily newspaper, volunteers could read about the opening of the construction site.[33] *Arhitektura* journal offered details about the work and showed images of the model of the city alongside the basic tools needed to build it (▶FIG. 7).[34]

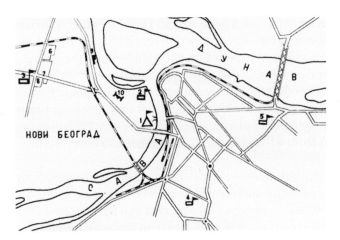

►5.1
Distribution of work stations around planned objects. From Ljubica Radojković, »Omladinske radne brigade na izgradnji Beograda 1947–1950«, *Godišnjak grada Beograda* V (1958): 379.

►5.2
Construction of temporary housing for volunteers. From *Beograd: grad akcijaša* (Belgrade: Publication from the conference organized by the Socialist Youth Society, 1985).

►5.3 Left: Construction of the first housing districts in New Belgrade, known as Paviljoni Tošin bunar, by voluntary actions. From Slobodan V. Ristanović, *Novi Beograd, Graditeljski poduhvat veka* (Belgrade: IA KSE-NA, 2009) 314. Right: View of the entrance hall once the housing was built. From »Život u Paviljonima nekada«, Stare slike Novog Beograda Facebook page, March 9, 2014. URL: https://m. facebook.com/photo.php?fbid=10152240271025943&id=265072550942&set=a.265223695942&refid=13&__ tn__=%2B%3D (last accessed: 29 November 2021).

▶5.4 Left: Construction of the Student City by voluntary actions in 1949. From Bratislav Stojanović »Novi Beograd«, *Beograd* no. 2 (November 1949): 9. Right: the completed Student City for 6000 students with international visitors. From *Novi Beograd 1961* (Belgrade: Direkcija za izgradnju Novog Beograda, 1961), 95.

▶5.5 Left: Construction of Hotel Yugoslavia by voluntary actions © Historical Archives of Belgrade, https://www.arhiv-beograda.org/index.php/sr/izlozba-ora. Right: Photograph of the Hotel Yugoslavia. From »Hotel Yugoslavija Hosted some of the most important people of the world«, Research project *Totally Lost*, 2013, URL: https://www.totallylost.eu/space/hotel-jugoslavija/ (last accessed: 10 August 2022).

▶5.6 Left: Construction of the area around the Federal Executive Council building (Savezno izvršno veće SIV) © Belgrade City Museum. Right: The recently opened building in May 1958 © Museum of Yugoslavia.

▶5.7 Left: Construction on the Danube embankment by voluntary actions, ca. 1948 © Historical Archives of Belgrade, Nemanja Budisavljević personal fonds. Right: The Danube embankment once completed. From Bratislav Stojanović, Uroš Martinović, *Beograd 1945–1975. Urbanizam arhitektura* (Belgrade: Tehnička knjiga, 1978), 51.

By supplementing the plan, the action took on the role of a different reality, responsible for bringing the fiction down to earth. This was a highly pragmatic undertaking, and what was happening at the site was different to what was on paper. The few existing construction enterprises were struggling to handle the work, and the overall coordination of the plan, the volunteers and the companies was led by a sector of the youth society (Council of the People's Youth of Yugoslavia).[35] The volunteers' interest in the buildings was fuelled by the desire to be part not of their design but of the activity needed to build them. In this sense, objectification held true in that the buildings could be seen as »crystalized forms of man's activity« rather than »external to and indifferent to the nature of the producer«.[36] The objects' relevance was in their role as mediators to form the group, and they ultimately facilitated the creation of social praxis.

Alongside the development of actions, and not without direct connection, the role of objects as social mediators was promoted in the *Praxis* circle, above all by Rudi Supek and Henri Lefebvre. Supek was a Yugoslavian philosopher and the main organizer of the summer school. He lived and studied in Paris, and had led a turbulent political life in the resistance movement in France and Germany. He was awarded the *Légion d'honneur* for his efforts to liberate prisoners, including himself, from Buchenwald concentration camp. Prior to organizing the summer school of philosophy, Supek spent years studying the construction of the highway between Belgrade and Zagreb, known as the Road of Brotherhood and Unity, built by voluntary work. The action of building the highway accompanied and succeeded the one to build New Belgrade, since part of the highway went through the city centre. Based on his time among the brigades, Supek eventually published a book about the psychology of the work action, based on diaries he wrote there and articles he published later. In the book, he explained the actions as a process of constructing the material image of a society whose ideal is lived out by the protagonists of the action.[37] This meant that, ideally, the volunteer was both builder and governor. According to Supek, this was possible due to the way the work was done. Making a distinction between work in an action as part of collective effort, and work in a factory, he writes:

> »Factory work is part of a complex production process that has a deep division. It serves a purpose that lives outside the factory according to the purpose

▶7
Front cover of *Arhitektura*. From *Arhitektura* no. 8–10 (1948).

of the final product. The work is divided, too, as the different phases are loosely connected for the individual worker who is unable to have the overall control that ultimately enables connection with work. The work has its set rhythm, often related to the rhythm of the machine (…). Conversely, work in which the individual sets the goal in limited space and time so that they are always conscious of it, where the tools of work are related with the way the person engages, where individual tempo marks the collective, and the collective is an expression of the individual's intimate connection with others, is work that grows like a work of art and has the characteristics of achievement. An aim such as the construction of socialism is general and abstract. Motives may be very personal (…). The process of work during the action therefore needs to relate us to its goal. The most personal motives ultimately merge into a symphony of collective effort and, only then, does the action become a life-learning experience. It reveals to individuals features of their sociability and many sides of their personalities. The fact that we are approaching an automated and professionally divided civilisation is an even clearer indication that this kind of work will become a way to enrich human existence. This goal is the ultimate purpose of the work action, not as a social and historical task, but as an individual's personal need for integrity. Society is called upon to provide only general frameworks for interpersonal relationships, and the broader and more democratic these frameworks are, the greater are the chances for each generation to introduce relationships that suit its needs and perceptions. The highway is, then, the chance for each coming generation to show how it intends to shape its social relations.«[38]

At around the time of publication of Supek's book of insights into the actions, he invited Lefebvre to the Summer School of Philosophy in 1964. The theme was Meaning and Perspectives of Socialism and, alongside Lefebvre, Parsons, Marcuse, Goldmann and Cerroni, to name just a few, discussed socialist practices from different perspectives. During his stay in Yugoslavia, Lefebvre wrote an article in *France Observateur* entitled »Le socialisme en vacances«, describing the search for socialism during the summer vacation. In the article, he depicts the atmosphere at Korčula and the existing plurality of Marxian positions on praxis:

»The Summer School becomes more interesting and significant every year (…). The consumers believe in various paths to socialism and interpretations of

Marxism (...). This year the topic is the search for meanings of socialism (...). The atmosphere is different to the regular colloquium or seminar. Fifteen days did not appear too long. Just to touch on problems (...). The theme of alienation was widespread (...). Then we moved on to discussions of philosophy (...). One of the various tendencies was that the role of philosophy was to create the image of the human present in its development. Philosophy, with its projection of an individual, was taken as a criterion for social development. This means that there is a need for a critique of existing everyday practice, including the socialist one. This thesis was argued by Yugoslavian philosophers Rudi Supek and Gajo Petrović (...). Herbert Marcuse also described present-day problems in this respect. He referred to American society. The individual does not feel alienated. Contradictions are absorbed, and Marxism has lost its capacity to act in developed countries (...). Serge Mallet reacted to this by saying that these analyses are questionable even for the USA, and are not relevant for Europe and France, even in the worst scenario. According to Mallet, social surveys appear superficial and the working class with its attitude does not justify Marcuse's radical pessimism (...). From all the discussions, we can conclude that Marxism proves its variety and vitality, offering theoretical analyses of different practices.«[39]

Lefebvre's summary suggests there was a strong tendency to analyse and operatively engage with different positions in Yugoslavia. Philosophy was tasked with addressing active citizenship. Lefebvre's lecture contributed his well-known preoccupation with the idea of the anonymous citizen. It was titled »Sur quelques critères du développement social et du socialisme«[40] and explained how everyday life has changed throughout history, but has always been relevant as a source of praxis. In Lefebvre's view, this meant that the everyday had to be involved in politics and urbanism, focusing on the anonymous citizen as an actor. To this end, sociology must be seen as production in Marxism, regarding objects as mediators. This argument was explicitly extended in his major works *Métaphilosophie* (1965) and *Sociologie de Marx* (1966). Marxian praxis, Lefebvre continues, should be read as old Greek *pragmata*, which means affairs in general, *things* addressed or managed by human beings in their active relations, or matters deliberated by members of society.[41] Lefebvre pointed to this meaning of praxis as a form of his critique of the division of *praxis* and *poiesis*. He writes:

> »The Greek word ›praxis‹ was reintroduced by Marx to avoid the confusions of the current word ›practice‹. It did not avoid contamination. Today ›praxis‹ encompasses several different meanings. It can denote any social human activity (...). It can also be contrasted with pure theory and knowledge (...). Finally, it can denote specifically social activity, relationships between human beings, distinguished by legitimate abstraction from relations with nature and matter (such as technology and *poiesis*). It is the final meaning that we are seeking to discern and define.«[42]

In his following book, *Sociologie de Marx* (1966), Lefebvre further stands against the detachment of praxis—seen as a solely managerial activity dealing with human relationships (politician, orator, trader)—from *poiesis* seen as the productive labour of man in modifying nature (agriculture, crafts and, later, industry). In the course of this vast process, Lefebvre writes, work comes into conflict with itself and gives rise

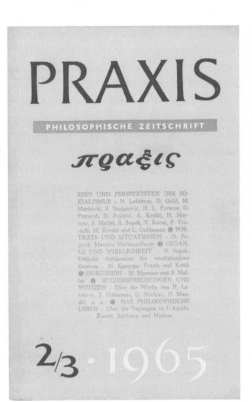

▶8   From left to right: *Praxis* no. 2/3, »Sinn und Perspektiven des Sozialismus« (1965) with Lefebvre's article
»Sur quelques critères du développement social et du socialisme« © Korčula City Library Ivan Vidali.
Praxis no. 3 »Aktuelnost Marksove misli« (1967) (International edition: *Die Aktualität der Gedanken von
Karl Marx*) included Supek's review of Lefebvre's book *Sociologie de Marx* © Korčula City Library Ivan
Vidali. Front cover of Rudi Supek's book about work actions, *Psihologija radne akcije. Omladina na
putu bratstva* (Beograd: Mladost, 1963). Covers of Lefebvre's books *Métaphilosophie* (Paris: Éditions de
Minuit, 1965) and *Sociologie de Marx* (Paris: Presses Universitaires de France, 1966).

to a specific form assumed by the product seen as a commodity. The divided work, which is necessary only when production is seen solely as a commodity, sharpens the division between city and countryside, and the division between the occupations of those who labour and others who think. Instead, praxis should subsume *poiesis*, as an »act, dialectical relation between man and nature, consciousness and things which can never be legitimately separated«.[43] The study of praxis, including *poiesis*, leads to a sociology of forms—that is, as a specific domain of Marxist sociology.[44]

A review of Lefebvre's book *The Sociology of Marx* was published soon afterwards in an issue of *Praxis* in 1967, as »Die Aktualität der Gedanken von Karl Marx«—the relevance of the thinking of Karl Marx. The review was written by Supek, who, as the sociologist of work actions and advocate of operative philosophy, stressed precisely how building practices (*poiesis*) could adopt praxis.[45] Marxist sociology, arguing that objects are material for social interaction, was part of the same reality of mediation by building that inspired Supek while writing his diary of work actions (▸FIG. 8). Moreover, it could be argued that Supek, influenced by his experience at actions, found in Lefebvre's philosophy an adequate argument to further promote links between collective production and praxis theory. And that, in this way, surrounding endeavours in construction contributed emerging theory in Yugoslavia.

From the reverse direction, looking at construction through the lens of Marxian sociology, the value of the actions lay in relating architecture to collective building by citizenship. They showed how architecture can share its domain. The combination of drafting a plan and distributing roles to volunteers was the innovative aspect of construction sites like the one in New Belgrade. Here, architecture was open to praxis: in mediating the different roles of participants through building. And the labour—though not the easiest—was related to mediation.

The Aesthetics of Group Production

The role of objects as mediators between participants became known in Marxian theory as social praxis. As these theories developed, social praxis became further related with the character of the group of producers, its internal regulations, constitution, negotiations and ties. What form did this take on a construction site organized by voluntary actions?

This question calls for an explanation of the way daily life was organized. Once at the site, participants would live in one of housing camps. Their temporary home was the brigade, which had its own centre (*štab brigade*) to organize its activity on site. Members of this centre could be volunteers recruited to the action or members of the People's Youth of Yugoslavia. Prior to organizing the brigade, they were taught the basics of architecture and construction, as well as rules about general behaviour. The average day was quite structured and divided into two parts. In the first or second half of the day, volunteers spent six to seven hours working in a specific location

on the construction site. The brigade would split into groups of between three and ten members, usually made up of craftsmen, young volunteers and someone from a construction company. Sometimes the work was divided according to the material: concrete, steel or brick, or transport. Building was risky and relied on improvisation in solving problems on site, which was probably the consequence of a general lack of experience. Since unspecialized work was combined with the testing process that followed, the work of the brigade members was paradoxically in line with Marx's ideal of avoiding a single occupation and viewed work as a voluntary activity carried out according to will, needs, abilities and talents.[46] What differed is that the participants would scarcely recognize themselves in Marx's initial image of artisan communism, picturing a utopic image of the process of production. It diverged from Marx's comparison of production to creation by the artist who, in work, »externalizes his own essential powers and appropriates the product once again in rapt contemplation«.[47]

The aesthetic of production was rooted not so much in contemplating built objects as in the possibility of taking part in a kind of mission to achieve an agreed goal. This was explicit in the way brigade members worked according to the short-term plans they undertook as daily tasks. They were discussed and assigned during evening gatherings, and known as norms. Alongside the short-term task related to a smaller group, a long-term norm was also undertaken by the whole brigade. Brigades would challenge each other, and participants were proud if they received a medallion for their efforts in the action that they could show off when they returned home.[48] This added a competitive stimulus to speed up production of the city that took the form of social recognition. The important thing was to complete the work, and the artistic values of objects, for the volunteers at least, took a secondary role.

However, the most outstanding quality of the aesthetics of production during the actions was the condition of commune. It was a reality where participants lived and worked together for a limited period, taking time out from their everyday lives. During this break, they would at once challenge their habits and the construction process (▶FIG. 9). For this sense of commune, the other part of the day was crucial. It was spent in a combination of learning, exposure to culture and socialization of members.[49] The programme was outlined by the headquarters (*glavni štab*), the organizational body for the whole action. As opposed to the brigade, which dealt with a specific building task, headquarters managed the process at a larger scale in connection with the companies responsible for constructing the buildings.[50] Apart from communicating with firms, its main goal was to implement the educational process of the brigades. This was illustrated in the statement that »the main success of the youth work action was the education of the individual«.[51] The education on offer was adapted to the different backgrounds of the brigade members, with the emphasis on literacy, which was still an issue in Yugoslavia. The participants could also take courses to gain credits in working with wood, concrete and brick, or other branches of the economy, with the possibility of being offered employment after the action. Finally, significant attention was devoted to familiarization with technology.[52]

Admiration for technology went hand-in-hand with society's call for emancipation. In this respect, Marx's was interpreted with preference towards technologically-oriented society rather than one of artisan communism. In *Praxis* issue »Un moment du socialisme Yougoslave«, Rudi Supek argued that for small states like Yugoslavia, the only healthy alternative for development compared to the semi-colonial dependence of big international capital was to find opportunities for technologically advanced industries by overcoming the boundaries of the national economy. In addition, this technology needed to fit to the concept of self-management. Supek saw the virtue of the Yugoslavian experiment in its anticipation that it was possible to merge the theory of self-management developed specially by Proudhon with the Marxian conception of socialism, bearing in mind that the two are usually considered unconnected.[53] In this trial, some well-known Marxist principles were intended to serve as the basis: the abolition of the technological division of labour towards a work community of manual labour, management and the production process.[54] German philosopher Jürgen Habermas in other *Praxis* issue argued that solutions for bringing praxis back to the loupe under the threat of rise of technocracy, needs to be found within industrialised society and not beyond.[55] His latter argument is useful in explaining how two different Marxian interpretations for the groups of producers might look. He wrote that Marx

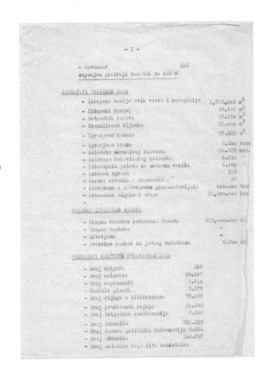

▶10.1 Typescript of the report »Savezna akcija Novi Beograd 1948« (Federal action New Belgrade, 1948), Fonds: SOJ 114-1, 1948–1955, Folder 152, Archives of Yugoslavia, Belgrade, 2,3.

▶10.2
Brigade members attending the literacy class on the New Belgrade construction site. From Slobodan V. Ristanović, *Novi Beograd, Graditeljski poduhvat veka* (Belgrade: IA KSE-NA, 2009), 294.

Federal Action New Belgrade 1948

Results of physical work

Excavated earth	1,723,906 m³
Walls built	69,535 m²
Concrete produced	36,140 m²
Granulated gravel	31,000 m²
Stone building	37,625 m²
Plaster	2500 t
Tack laid	24,329 m
Masonry buildings	128
Timber buildings	99
Material loaded and unloaded	400,000 t

Results in educational work

Number of brigades	318	
Number of youths	49,807	
Number of illiterate participants	3610	
Number who learned to write	3329	
Number of books in libraries	78496	
Number of books read	55,933	
Number of youths reading newspapers independently		26,925
Number of lectures given	984	
Number of stage performances by brigade members		455
Number of performances given	395	
Number of films seen	1446	
Number of festivals held	2	
Number of camp fires	686	
Number of choir rehearsals	3830	
Number of dance rehearsals	2087	
Number of literary circles	421	
Number of fine arts circles	266	
Number of posters made	2917	

...

Results in physical education

Hours of gymnastics	13,114
Volleyball matches	6624
Basketball matches	1822
Football matches	3121
Wrestling matches	27,541
Boxing matches	13085
Chess games	34,186

»eventually gave up his orientation to the prototype of craftsman-like praxis taken from the past« for another one of a post-industrial, technological society.[56] The group in which producers can take part is, then, not solely one of sentimental socialism. On the contrary, praxis emerges as a possibility of production in the current social order with all these particular everyday aspects. It may be more alienated or more dis-alienated, depending on the particular narrative of the two alternatives. However, this appears to be a question not of tools but of the quality of the encounter.[57] In this light, modernization—to which the actions aspired—can be seen as a participatory process, despite the goal of industrial production. It could be said that this ambiguity in reading Marx's preferences between craft and technology[58] serves actually beneficial when related to the case of the actions. For those involved, creativity appeared around very industrially-driven goals, just as elsewhere it could around pastoral sentimentalism. The collective production was ultimately dependent not on the means of production, but on the constitution of the group.

Habermas further explains that Marx deliberately does not define the principle of labour too narrowly, because he wants to position praxis within the rational concept of anonymous citizen. This means that participation should be a broadly accessible experience to include a variety of participants. This argument is applicable in the case of voluntary building in terms that all efforts and levels of proficiency were welcomed. What might be further questioned is whether citizen participation in labour was based on a self-reflective process. Habermas argues that the assimilation of labour into a model with a normative character—meaning a model that accommodates creativity and a sense of purpose for the participant—is what distinguishes between »satisfied praxis that returns to itself and a praxis that is impeded and fragmented«.[59] Whether the group in question is successful depends on the freedom of its internal constitution and its reconciliation with the socially institutionalized context of life. The existence of a social bond that is »the community-forming and solidarity-building force of *unalienated cooperation and living together* (...) ultimately decides whether reason embodied in social practice is in touch with history and nature«.[60] Seen from the viewpoint of volunteers, Habermas's point raises the question of how free the action was. Solidarity or ideology?

There was, certainly, a place for ideology in the history of the actions. Daily events were extensively based on the promotion of cooperation. Lectures on cooperative modes of production were regularly given, political education was high on the list of priorities, and the international press circulated, accompanied by international visits. Ritual and socialization were inseparable parts of the promotion of collective values. Participants could watch plays, films or dance performances, sing in a choir, gather around evening fires or explore the city. A basic library, a student cultural centre and sports facilities were built by volunteers. These aimed to create a communal experience of culture intertwined with life and work into a package that stood out from everyday routine.[61] Sound stations and daily bulletins answered everyday questions.[62] The programme they announced aimed to merge the physical, political and cultural education of individuals in order to include them in the economy.[63] Extensive lists were announced of how many books were read, the length of walls built, the number of plays seen, how many football matches

▶11
French brigade on the construction of Student town in Zagreb, 1950, HPM-79981/56
© Croatian History Museum, Zagreb.

were played and how many people were taught to write (▶FIG. 10). All served as proof of success.

In addition to the active promotion of cooperative values and the assurance that Yugoslavia was on the right path to socialism, the actions prompted a broad, fairly authentic reaction from citizens that went beyond ideology. American activist and UNESCO member Arthur Gillette wrote about this in his book *One Million Volunteers* (1968), which follows the story of volunteer youth service worldwide:

»Among the most outstanding feats of volunteers in the Eastern countries were those of Yugoslav young people and the international teams that joined them in the late 1940s and early 1950s. [...] It can be pointed out that one of the most vivid memories sticking in the minds of observed or participated in work drives is the enthusiasm of the local young people. And enthusiasm is as difficult to simulate as apathy is to hide.«[64]

Constitutionally, the brigade was envisioned as a democratic unit, coinciding with the introduction of self-management in industry. The form of governance was based on brigade conferences and involving up to half of any given brigade in elective positions of authority.[65] The fact that the action was a reality of its own with level of autonomy was also visible in the mix of participants, and the frictions and alignments between them (▶FIG. 11).

As well as peasants and local students, participants were volunteers from France, Canada, Norway, Great Britain, Denmark and elsewhere. Visits were due to the strong organizational efforts of youth society to internationalize the actions. Initially, this was in publications such as *Novo pokoljenje* (New generation). The journal organized an exchange by publishing issues for abroad and gathering international articles for local public distribution.[66] Additionally, the Yugoslav bulletin *Omladina u svetu* (Youth in the world) started to be distributed regularly by all kinds of local social organiza-

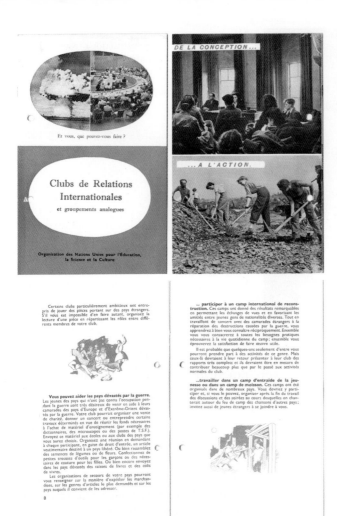

▶12
United Nations booklet *Clubs de Relations Internationales et groupements analogues* (UNESCO Publications, 1949) on the promotion of work actions via UN clubs © Archives of Yugoslavia, Belgrade.

tions and publishers connected with the youth movement.[67] Contact was made with foreign youth organizations via the World Federation of Democratic Youth (WFDY) that was created in London in 1945, as a means to spread participation in international projects. The actions were an important link in this connection.[68] International participants responded to an open call issued under the slogan of »turning consumers into makers«.[69] The application form included a point explaining that the group's organization would be led by its elected committee.

Photographs and posters from the New Belgrade construction site followed calls to international volunteers. Meanwhile, in 1949 Yugoslavia had joined the United Nations, which seemed to promote a similar agenda. A UN Information Centre opened in Belgrade, UN radio was introduced[70] and Yugoslavia participated in various UN conferences that tried to reduce Cold War tensions.[71] UN brochures were distributed in Yugoslavia's schools with the slogan »To Combine Our Efforts«,[72] and UN clubs were opened. All of this promoted interconnection. Taking part in reconstruction or

travelling to the student camp were among the aims of the UN clubs that started to appear internationally and in Yugoslavia as of 1954.[73] Architecture was used in promotional sketches in order to connect international brigades aiming to experiment, travel and engage (▶FIG. 12).[74]

This international activity in the early post-war years empowered the local youth movement that was struggling with the loss of political power from the East. Moreover, the bonds created served to assure participants from abroad that the place was safe and worth visiting. Having international brigades on the sites was beneficial as a proof for both those within and outside the country of belief in this rather unusual social experiment in production. International youth ended up in the local press talking about months in Yugoslavia packed with experiences quite unrelated to the noise of the Cold War. Although they mainly worked on building the Road of Brotherhood and Unity and the railway, they also visited the New Belgrade site.[75] Their engagement with local volunteers was far from homogenous. Sometimes it was a source of inspiration, as in the case of the well-known British historian, sociologist and Marxist Edward Palmer Thompson who published the book *The Railway: An Adventure in Construction* about his own and the British brigade's experience of building the Šamac-Sarajevo railway in Yugoslavia in 1947 (▶FIG. 13). Later, in 1973, in an open letter to Polish philosopher Leszek Kołakowski, coloured with a dispute they had, Thompson briefly recalled this experience in Yugoslavia as fitting Marx's idea of the collective.

»Marx [...] appears to propose [...] men who within the context of certain institutions and culture can conceptualize in terms of ›our‹ rather than ›my‹ or ›their‹. I was a participating witness, in 1947, in the euphoric aftermath of a revolutionary transition, of exactly such a transformation in attitudes. Young Yugoslav peasants, students, and workers, constructing with high morale their own railway, undoubtedly had this new affirmative concept of *nasha* (our), although this *nasha*—as may have proved fortunate for Yugoslavia—was in part the *nasha* of socialist consciousness, and in part the *nasha* of the nation. The fact that this moment of euphoria proved to be evanescent—and that both the Soviet Union and ›the West‹ did what they could to reverse the impulse—does not disallow the validity of the experience.«[76]

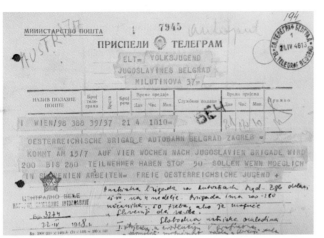

▶14 Telegrams reporting the arrival of foreign brigades at construction sites in Yugoslavia, 22 April 1948, 8 April 1948 © Archives of Yugoslavia, Belgrade.

In similarly affirmative mode, members of the Austrian brigade sent greetings when they published an account of their experience in Yugoslavia.[77] On the other hand, the work of international brigades on construction sites in Yugoslavia was also ›a collision of different worlds‹. This was the case of the Danish brigade, where socialism signalled sexual freedom, pop culture and daily contingency distant to the mainly conservative behaviour of the local rural youth.[78] Whether collision or alignment, international presence, traceable in frequent postal correspondence, furthered this experimental approach to construction that marked the borderline of the Cold War (▶FIG. 14).

The main argument for viewing the actions as free experimentation was the solidarity of the many participants who were willing to return. Oral testimonies present the actions as a favourite phenomenon. Slobodan Ž. Marković, who was part of the New Belgrade action, wrote how he participated construction as one of philosophy students:

»We worked on the construction of the government presidency building and the Hotel Yugoslavia. We were assigned to help construction workers on concrete reinforcement. There were two types of systems: *avramenko* and the so-called P system. We soon started to produce construction elements by ourselves. The

▶15
Members of the brigade from
the Faculty of Philosophy in
Belgrade, who worked on the
New Belgrade construction site.
From Slobodan V. Ristanović, *Novi
Beograd, Graditeljski poduhvat veka*
(Belgrade: IA KSE-NA, 2009), 379.

engineer in charge of the process was Branko Žeželj, who, for the first time, was testing the new method of prefabrication. We returned to the New Belgrade construction site after the summer. This time to help build the Student City. We worked on the interior walls and painting the inside (…). When our first winter came, we made fires in tin barrels at night to dry the walls. We also used these fires to have barbecues that we all remembered for decades.« (▶FIG. 15).[79] When the first push to set up production was over and technology began to take off, the actions stopped being economically feasible and even started to cost money and time compared to conventional construction. This was when they were to get abolished by the state. However, due to high demand from young people, they continued as self-organized actions, building more slowly and with less ambitious goals.[80] This moment further illustrates the autonomy actions had in generating bottom-up realities. In this respect, the New Belgrade construction site was one of the first where participants offered labour for the sake of collective production. What did they ask for in return? Although there was the possibility of education and the chance of new prospects, this was above all a social exchange. Viewing youth action from today's distant vantage point means learning about the gratification of individuals, symbolic exchange and the necessity of keeping the building process accessible to people who were unskilled.

Conclusion

Offered argument aimed to relate the emergence of praxis theory to the construction methods employed in building Yugoslav cities, roads and railways by peasants, students and international brigades. It traced to what extent readings that emerged in and around the *Praxis* circle in Yugoslavia were mimetic to collective building by work action. Did the flourishment of praxis theory come as a consequence of the enthusiastic building of New Belgrade and associated sites? Or the building was a testing site for intellectual and theoretical debate publicly perceived as a guideline? Stating either option would be possible to prove but reinforced. Rather, it was an exchange between theory and practice, which enabled moments in which the first was instructive to the latter, and the other way around. To name just one among many possible interlinks, it can be said that Supek's years at construction sites certainly contributed to his theory and selection of philosophers he performed as editor of *Praxis* journal and organizer of the summer school. On another side, Petrović's high school class book *Logika* (Logics) on which generations were educated influenced adolescents joining work actions during their forty-year span. In this sense, it could be pointed to the mutual highlight of construction and philosophy. This was, after all, the main preoccupation of extensive re-readings of Marx in Yugoslavia: how to make the theory operative while acknowledging the inevitable tension between philosophy and praxis.

Experimental construction methods succeeded in a double task: to revisit Marxian theories and to initiate building in a twice-ostracized and technologically poor set-up. This was not possible solely due to the establishment of camps, but also due to the proximity of the *Praxis* journal at the end, where theorizations of praxis by local and sympathetic Western theorists circulated and found an audience. Next to being valuable to Marxist theory, building campaigns were anti-Stalinist directed and indicative of the highs and lows of Yugoslavian socialist trials. Parallel with the theory of praxis collective construction techniques advanced assertions of Yugoslav independence from Soviet power. With slogans of turning consumers into the makers, actions were also relevant in pointing to Marxian production as one that is based on share and exchange at the moment when philosophers addressed the global step-in to the massive age of consumption. Finally, they offered an original scenario for building with oral histories filled with appraisals of communal living and working. In this process, objects served as mediators, which could be regarded as one of the best outcomes of the actions: the possibility of establishing social bonds through construction and voluntary building as part of architectural production. In addition, it is quite obvious that much more could be done to further connections between the processes of design and construction. Finally, it was generally beneficial to appropriate a public prospect for local and international engagement in the construction of the city, despite the existing excess of rhetorics in the official state propaganda. In this sense, work actions proved capable of serving as both an inspiration and a reflection of the philosophy of that moment.

Praxis and Imagination: Towards Participation in Prefabrication

»Imagination is the power to make appear representations [...] whether with or without an external incitement. In other words: imagination is the power to make be that which realiter is not.«[1]

The aim of the first chapter was to show how youth work actions were important for bringing collective production into construction. They relied on unspecialized work, volunteerism and testing processes. Building by actions was questioned by theoretical readings of Marx as part of a lively debate in the country's philosophical *Zeitgeist*. These readings offered guidelines as to how the link between producer, objects and groups of producers worked as praxis. In the comparison between philosophy and building, praxis was seen as creative, reflective and purposeful human action in regard to material culture. Praxis in Marx was based on labour with broad, egalitarian involvement in terms of active citizenship.[2] Criticizing and developing his thinking, Marxian philosophers shifted praxis from one based on human labour towards praxis that is generated by language. The shift was present in Yugoslavia, too, where new voices of the philosophy of praxis were beginning to be influential. Among the first to talk about praxis and imagination as a form of social language were Ernst Bloch and Cornelius Castoriadis. Though very different to each other, their voices overlapped with the philosophical discourse in Yugoslavia. To shed some light on historical connections and the flow of ideas, it might be useful briefly to describe in what way the development of philosophy in the country resonated with their work.

New Voices in the Philosophy of Praxis

Cornelius Castoriadis crossed paths with the Yugoslav case on several occasions. As early as 1951, he published an article on what he called Yugoslavian bureaucracy in the leftist review *Socialisme ou Barbarie (SouB)*. In addition to a critical view of the early post-war constitution of the country, which had not yet fully transformed to self-governance, the article highlighted the rising role of technology. According to Castoriadis, this was due to the country's particular geopolitical position in the middle of the Cold War conflict. In an attempt to escape dependence on the Eastern bloc, the country shifted its means of production from predominantly agrarian to the development of its own technology. The rise of industry was seen as the way to achieve autonomy, in which Castoriadis recognized the moment of authentic force that existed in the country. This was explicit in citizens' willingness to get involved in the formation of new industries, which was a reality present in the work action movement, among others.[3]

Not long after, in the mid-fifties and in the same journal, Castoriadis's writings argued the idea of workers' councils as a democratic way of constituting society.

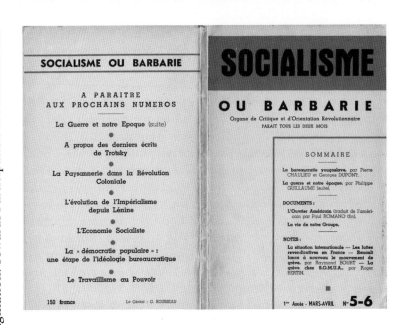

▶1   Cornelius Castoriadis on Yugoslavia in *Socialisme ou Barbarie* no. 5–6 (March April 1950)
© URL: https://soubscan.org/ (last accessed: 2 September 2021).

Among other things, he wrote that the proletariat's objections could no longer centre solely on the demand for nationalization of means of production and planning, and should extend to worker management of the economy. To organize the collective, socialized governance of production, Castoriadis championed »the masses' conscious and perpetual self-managerial activity« that »cannot be ›objectively‹ inscribed [...] in constitution, nationalization of the means of production, planning, nor even in a law instaurating workers' management«. Conversely, production appears to be possible by means of »the unleashing of the free creative activity of the oppressed masses«[4] by historical development. Here, Castoriadis pointed to the work union based on creativity as a model for social production—the theme that was to mark the development of his theory. At that time, the creation of workers' councils was actually happening in Yugoslavia thanks to the law of self-governance of society. There were many points on which Castoriadis was critical of the further development of the Yugoslav attempt, and these were connected with an excess of rhetoric and rigidity in the governing system.[5] However, points of agreement existed alongside these—mostly in the philosophical debates of the country, where Castoriadis's theory was present. His books were published and translated by the philosophical journal *Theoria*, and he came into contact with the Yugoslavian *Praxis* circle of philosophy, though actively when it had dissolved and reformed.[6] An opinion that Castoriadis and philosophical debate in the country did have in common was the importance of creativity for social production. By way of example, the 1967 Summer School of Philosophy was devoted to the theme of creativity and reification with its title *Schöpfertum und Verdinglichung* (*Créativité et réification*, ▶FIG. 2).

OPĆA TEMA

STVARALAŠTVO I POSTVARENJE
(Créativité et réification)

Plenarna predavanja na gornju temu održat će slijedeći predavači:

E. V. ILJENKOV, Moskva, Filozofski Institut AN SSSR-a
JÜRGEN HABERMAS, Frankfurt, J. W. Goethe-Universität
LESZEK KOLAKOWSKI, Varšava, Filozofski Institut AN Poljske

LELJO BASSO, Rim, urednik »Revue International du Socialisme«

ERNEST MANDEL, Bruxelles, Ekonomski fakultet
KAREL KOSIK, Prag, Filozofski Institut AN Čehoslovačke
DANKO GRLIĆ, Zagreb, urednik »Jugoslavenske Enciklopedije«

MILAN KANGRGA, Zagreb, docent Filozofskog fakulteta
VELJKO KORAĆ, Beograd, profesor Filozofskog fakulteta
GAJO PETROVIĆ, Zagreb, profesor Filozofskog fakulteta
LJUBOMIR TADIĆ, Beograd, profesor Filozofskog fakulteta
PREDRAG VRANICKI, Zagreb, profesor Filozofskog fakulteta

Sva plenarna predavanja bit će popraćena diskusijom. Predavanja na stranim jezicima bit će ukratko rezimirana na srpsko-hrvatskom jeziku.

SIMPOZIJI

1.

SLOBODA I PLANIRANJE
(Liberté et planification)

Predsjedavajući i uvodna riječ: D. PEJOVIĆ (Zagreb)
Učesnici: B. BOŠNJAK (Zagreb), M. FILIPOVIĆ (Sarajevo), G. FISCHER (New York), B. HORVAT (Beograd), H. D. KLEIN (Beč), V. MILIĆ (Beograd), V. STIPETIĆ (Zagreb), A. VIDICH (New York), G. WETTER (Rim)

2.

BIROKRACIJA, TEHNOKRACIJA I LIČNE SLOBODE
(Bureaucratie, technocratie et libertés individuelles)

Predsjedavajući i uvodna riječ: M. MARKOVIĆ (Beograd)
Učesnici: N. BELU (Bukurešt), R. COHEN (Boston), L. GOLDMANN (Pariz), D. C. HODGES (Tallahassee, Florida), B. IBRAHIMPAŠIĆ (Sarajevo), I. KUVAČIĆ (Zagreb), H. MARCUSE (New York), Z. PEŠIĆ-GOLUBOVIĆ (Beograd), F. RAPP (Fribourg), G. SEMERARI (Bari), V. SUTLIĆ (Zagreb), A. TANOVIĆ (Sarajevo)

3.

SAMOUPRAVLJANJE I RADNIČKI POKRETI
(Mouvements ouvriers et l'autogestion)

Predsjedavajući i uvodna riječ: R. SUPEK (Zagreb)
Učesnici: I. BABIĆ (Zagreb), L. BASSO (Rim), V. CVJETIČANIN (Zagreb), D. C. HODGES (Tallahassee), K. KOSING (Berlin, DDR), A. KÜNZLI (Basel), S. MALLET (Pariz), V. RUS (Ljubljana)

4.

KULTURNO STVARANJE I DRUŠTVENA ORGANIZACIJA
(Création culturelle et organisation sociale)

Predsjedavajući i uvodna riječ: M. ČALDAROVIĆ (Zagreb)
Učesnici: A. DIEMER (Düsseldorf), M. EAMES (Carbondale, Illinois), O. FLECHTHEIM (Berlin, BRD), V. FILIPOVIĆ (Zagreb), C. I. GULLIAN (Bukurešt), T. KERMAUNER (Ljubljana), W. A. LEVI (St. Louis), V. Ž. KELLE (Moskva), A. HELLER (Budapest), K. PIRJEVEC (Ljubljana), J. STRINKA (Bratislava), Z. TORDAI (Budapest), I. VARGA (Budapest)

Predviđa se mogućnost da neki učesnici učestvuju u drugom simpoziju od onoga u kome su sada navedeni.

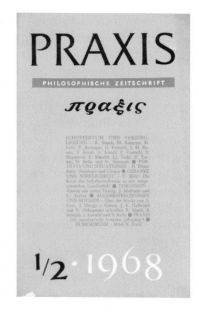

▶2　Short program for the 1967 Summer School of Philosophy on the subject of creativity and reification (*Créativité et réification*) and front cover of *Praxis* no. 1/2 (1968) with a review from the school © Korčula City Library Ivan Vidali.

Most of the speakers were from the Marxist milieu in Paris, like Castoriadis. One was Kostas Axelos, who was on the same ship on which Castoriadis left civil war in Greece for Paris in 1945, following the defeat of the communist wing. Axelos was part of the *Praxis* circle in Yugoslavia and a central figure in the publication of Marxist literature in France. As editor of the Parisian journal *Arguments* and a series of books of the same title about critical positions in Marxism, Axelos facilitated an exchange between this literature and *Praxis*. His own work was also built around the topic of imagination, introducing the concept of play as an ideal in an unalienated society (*Le Jeu du monde*, 1969, Arguments series). Along with Axelos, other lecturers at the 1967 school included André Gorz and Serge Mallet, the latter of whom also published in *Arguments* and *Les Temps modernes*. Mallet was known for his study of the sociology of work and the new working class, most explicitly in his book *La nouvelle classe ouvrière* (1963, Éditions du Seuil), with arguments that were taken up by *Praxis* journal. The French surrealist writer Pierre Naville, in search of a relation between surrealism and Marxism; the Trotskyist and Marxian economist Ernest Mandel, and Eugen Finke, the German philosopher on the imaginative potential of play (*Le Jeu comme symbole du monde*, 1960 Arguments, Les Éditiones de Minuit), all lectured and published in *Praxis* on different aspects of creativity. Contributors to *Arguments* and *Socialisme ou Barbarie*[7] who visited the summer school thereby furthered the relation between praxis and creativity, and the exchange with Castoriadis's work.

　　The intellectual link, then, existed before Castoriadis was eventually invited to lecture in Yugoslavia on creativity and the human world, and theories of modernity. His lectures were part of annual philosophical gatherings held at the international university centre in Dubrovnik set up by philosophers following the dissolution of the Summer School of Philosophy and *Praxis* journal.[8] The centre was known as the Inter-University Postgraduate Centre and was founded by member universities and international academic institutions. On the initiative of Gajo Petrović, a leading member of the *Praxis* circle in Yugoslavia, the course Philosophy and Social Science was set up. Petrović asked the German philosopher Jürgen Habermas to co-direct the course,[9] and Dubrovnik was where Castoriadis met Habermas, who, in his *Excursus on Cornelius Castoriadis*, wrote: »His [Castoriadis's] work has a central place among the new departures in praxis philosophy that have been evolving since the mid-1960s [...] in Prague, Budapest, Zagreb, and Belgrade, and that for a decade enlivened the discussions at the Summer School of Korčula.« Calling the school »the most original, ambitious and reflective attempt to think through liberating mediation of history, society, external and internal nature once again as praxis«,[10] Habermas pointed to the relevance of the philosophy of praxis and Castoriadis's work for the social discourse in Yugoslavia.

This relevance was probably most explicit in Castoriadis' reading of praxis as creative and emancipatory politics in historical moments when movements in society create new institutions by breaking with old ones. The movement in society was very much present in post-war Yugoslavia and was followed by the search for a new interpretation of the world. The new economy was followed by a material shift in cities, housing and work. Castoriadis wrote about the act of new material interpretation as a »world-disclosing meaning« and related it to the subject's capacity to imagine.[11] The argument that the powers of imagination of individuals create institutions is Castoriadis's main theoretical concept for comparison with the material production trial in Yugoslavia.

Ernst Bloch was another philosopher who was even more relevant for the development of praxis thought in Yugoslavia. Bloch himself was less critical and rather positive about the country's political trials, and one of its best-loved philosophers. His book *Subjekt-Objekt, Erläuterungen zu Hegel*[12] was published in Yugoslavia in 1959 and, alongside Marx's *Early Works* and György Lukács' *History and Class Consciousness*, was a fundamental influence in the shift towards the philosophy of praxis that inspired young teachers in the *Praxis* circle.[13] Bloch himself participated actively in the journal's philosophical circle and summer gatherings in Korčula. As a member of the editorial board, he wrote articles, gave lectures and led discussions at the summer schools. Bloch actively wrote in *Spiegel* when the philosophical movement in Yugoslavia was met with censorship. He maintained that socialism in Yugoslavia made the country distinctive in the world and that the political shift of the seventies was like shooting oneself in the foot.[14] Courses on Bloch's reading of praxis were later held at the Inter-University Centre in Dubrovnik. Almost all of Bloch's books, including *Das Prinzip Hoffnung*, were translated, making him one of the most-read philosophers (▶FIG. 3).

Although both Castoriadis and Bloch developed praxis as rooted in imagination, they did it in a rather distinctive way.[15] One thing they had in common was that their readings were based on the link between citizens' imagination and the surrounding materiality. For Castoriadis, the result of imagination was a new social formation within cities. Referring to the Greek *polis*, Castoriadis wrote that philosophy in the city

►3
Herbert Marcuse (right) with Ernst Bloch in Korčula, Dalmatia, 1968, summer seminar of *Praxis*. From George V. Ritzoulis, »Is there Human Nature and Humanism any more?« URL: http://aftercrisisblog. blogspot.com/p/blog-page_13.html (last accessed: 26 June 2021).

emerged twofold: with words and with community action to question institutional order. This philosophy of action raises the question of who establishes the *nomos* of the city, constituting the government and instituting community. The institution of community was the consequence of the particular imagination of a society that led to both material and social construction.[16] Bloch, on the other hand, saw imagination as closer to the surrounding material world. Imagination was a tool that led the process of forming and transforming materiality towards what Marx called »a dream of the thing«. As in poetry, Bloch writes, this process requires precise imagination to portray it.[17] In the imagination of the ideal (a supreme good), the role of utopia is to give the ideal a concrete materialization. Although ideals cannot be taught by the factual world, they must have a close relationship with what is yet to become factual. For Bloch, this takes place through anticipation, seeing ideals as models, aesthetic and anticipatory illuminations that indicate their possible realization.[18] Unlike Castoriadis, for whom imagination led to the institution of society and was primarily a social act, for Bloch it was bound up with utopia in terms of its material construction. Another characteristic they shared was that both Bloch and Castoriadis were dissidents and critical of dogmatic readings of Marx. They tried to break with this legacy by pointing out new possibilities in the interpretation of materiality.

Bearing in mind the light that the two philosophers shed on the concept of imagination and their proximity to philosophical discussions in Yugoslavia, their voices serve to describe how material production in the country was bound up with social imagination. Or, more precisely, how work action was followed by early building enterprises, and how the imagination that preceded further accompanied this process. First, however, it may help briefly to explain how building practice had developed since the time of the actions.

When actions started to shift towards a smaller scale, construction began to address creation of early industry, as Castoriadis pointed out in the Yugoslavian case. Industrial development was based on the legacy of the actions, as it continued to involve unspecialized work. In this way, early building enterprises were to achieve a two-fold dream. The first was to form a work cooperative, that all enterprises, including those devoted to construction, were to contribute to. The second was that

►4
Josip Bosnar, *Workers' Council* 1952
© Goran Malić Archive.

the city, rather than the countryside, would become the centre of social life with enterprises and housing that needed to be built. The first dream was based on the political experiment of establishing self-governed production. State property was thereby abolished and became the common property of enterprises envisioned as autonomous work cooperatives. The second, related to housing, relied on the hybrid of a social housing policy of »an apartment for everyone« and the means of modern architecture. For anonymous citizens, these two dreams reinforced their contribution to construction. What emerged was participation in prefabrication that transcended institutionalization as an architectural discourse. Explaining the processes of building and imagining these two dreams offers the answer to the main question of this chapter: How was prefabrication bound up with the collective imagination?

The Imagination of the Work Cooperative

Starting with the first dream of work cooperatives, what expectations did this prospect create for citizens? Expectations were different from those of the usual cooperative associations, formed freely by people with a common economic interest. The scenario was closer to Robert Owen's utopian socialism, where cooperative work also meant experiments in communal life and called for the participation of all. The closest to it was Marx's view on cooperatives, which, for him, made sense only if they were part of an explicit public contract.[19]

The implementation of cooperative work started in 1950 when the Yugoslav Assembly voted to hand over production to the workers' councils. According to the law, a citizen would be given the opportunity to manage enterprises directly or through a

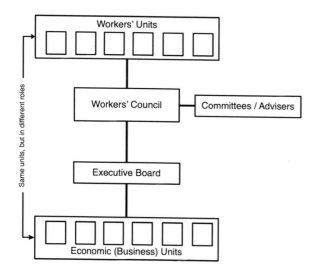

▶5

Self-governance scheme.
Reproduced from Branko Horvat,
The Political Economy of Socialism
(New York: M. E. Sharpe, Inc.,
Armonk, 1982), Yugoslavian edition
Politička ekonomija socijalizma,
(Zagreb: Globus, 1983), 203.

body of her choice. She would organize production and decide about the exchange of products. She would take part in decisions about assets, income, staffing and changes in work organization.[20] This promising law ushered in an era of lengthy attempts to organize production and strengthened the collective imagination needed to achieve it. The attempts varied in success, and the trial itself had its highs and lows. Far from signalling the overall success of the experiment, its value was most apparent in creating pop-up realities. These were enterprises that captured background echoes and furthered the internal organization of production.

And the background echoes were emancipatory. According to one of the country's most influential theoreticians, Edvard Kardelj, self-governance was not the invention of Yugoslav practice that some attribute to it as a merit and others as a sin. On the contrary, the idea of self-government is as old as the international proletariat, its class struggle and socialist practice. The scope of this practice was at different scales, with completely different forms, according to the specifics of the case. It is not possible to talk about a common base for self-governance.[21] Particularity was the first precondition, followed by an outline for the economy that was abstract enough to fit multiple scenarios. It typically looked as shown in ▶FIG. 5.

The squares represent workers' units that together formed the enterprise. In legislation, these were known as cooperative work units and aimed to be small enough to enable individual influence. The units were economically independent and had a twofold role: to make political decisions and carry out the work. They were political insofar as they decided how the enterprise would develop. This meant that the units voted their representatives to form the workers' council. The Council summed up the decisions of the units and made an overall decision. It then negotiated with the Board to produce a plan for implementation. The Board, together with the Principal, negotiated a plan for development and returned it to the Units, which then appeared in their economic role. The Board was also voted by the workers' council, apart from the Principal, who was to be assigned mostly by the state with the workers' necessary electoral approval. Between the Council and the Board there were built-in systems of protection and advisory commissions for consultation. Conflicts at this level were foreseen and delegated to advisory bodies.[22]

This scheme was the model for forty years of trials, accompanied by struggles and successes. It was not a static system, and there were constant adjustments. Nevertheless, there were three main versions of the way the economy worked. Briefly, the first marked the fifties (1953 Constitution), when enterprises worked on the principle of a limited market. This meant that they had autonomy in forming prices, investment, exchange, employment and work plans. At the same time, they had to pay relatively high taxes to the state, still present in the role of profit distribution. In return, the state would create new enterprises and funds for health, social protection, education, housing, etc. Salaries served as an indicator of the bond between companies and the state. The citizen, then, would receive part of the salary that was fixed by the state, and a variable bonus according to the enterprises's success. Growth went well in this phase, and Yugoslavia had the second highest GDP in the world after Japan, without international loans. In 1957, the workers' councils demanded they be given the right to full operations and decisions about the distribution of profits.

This influenced the new phase in the early sixties (1963 Constitution). The limited market was at an end, and there was national and international free exchange, with state funds being cut off. The state withdrew from investments except to support the developing banking sector that also worked on a self-governing principle. After a decade, this caused another problem of class stratification and inequality, creating a new network of rebellion in poorer companies and regions. Worker influence started to decline in favour of experts, provoking the 1968 students' riots against technocracy, among other things. As Gal Kirn pointed out, economic rationality meant that egalitarian criteria had to be reconsidered, and redistributive institutions had to be dismantled. Debate revolved around the question of how much (more) market and how much (less) state should be involved. Some saw the defeat of the solidarity model with the decision to cut off investment funds in favour of banks that increased competition and exploitation of labour. Others wanted to keep going.

As a result of these frictions, a new constitution appeared (1974), again calling for planning, but this time from the bottom up. The entire administration became fragmented, and cooperative units were given the right to be completely independent in the market and to mix, leaving their boundaries as a single enterprise only loosely defined. This meant that if a citizen was part of a poorer enterprise, they could still work for a better one according to five-year contracts called social agreements. Instead of the state funds in the fifties that provided the role of social protection and development, unions of citizens formed in new legal nucleuses of the self-governing system called self-governed interest units (SIZ) and dealt with culture, housing, education, health, etc. They were based on the temporary involvement of workers and inhabitants. This very particular legal framework did not have an easy start. This phase was marked by loans that poorer enterprises obtained from international banks and debts that were eventually covered by the state at high interest rates due to the oil crisis. The resulting inflation meant that the last phase did not equal the economic growth of the fifties, creating an argument for those who saw the liberal market as an enemy.

Others, meanwhile, argued that the problem was not leaving it free long enough for workers to acquire shares as their private property. All in all, self-governance was a trial in negotiating the degree of operativity of the state and emancipation of citizens. From both it called for extremely high levels of solidarity, patience and trust.[23]

These causes were not so explicit at citizen level. This explanation offers a rather simplified scenario when seen from perspective of everyday culture. Time did not pass so quickly, and the process of the trials was not perceived without the impression that life was getting better. Following ongoing attempts to organize production, interpretations in philosophy and in everyday culture came up with their own versions. In addition to the legal trials, philosophers in Yugoslavia pursued the same idea of participatory democracy in Marxism. They belonged to the humanist bloc that advocated the operative role of theory in everyday society. To this end, they sought international support. Before the *Praxis* circle of philosophy was well established, some of its members corresponded with Marxists worldwide. One of the first was Ernst Bloch, as explained in the writings of *Praxis* philosopher Gajo Petrović (▶FIG. 6). Petrović wrote that Bloch's thinking was introduced into Yugoslavia in the fifties, when *Praxis* members visited him in Germany. Following their talks, Bloch's work was published in a special issue of *Praxis* devoted to his philosophy. In the sixties and seventies, Bloch himself took an active part in the *Praxis* circle, lecturing at the summer school, publishing and forming part of the editorial board.[24] In all of his interventions, Bloch reinforced the same idea of active engagement with the material and visible transformation of the real world in keeping with the local *Zeitgeist*, driven by an attempt to establish new production. Bloch described this idea as a warm breeze of Marxism and called it *Novum*, intended as a completely new place to emerge as a result of the attempt to construct utopia. Bloch presented the argument in his lecture »Marx als Denker der Revolution« given in Korčula in 1968, where, completely devoid of nihilism, he argued that revolution in Marx was an opportunity to construct a concrete rather than an abstract utopic setting.[25] The construction of imagination was, then, Bloch's reading of praxis, and utopia was a tool to change existing reality. To prove his argument, Bloch pointed to many attempts to depict phantasy explicitly, such as fairy tales, circuses and ornaments. He did not seem unaware of the possibility of failure, since imagination has a certain superiority over attempt. Yet this attempt seems to have been relevant, in that Bloch, in his lecture, advocated utopia not as an object for discussion but rather as a medium for active collective imagination.[26]

In the case of Yugoslavia, this tangibility of imagination in the form of construction was under discussion, as things needed to be shifted physically in order to establish self-governance. Cities were promoted, housing and industries needed to be built. This was one of the reasons why Bloch's work was well received. It was rather optimistic—the principle of hope—and encouraged transformation directly and visibly. This drive for a physical shift was, then, on the table both politically and philosophically at the same time as enterprises started to implement it in reality. This involved the construction sector, which, to this end, was promoted as a driving force.

One of these new enterprises was the Institute for Materials Testing (IMS) that emerged as part of the process of dissolving the government and the Ministry of Construction into institutes, enterprises and laboratories to enter the market independently

▶6   Ernst Bloch's contributions to *Praxis*. Right: Special edition devoted to Bloch's work with the
        contribution of *Praxis* philosopher Gajo Petrović, explaining his relation with Bloch © Korčula City
        Library Ivan Vidali.

based on the principle of cooperation. It was envisioned as a trial space at public level
and as a home for the construction of utopia in Bloch's terms. It was projected as a
scientific body where economic development went hand in hand with the development
of social politics.[27] In the context of general lack of expertise, the participants who
founded the Institute were chosen from those who could offer specific knowledge.
Among them was the recently retired ETH Professor of Material Science, Mirko Gottfried
Roš. Roš was part of a well-known pre-war Belgrade family whose palace in the city
centre was assigned to the Soviet Embassy just after the war. Internationally educated,
Roš obtained numerous honorary doctorates from universities worldwide. From 1924
to 1949, he headed the ETH Institute for Materials Testing, and engaged in scientific
work in line with Eugen Frayssinet, Gustaaf Magnel and Robert Maillart, with whom

Roš was friends. While in Zurich, Roš received photographs of work actions in New Belgrade. They were sent by the Ministry of Construction, asking Roš to return to the country to help set up an institute for construction and materials testing.

With his insightful experience, Roš made it possible to transfer knowledge about concrete, a necessary precondition for the building process. The newly established Institute for Materials Testing (1952) was initially to be part of the Academy of Sciences, becoming independent a year later. That year was spent on initiating scientific research.[28] Departments were created for particular materials: Stone, Concrete, Geomechanics, Wood, Metals, Physics and Chemistry, as well as for the Development of Machines. Each department was designed as a small centre equipped with »offices for researchers to carry out their scientific work, conduct personal relations and receive groups of scientists from abroad«. To fit out the interior, Roš headed the process of importing *Amsler* machinery from Switzerland, equipping the Institute with technology that not many people knew how to use at the time.[29]

The subject of testing was explicit in the Institute's interior. The building was part factory, part representational architecture, with elements reminiscent of churches. The house, a pre-war stamp factory, was enlarged by testing halls, with the addition of two sculptures of producers at the entrance and a huge stretch of stained glass telling the story of production (▶FIG. 7). All research was kept under one roof to promote communication between departments, and future extensions were foreseen to avoid dividing up the Institute. In this first period, the departments functioned in a similar way to the university, as the heads of department were members of the Scientific Council that was the ruling body, together with the Principal. Each department was assigned its own budget as a trial run, as there was no clear idea as to how it would develop.[30]

Once the Institute was set up, Roš's role started to fade. In 1953 the Institute became a detached unit with its own funding and independent research, and Roš's promising young deputy and head of the Department of Concrete, Branko Žeželj, took over his position as Principal.[31] Once the physical space was complete with the laboratories and testing halls needed to produce the new materials, social relations were established according to the principles of a cooperative. Within the Institute, the departments of materials started operating as work units, running their programs, yearly plans and selection of personnel and equipment.[32] Decisions were made by vote after discussions that were public and free to access.[33] Extensive examples of meetings can be found in the IMS archive, covering a vast range of topics from new patents, apartment shares, trips abroad, financial plans, laws on the organization of scientific work, new jobs, etc. In one meeting in 1961, representatives of the departments of materials were asked to propose new developments for discussion with the Council.[34] Another was about funding, choosing a principal for the Department of Concrete, and the employment of new staff.[35] Topics such as loans and help to Skopje after the earthquake in 1963, technical assistance to Eastern Europe countries and annual production plans were often present. International exchange policies started to be promoted. Themes appearing frequently in archive records were exchanges of publications, foreign research specialization and participation in symposiums of the European Committee for Concrete.[36]

The legal process promoting cooperatives assured the public that the Institute was a place for cooperation in building, bringing together the collective and the individual imaginary. More than a superstructure, it was an accessible place where decisions and negotiations accompanied building. Technology was to be viewed through the lens of social production and could be compared with Castoriadis's use of the word *teukhein*. Castoriadis explained *teukhein* as an Ancient Greek notion meaning assembling, adjusting, prefabricating, constructing and making appropriate. In its historical development, the word *techne* comes from *teukhein* (making), and technique and technology in the contemporary sense are particular manifestations of it. Nevertheless, this broad meaning of *techne* tends to get lost in the contemporary notion of technology because *teukhein* is often understood without another important concept for social representation: that of *legein* (saying). Castoriadis, conversely, argues that the two concepts of making and saying go together as a means by which social institutions are created. Before objects are made as the product of technology, the social imaginary must create itself as a society, as a group for doing based on the process of saying. The institute in question aspired to bring together making and saying by combining technology with a social contract. For Castoriadis, the process also works the other way, with making followed by saying. This means that the shaping of individuals by society in the course of their socialization is based not just on language, but also on a kind of craft. Society makes subjects as social individuals that adopt certain roles.[37] In the history of the Institute, this reverse direction was explicit too, as by including people in production, it was counting on a new kind of citizen as a result of the wave of migration.

Indications of this scenario can be seen in the photo captions from archive material as shown in ▶FIG. 8A. The group is testing the dome for Belgrade Fair, which, at that time, had a span of 109 m, making it the world's biggest hall made of reinforced concrete. The dome was among the Institute's first building ventures with models used for construction. Far from a bureaucratic practice, the group on top of the model represents the process of making that was going on. The absence of posturing, the various skills visible in their clothing, a certain nonchalance and the familiarity between them and with the material all suggest the novelty of the testing experience. Their

apparent belief in a successful result points to a process in which tools, arrangement and actors were employed in a single imagination with an unknown outcome. With testing at the centre of the trial, the individual was tasked with turning the process into a dynamic relation with the material. The work process that started with the installation of the dome soon moved on to testing the prefabrication system for housing. After cooperative work, housing was the next imaginary of citizens.

Imagining a Modern Kind of Housing

In producing new housing, the Institute aimed to bridge two existing realities. One was the pre-war salon apartment with the influences of Vienna, Budapest and Paris, the mark of civic culture in major cities. The other, far more widespread, was the rural

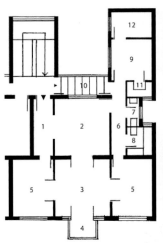

▸9a   Typical layout of the saloon apartment, characteristic of city culture between the World Wars, Djordje
       Alfirević, Sanja Simonović Alfirević, »Salon Apartment in Serbia between the Two World Wars.
       Reassessing the Rationale behind the Term«, *Arhitektura i urbanizam* no. 44 (2017): 12.
▸9b   Rural house made out of wood in the mountain region of Yugoslavia © Collection of Obrad Pješivac.

low-tech house built by the owners themselves, almost entirely of wood or stone, which
in most cases the new generations were trying to leave behind (▸FIG. 9A, B). At this
time, Yugoslavia was top of the list for overcrowded dwellings in Europe. According
to a UN report on housing, in 1956 an average of five people were living in a two-room
flat.[38] Emerging housing policies made the task even more ambitious, as the housing
law ensured everyone the right to a flat.

     This took the form of three versions that corresponded to changes in the con-
stitution of self-governance. In the fifties this relied on the state housing tax that was
paid by enterprises, institutions and, in some cases, citizens. To this end, a set of laws
was passed (1959) to link the commune in the role of the developer, and the housing
stock. Communes were organized on various levels from district, city, region and finally
republic in order to organize housing production and distribution. The overall aim was
for the district to be able to create its own housing policy based on the cooperative and
an investment fund.[39] However, the role of the commune was not fully exploited due
to the liberation of the market in the sixties, which was followed by the cutting of state
funds, including for housing. Housing shifted towards market-based production, with
one significant difference from the Western understanding: enterprises continued to
bear the main responsibility for meeting housing needs. In practice, this meant that
if a citizen became part of the enterprise, they would be on the list for an apartment.
The enterprise provided flats from its own fund, and they were allocated to employees
along with a contract regulating a minimum agreed duration. At the end of the contract,
citizens could change enterprise and keep the apartment. If they wanted to apply for
another flat, they had to return the original one to the new enterprise. Otherwise, it
belonged to them indefinitely. As a rule, enterprises would buy flats from the building
sector either in the form of apartments spread throughout city, or as whole buildings.
Sometimes citizens would get a flat promptly, while on other occasions it took time

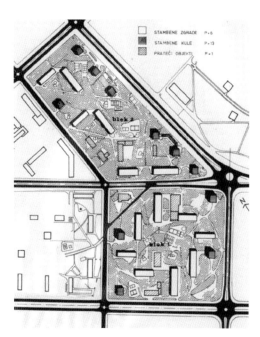

►10
Site plan of the Experimental Housing. Reprinted
from the journal *Urbanizam Beograda*, no. 2
(Belgrade, 1969), 14. Architect: Branko Petričić, 1958.

and effort, but as a rule employees obtained accommodation. With the final change in constitution (1974), the link between enterprises and the housing sector was mediated by self-governed interest units (SIZ). The ones that dealt with housing were regulated by the constitution as set up by workers directly or through the enterprise, and based on solidarity in gaining personal or collective benefits in the field of housing.[40] The SIZ were made up of a mix of people for temporary periods. They collected money, established a program of housing construction, allocated and distributed apartments, and carried out maintenance. Once in the possession of enterprises, apartments were distributed to employees by the workers' councils and commissions that created lists according to duration of employment, family status, income, etc. In the attempt to establish housing as a right, associated with employment, Yugoslavia built two and a half million flats in its first twenty-five years of self-governance, housing around eight million people.[41] Throughout all of these changes, starting from greater state control, to the one of market and finally moving towards a bottom-up system, work was immediately associated with housing. In Castoriadis's terms, an apartment was a socially instituted *eidos* (form): a product that does not necessarily still exist in reality, but becomes real in the social imaginary. For this *eidos*, cooperative building was a way to transform reality by means of the process of making (*teukhein*).[42]

The work of the Institute for Materials Testing stood at the beginning of these processes, and its response to the new vision of housing was the search for an open system of prefabrication. To fit within the abstractness of a social form, the new housing system had to be adaptable for infinite uses. It was necessary to mimic cooperative production, with the ideal combination of laymen and engineers engaged on site. To provide this image, the Institute proclaimed itself ready to go out into the field whenever required, with laboratories set up at construction sites. Collaboration with the universities was created with a two-year course to prepare students for the role of

▶11   Branko Turin, *Novi Beograd*, 1962. 24 × 18 cm, 18 × 13 cm. Ur_12170, Ur_12180 © Belgrade City Museum.

field engineer.[43] The search for an open-system patent lasted from 1956 to 1960, with experimentation on a construction site.

The test site was New Belgrade, with a housing development called Experimental Blocks 1 and 2, built between 1957 and 1963. When it entered the site, in the Institute was noted that the construction was accompanied by a shared desire for the city to be something new and beautiful.[44] The housing development was from the outset recognized as a »laboratory of experimental work whose findings were of major significance for the development of the construction sector«.[45] The new buildings were the first local community on the vast construction site that had lain empty for years after the work actions. It was surrounded by tonnes of sand long after first inhabitants moved in. The urbanism of the new settlement was designed by the Town Planning Institute in 1958 and conveyed an obvious French influence (▶FIG. 10).

This was not by chance, as the plan was drawn up by the group around the architect Branko Petričić, who had collaborated with Le Corbusier on the Plan de Paris 37, a project that sought to apply the thesis of the *Ville Radieuse* to the scale of the housing block. The Institute for Materials Testing was in touch with the planning group, as one of its architects had worked on the first buildings. This was Dušan Milenković, who designed dwellings in 1957/1958, prior to the adaptation of the plan as a sort of model for it.[46] It is not easy to say which came first, the testing of the system or of the urbanism, as the two were synchronized and accompanied by a degree of improvisation. One of the aims, largely transmitted by architecture culture, was the commitment to the joint development of a housing policy of the right to a dwelling by the language of the modern movement. The latter offered the perfect option for participatory discourse in Yugoslavia: open blocks with community centres inside. The scenario that was promoted and largely considered to be desirable is shown in the images taken by Belgrade photographer Branko Turin as the building went up (▶FIG. 11).[47]

Depicted, a man sits in the restaurant and looks out through a large window towards the central courtyard that was to become green in the coming years. Dressed in a suit, he is surrounded by marble columns and wooden walls featuring a picture commemorating the youth work actions. The use of luxury materials for communal spaces became a developing tradition in Yugoslav architectural practice. The restaurant is part of the local community centre, surrounded by a playground and a school. The buildings are neutral, while significant attention is paid to their appropriate lengths, heights and layouts amid the vegetation of the cascading ground floor. The role of greenery was to be radically reinforced as freestanding objects took almost a secondary role in the overall *imago* of social life. Although this image reflected the well-known view of the modern city set amid trees, the picture was novel for the local population. The use of the word *experimental* to describe the development was true for various reasons: both the system and the form of urbanism were being tested, and the way of living in these apartments was also new. For the occupants, the apartment as a social *eidos* was associated with features of modern architecture such as green, open blocks, community centres and running water. In the creation of this *eidos*, the initial phase was devoted to discovering how, in Castoriadis's terms, the institution of the building cooperative materialized the imagination of communal housing.

Praxis on the Construction Site: Can Prefabrication Be a Craft?

Castoriadis argued that the creation of a common goal for a group or society has its source in individual and social imagination. In order to create these institutions, individuals are responsible for saying and making. The modality of this making is praxis. Drawing a parallel, one might ask: if the building process emerged as a social institution with its source in the imagination of communal housing, what form did praxis take on the construction site?

There are several lines from Castoriadis that may be helpful in understanding how a construction site can function as a place of praxis. First of all, for Castoriadis, as for Marx and Lefebvre, praxis includes *poiesis* (making, in antiquity). These spheres are not separate, and praxis is not reserved for intangible activities of language and politics, as in the philosophy of antiquity. On the contrary, praxis is the possibility of making new objects using new social forms by means of the creative process.[48] Creativity is involved in the way praxis relates to the acquisition of knowledge, which, according to Castoriadis, should be provisional, fragmentary and take place throughout the process. He writes: »To do something, to do a book, to make a child, a revolution, or just doing as such, is projecting oneself into a future situation which is opened up on all sides to the unknown.«[49]

In the process, knowledge does not presuppose law-like propositions used to achieve predetermined goals. Rather, it remains fragmentary within a concrete intercourse of action, without ever becoming a theory about an object. As such, praxis

▶12a The production of floor slabs for the IMS system at an Experimental Housing construction site, Album of the Department of Concrete (II) 1960 © IMS Archive.

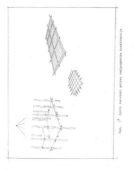
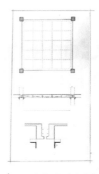

▶12b The IMS structural concept from »Study of the Testing of Prefabricated Floor Slabs« (1960), scientific work of Department II: Concrete, the Institute for Materials Testing FRS Belgrade © IMS Archive.

is neither the materialization of absolute knowledge nor a technique; it is based on the dynamics of the process. This is due to the progressive nature of praxis, which, in itself, constantly gives rises to new knowledge. By doing, we learn anew, and clarification and transformation of materiality advance together in praxis, each conditioning the other. Activity precedes clarification, and, for praxis, the ultimate goal is not the final form, but the transformation.[50] Castoriadis thereby assigned the possibility of creating new objects to new social forms by means of a testing process on a one-to-one scale. This resonated with the experimental site in New Belgrade, primarily because trial was the only possible consequence of the general lack of expert knowledge and the austerity of the time. Recalling construction difficulties, Branko Žeželj mentioned that the soil was unexplored and sometimes impassable, and that there was a lack of electricity, phones and basic materials such as cement and gravel. Moreover, there was little mechanization, with only a few small cranes. Since transport from the factory was expensive, it was decided that elements would be produced on the construction site.[51]

Restricting factors made for greater inventiveness to find a solution. A lightweight construction was the first aim, as the floodplains called for the removal of any surplus weight. This led to minimal construction with thin elements of high-quality prestressed concrete. The system consisted of columns and floor slabs as the lowest common denominator within the building. It was a homogenous and fairly simple solution, with a pillar and slab forming a 4.2×4.2 m square. Its main quality was an ingenious join of the slab and column that was regulated by prestressed steel wires. Due to the various possible degrees of reinforcement, the system offered a high level of flexibility and spans (▶FIG. 12A, B).

The floor slabs were made of internal ribs sandwiched between layers. The ribs were accompanied by cables that transmitted the introduced force through each floor. The top layer of concrete was fixed to the ribs as a monolithic piece. The bottom slab was made of two layers of plaster with mesh net between them and was the final solution for the ceiling, integrated into the prefabricated element. Due to of the absence of a beam and the integration of the ceiling, the structure formed a clean base for further work. The production of the floor slabs was also simple, using paper instead of steel moulds. Using cardboard to mould the slab was prioritized for economy and the simplicity of assembly, as it enabled the ribs and the slab to be made in a single process. This avoided a two-phase operation of joining first the ribs and then the slabs. In addition, the final floor appeared more monolithic and structurally resistant as there was no subsequent joining of elements into a single system.[52] The solution achieved the aim using slabs that weighed 30% less than any known system of prefabrication and actually made it possible to build on sand.[53]

The floor slabs were intertwined in different continuums by intersecting the cables running through the ribs. The applied force was adjusted on site using equipment produced as part of the solution. A start was also made on organizing training in the process. The attempt to condense construction to the minimum significantly contributed to the image of the open system, the characteristic that was to bring Žeželj many international awards as author of the patent.[54]

Apart from the importance of testing, work on the construction site was also in keeping with praxis in the way the community of builders was employed. As the Institute worked with a mixture of scientific, skilled and unskilled staff, the construction was quite eclectic.[55] As a 1960 album of the Department of Concrete shows, the structure of the Experimental Housing was constructed by a range of builders, from laymen and semi-skilled workers to engineers. This process of moulding, cutting and weighing with very basic machinery and without even helmets can be described as the crafting of industry by actors who sought a place in society by building it. At this time, the way towards industrialization had the potential for participatory, low-cost, adjustable prefabrication, with the direct involvement of people with material. Castoriadis's idea of praxis as non-specialized knowledge suited the construction site, as actors were not assigned to a single role in their work, but to the fragmented acquisition of know-how. The work was, then, a kind of flirtation with semi-specialization. Talking about their experience afterwards, participants described the guiding idea as

▶13   Left: School in Experimental Housing, photograph by Branko Turin, *Novi Beograd*, 1962. 18 × 13 cm,
Ur_12179 © Belgrade City Museum.
Right: Perspective view of a segment of Experimental Housing with the community centre building.
24 × 18 cm, Ur_13223 © Belgrade City Museum.

simple: »We needed to find the minimum number of structural elements out of which
it would be possible to make an infinite number of different flats.«[56]

What participants did on the site was retroactively returned to the plan. Planning
followed the experimental building, as affirmed by the plan's author, Branko Petričić,
who wrote that in order to meet the vision of the IMS, defined spans, heights and
modules were needed. Petričić worked on spans, recalling that »we adopted a span of
4.2 × 4.2 m and, as well as a new urban vision, we came up with an original structural
system. It seems that the extremely difficult site conditions were crucial to this«.[57]
Architects discussed and defined the main criteria for the evolution of the system in
terms of its acceptance in architecture. The system was required to contain a varied
number of floors (4–18) and engage with all the needs of city planning. Additionally,
it was not to be associated with a specific number of flat layouts, but to be able to
work with existing typologies and emerging solutions. It was required to enable the
construction of buildings with different levels of finish and equipment, from luxury
to low-budget.[58] The plan simultaneously adopted the results of first buildings for
the construction of the rest of the experimental housing, from 1960 until 1963, as an
initial trial of modern living (▶FIG. 13).[59] The solution brought relief to the housing
sector, as by the late 1960s most of the further buildings in New Belgrade had been
designed and built using the IMS system.

The relation between the open system and the urban project offers the third
argument for understanding the construction site as a place of praxis. In Castoriadis's
terms, the project serves as an element of praxis that connects it to reality and triggers
collective imagination of it. The project inspires activity, defines the objectives of praxis
and specifies mediation for transforming the material. However, the project should
avoid being fixed in »clear and unambiguous ideas« that consider realization as the

only essential moment. Instead, it should include the unregulated conditions involved in the process. The way in which the urban planning and building processes shifted at the New Belgrade site was important for the resulting collective production.[60] The possibility of switching between planning and building was beneficial to the way the Institute adapted the architectural plan. This was possible due to the ambivalence of its role, with one foot in the pragmatics of construction, and the other in the planning and imagination of the future city. With regard to Marx's »everyone does everything«, this exchange of competencies was an important precondition for collective production.

Imagination as Part of Material Culture

Ideas about praxis and imagination that were being developed internationally became part of the cultural and political debate in Yugoslavia. Part of this discourse was mirrored in the building sector and inspired its search for the open system that ultimately mimicked the objective of a participatory society. Once the Experimental Housing was complete, how did praxis continue? Did imagination inspire just the actual making of the prototype of the open system, or was it developed further in everyday material culture? What did the new inhabitants then do in their homes, and did their use offer any proof of further collective production? If Castoriadis was useful in reinforcing the link between imagination and making in social institutions, Bloch further helped to understand how the advance of imagination affected the new housing developments. His theory goes to show how the material served as a testimony to collective production and a further source of imagination.

Bloch offered a poetical interpretation of time, objects and imagination in his lecture at the summer school of philosophy devoted to the contemporary relevance of Hegel (*Hegel et Notre Temps*, 1970). In his interpretation, Bloch compared the process of imagination with the experience of travelling. He explained that Hegel's philosophy is conditioned by the outcome and the object as motive for travel (*Fahrtmotiv*). During travel, in the relation with the surrounding material, food must be eaten, the world must be consumed and received (*aufgenommen*), with its artistic, plastic and optical effect, with contemplation and a lot of just seeing, and the easiness that travel brings, without fear, though the outcome is unknown. By means of this process, Bloch concludes, *Das Motiv einer Fahrt* changed the subject and the way travelled (*das Durchfahrene*), while the objects experienced, despite also changing, remain the traveller's allies.[61]

Bloch promoted active engagement with the material as a practice that is ongoing rather than stopping when the goal, such as the production of a particular object, is attained. Engagement then becomes a certain cultural attitude. The changed objects remain the allies of the traveller as they continue to follow the imagination

Children playing in the sand of Experimental Housing. Clip from the series of documentary films on the construction of New Belgrade, part IV, *Prepreke su mnogobrojne*, directed by Miloš Bukumirović (Belgrade: Slavija film I, 1959–1962) © Yugoslav Film Archives.

process. In this way, making with the imagination becomes an everyday practice, a kind of daydream. Here we find an aspect of everyday life in Bloch's thinking that he attributed to the hope of an individual who, through active daydreaming, questions the political environment. What emerged was a dynamic idea of praxis, seen as an everyday culture of transformation based on imagination. Placing this idea in the context in question, we can argue that if building on the experimental site managed to convey something of this to the material culture of future usage, it might be said to have the quality of social innovation. This can perhaps be shown through the documentary material of the captions, which give an indication of the extent to which this dynamic idea of praxis continued to be present. Which sequences strengthen this argument?

1.
—

The first photo is from a series of documentary films about the years spent on the construction of New Belgrade, entitled *Život na pesku* (Life on Sand, ▶FIG. 14). It shows that maybe the most explicit development of making in everyday culture was the on-going state of construction that continued to surround the Experimental Housing decades after it was first occupied. The housing area was just the start, to be followed by further building of the city. The condition of the site as both place of residence and further building promoted making on an everyday level and affected the childhood of those growing up there. The sandy ground became a huge playground where the children built cities of sand, imitating their existing reality.[62]

2.
—

The second pair accompany the history told by one of first inhabitants of the Experimental Housing (▶FIG. 15). This is Mirjana Obradović of the Historical Archives of Belgrade, who, while working on the archive photographs with me, also showed me

▶15   Left: Mirjana Obradović as a child with family in the Experimental Housing; Right: Children playing in
the surroundings of the Experimental Housing, 1968 © Personal collection of Milenković family.

her own. As a child when her parents were first-generation settlers, she explains how
the inhabitants appropriated the emerging materiality.

»My parents moved into their new flat in spring 1965. They told me that the paths
in the housing block were first laid out at right angles according to the architects' plan.
But people then made their own paths, and workers from the city came to consolidate
these new ones. We children would gather around a sculpture of a polar bear that was
made and placed in the middle of the block by the father of a school friend who was a
stonemason. The inner courtyard was large and filled with playgrounds and benches,
and pines, chestnuts, birches and plane trees. The school and kindergarten were part
of it and had no fences; everyone could use everything. Almost all the inhabitants
gathered in the yard. There was a building called the Community Centre that we called
the Fountain because of the fountain in the middle. Nearby were a grocery store,
chemist's, post office, florist's and restaurant on the ground floor. There was also the
cinema, where children often went and saw their first films. On the first floor was a
hall where residents could meet. I used to go there with my mother to the women's
evenings, where women from public life talked to residents on particular topics. My
parents, along with others, organized various activities in the hall. The centre also had
a part with shops such as a tailor's, a shoemaker's and an electrician's, and a library.
The library was part of the city library, which was decentralized to various sites, and all
the blocks in New Belgrade had one. The buildings were quite neutral; the flats were
not too big, three rooms at most. What I remember of them was lots of sun and light,
big windows in the façade through which you could see leaves, rain and snow. The
family of the concierge lived on the ground floor and looked after the entrance hall
and its residents. Next door there was a room for celebrations and birthdays, and the
whole entrance had a lot of glass and atriums overlooking the neighbouring entrance
halls. We, the occupants, grew plants there until it eventually became a greenhouse.
Roma brass bands regularly played in the atriums, and we would throw them coins
from the windows of our flats above. The top floor housed common utilities such as

▶16
Making IMS prefabricated floor
slabs © IMS Archive.

washrooms, where we often played next to our parents. It was surrounded by a construction site for quite a long time. The sand was full of pools with bulrushes, fish and
ducks. We played hide-and-seek in the infrastructure pipes that lay around for years.«[63]

3/4.

The third photograph shows how the Institute further developed imagination and
making by adopting the new work culture. The experience of the experimental site was
taken as a discovery for the system as a means of social production. This emerged in
the context shown in the photo (▶FIG. 16), where a mixed community attempts to make
the floor slab work. The attitude towards materiality shown here was transmitted in
further construction of housing in Yugoslavia and internationally. More than just a
patent, the Institute started to offer a new vision for the production of flats based on
social engagement. The aim of the workshops was to be organized on sites as mobile
units, which, when finished, were dismantled and rebuilt in a new area. The overall
goal was to produce flats with a small number of structural elements, and a variety of
floor plans and number of floors, using local raw materials.[64]

To work on this, a new department was set up. The role of the Buildings Department (*zgradarstvo*) was to study the compatibility of systems in different emerging
residential buildings. It was associated with studying the apartment and adapting
patents. Its main value was that architects, engineers, lab technicians and builders
worked together near the construction site. Eventually, the Buildings Department
evolved into the more specialized Centre for Housing that was set up by architects
working at the Institute in 1967.[65] The Centre further promoted the idea of the open
system. Architects therefore viewed the apartment as a dynamic field that responded
to the open structural system, and promoted participation by means of projections of
future uses by the occupants. In this way, the initial material preoccupation with open
production that emerged on the construction site continued in the schemes produced
by the Centre for the development of housing in Yugoslavia. In the floor plan of an

▶17 Floor plan for an apartment in New Belgrade using the IMS system (Block 23, architects Aleksandar Stjepanović, Božidar Janković, Branislav Karažić, designed 1968, built 1974), *Informativni bilten CS IMS* 15/74, front cover.
Top: Block 23, *Centar za stanovanje* no. 27 (1980), n.p.
Bottom: Block 23, 2017. Personal archive, photograph by Aleksandar Knežević.

apartment on the front cover of Institute's journal (▶FIG. 17), the pillars of the IMS's system are the only fixed points in space, while barely existing partition walls indicate many possibilities for transformation. The plan in question represented the Centre's quest for flexibility that eventually led to the concept of the »neutral apartment«, where vague corners were determined only by furniture.

5.

The fifth set of photographs is an example of how the practice of the open system as part of the social contract started to be exported abroad, along with the necessary tools. Its export showed above all that this scenario was not only possible in Yugoslavia due to the strong social contract that existed, but that links could be made in other ways. The transfer of technology to produce residential buildings began in Italy, with the construction of apartment buildings around Milan. These were soon followed by Budapest in Hungary, the USSR, Cuba and China. The system also travelled to Angola, Egypt, the Philippines and Austria, and the Institute had collaborations with Ethiopia, Iraq and Iran.[66] Though each place brought its own particularities, the common denominator was the involvement and education of local people and materials. In this respect, the Institute exported not just technology, but also the social aspect of

▶18
Top: Experimental Housing, Luanda, Angola. 1978. Lead architect: Ivan Petrović for the IMS. Published in *Toward a Concrete Utopia: Architecture in Yugoslavia, 1948–1980*, ed. V. Kulić, T. B. Klarin, Martino Stierli (New York: Museum of Modern Art, 2018), 23.
Bottom: Experimental Housing, Luanda, Angola, 1977–1980. Published in: Jelica Jovanović, »From Yugoslavia to Angola: Housing as Postcolonial Technical Assistance City Building through IMS Žeželj Housing Technology.« *Architektúra & Urbanizmus* 3–4 (2019): 175.

production. New geographies once again affected materiality. On the one hand, up until 1978, the search for the open system was still visible, as seen in ▶FIG. 18. The experimental housing block for Luanda in Angola developed by the Centre for Housing appears as a skeleton of structural elements with independent infill.

On the other hand, this transfer also influenced new housing schemes, and their materiality could hardly be linked with the image of modernity preserved in Yugoslavia. These were schemes for low-tech single-family and semidetached houses built by local labour, corresponding to the idea of an open system in this new context. The drawings in ▶FIG. 19 show elements of the system that became unrecognizable after the application of local materials by local constructors.[67] The architect Ivan Petrović, who worked at the forefront of the Centre for Housing on the Luanda project, explained what happened on the site.

»IMS is well suited to construction with transitional conditions of technological development, most probably due to the low initial costs, simple production and its openness to construction and design by laymen, and the use of local materials… The finalization of the facilities remains entirely at the discretion of the user and can range from full prefabrication to individual construction by inhabitants using local materials.«[68]

The sequences of photographs suggests that, from the beginning on the construction site, imagination unfolded in the transformation of material in the second,

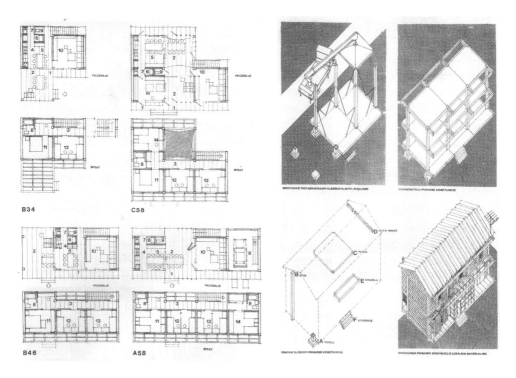

B34   C58

B46   A58

▶19   IMS drawings for semidetached houses in Luanda, Angola, 1980. Arch. Ivan Petrović, *Bilten IMS* no. 1–2 (December 1980): 10, 14.

third and fourth cases: through the regular activity of construction that inspires children's play, through the newly discovered use of the courtyards by residents, through the attempt to implement the system in the apartments as a tool to achieve a neutral, flexible support for activity, and, finally, through the open transformation of materiality when exported. As Ernst Bloch writes in *Experimentum Mundi*, the building of a certain idea appears as an open-ended process that constantly reinvents itself as both the dogma of instability and a degree of emancipation of the subject.[69] In this sense, there is a link between Bloch's dynamic idea of praxis and the possibility of emancipation seen in a form of spatial concern that persists in material culture and engages the participant. Emancipation existed in this particular case in that the actors saw their spatial setting as one that corresponded to their social setting, and intervened in it by means of the process of making. The ability to accept this process as open-ended, more even than the open structural system, open work unit and open housing block themselves, together with the contingency it brings, is perhaps the ultimate modernity contained within the makers' efforts.

The Question of Autonomy

As we have seen, those protagonists who engaged directly with the construction site expanded the contract of making to architects, residents and an international audience. At the same time, they were all surrounded by a philosophical and societal debate. The network of actors involved in organizing participation comprised the plural positions of brigade members, workers, philosophers, engineers and architects, and, finally, residents. The proximity of their roles reflected the quality of collective production based on praxis. Relations between them were sometimes more than occasional, as some members of the *Praxis* circle developed a direct collaboration with the Institute for Materials Testing. However, apart from particular historical cases, the new public atmosphere was open enough to communicate influences. To illustrate this, communication between the actors in their general roles could be described as follows:

Philosophers talked about the ideal of participation in existing society. They argued that philosophy had an operative role in participation and were critical if the attempt remained purely rhetorical. At the same time, they also promoted its potential for the emancipation of society. Their work resonated with political attempts to establish participative production in a context of Cold War frictions. This took the form of legislation accompanied by changes. Messages from both politicians and philosophers were picked up by enterprises, the building sector and, finally, citizens, in their dual role as residents and workers. The messages were not always coordinated, and citizens had to decide how to proceed by themselves. In the case of the Institute, workers and engineers decided to create an open system, architects designed open layouts and residents promoted the open courtyard. These three protagonists stood in close proximity, often part of the same enterprise, work unit, testing hall, construction site or meeting. To what extent were their actions autonomous? Were they ideologically driven?

Here, Castoriadis's work offers a point of reference, as autonomy is inseparably tied up with his reading of praxis. For Castoriadis, creating an institution by saying and making is not about reinforcing supra-individual phenomena or the primacy of collectivity, but the specific structure of human collectivity and individuality.[70] He writes that instituting is: »a state in which the collective knows that its institutions are its own creation and has become capable of regarding them as such, of taking them up again and transforming them.«[71] In their important role in creating institutions, Castoriadis calls individuals autonomous. What is an autonomous individual?

Castoriadis replies:
»It is someone socialized; he has, in a certain way, internalized the institutions of society. [...] He internalizes free inquiry [...], free reflection, free research [...]. This has to be learned as well. There is an education in autonomy [...] and there is a tradition of autonomy, which must always be reflexive [...]. I am not saying that, in an autonomous society, the content of the life of everyone must be an artistic creation; that would be madness. But these are the questions of the content of life that an autonomous society will have to resolve for itself. Autonomy does not suffice: we want autonomy for itself, but we also want it in order to do things.«[72]

For Castoriadis, autonomy is an emancipatory attitude and later, in the course of the twentieth century, influenced by the environmental debate, it also appears as a form of self-limitation. As such, autonomy means exactly what the word says: »I lay down a law for myself« as, at the same time, the ability to act freely and to define limits for myself.[73] Historically, autonomous individuals are aware of the social material existing around them, because they built on the basis of what already existed. »Every symbolism is built on the ruins of earlier symbolic edifices and uses their materials even if it is only to fill the foundations of new temples, as the Athenians did after the Persian wars.«[74] In doing so, autonomous individuals push existing boundaries and build within a social life full of interstices and degrees of freedom.

According to this interpretation, the work of the Institute can be seen as one of the pop-up realities of the Yugoslav trial. There, in the context of existing debate, the groups managed to push production towards a higher level of autonomy.

Whose were the voices of approval or disapproval?

In an interview we conducted, one of Institute's members, sociologist Ksenija Petovar of the Centre for Housing, first explained that the place was not dependent on state politics. She described it as a very specific institution that, soon after being set up, started to work at international level and was given the opportunity to exist with complete economic independence. It included among its members voices that were critical of state politics, such as one of its major researchers in concrete, Boško Petrović. Petovar had come to the Institute as a prominent student in the annual programs. None of the group in which she worked belonged to the League of Communists, which was no impediment to them winning housing competitions.[75]

Another Institute member, engineer Branimir Grujić who was working on international transfer, explained that decisions about the use of the system had to do only with the performance of the patent. He disregarded any political priorities and connected the success of the work to the economic interest in building—that is, the time in which housing was paid off. About his beginnings at the Institute, Grujić says:

»In the mid-fifties, I started work at the Institute on construction testing. At the same time, I collaborated with Žeželj on the prefabrication of the IMS system. The experimental housing using the IMS system was built in New Belgrade to test the structure. I led construction work, for which I received an apartment. When building was complete, 30 apartments were distributed to the workers of the Institute according to the list. Afterwards, I started setting up the distribution department (*Sektor za plasman*), which dealt with the research, design and export of prefabricated components and pre-stressing technology.«[76]

Technologist Milan Pajević worked in the laboratory on new materials made from construction surplus and used to fill in the façades of the Experimental Housing Blocks (▶FIG. 20). He wrote that he knew languages, and that the library was full of resources he could try out in the laboratory. At that time, Yugoslavia's declaration on neutrality in the world included cooperation with the United Nations.[77] The experience at the Institute took Pajević to the UN in 1962, to set up new institutes to develop materials that were assigned to centres for housing in Indonesia, Thailand, Iraq and Iran (▶FIG. 21). The IMS provided a service to set up these centres in Iraq and Indonesia by training local people for open industrialization, incorporating traditional materials such as canvas.[78]

▶20
Building the façade of the experimental housing. Clip from the series of documentary films about the construction of New Belgrade, part IV, *Prepreke su mnogobrojne*, directed by Miloš Bukumirović (Belgrade: Slavija film I, 1959–1962) © Yugoslav Film Archives.

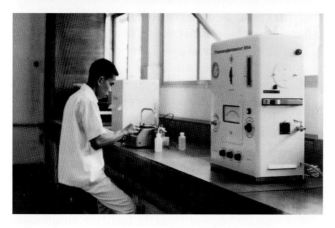

▶21
Laboratory training for local people to develop materials at the regional Centre for Housing Construction of Southeast Asia (BMDL), Bandung, Indonesia, mid-1960s. Photograph courtesy of Milan Pajević.

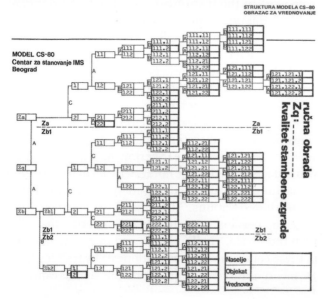

▶22
Diagram for housing evaluation from the study by Mihailo Čanak and Zorana Luković, »Uporedna analiza funkcionalih mogućnosti skeletnih sistema i sistema sa poprečnim nosećim zidovima«, 1978, published in *Bilten Centra za stanovanje* no. 27 (1980), n.p.

In projects that actually promoted the modern idea of progress, like the one in Iraq, Pajević worked on setting up the Institute as part of the University of Bagdad on which construction was underway, led by Walter Gropius and TAC (1957–1969). On such occasions, he observed: »The UN's way of working was first to negotiate with governments, and then to assign projects with local and international people. The locals would take training courses, some of which were organized by the IMS. In Bagdad, the IMS exported technology, and gave lectures and training for four years. At the time, Iraq ran modernization projects with many modern architects involved. Gropius designed the university campus that included our institute. For the work on this project, we were offered facilities designed by Dioxiadis as part of a former UNDP project.«[79]

On his return from a fourteen-year period in Asia, Pajević continued at the IMS, establishing further open industrialization projects, this time at the significantly smaller level of semi-detached houses.

Yugoslav *Praxis* philosophers crossed paths with the Institute at around the time when the progressive phase of self-governance was receding after frictions due to student unrest in 1968. Philosophers were blamed for the strikes, and there were plans to replace them at Belgrade University. They were only replaced six years later in 1974, due to the support of the university, which had in the meantime become self-governed and was not easy to influence. At the same time, due to its dissolution, the *Praxis* group gained strong international support from philosophers worldwide.[80] Shortly afterwards, some of the banned philosophers started to cooperate with the Institute for Materials Testing. Miladin Životić was among those supported by Bloch in the international press when he started to work with the Centre for Housing. At that time, the Institute was developing tools to work with the open system in housing design. Životić introduced into its study a series of criteria for assessing the value of the apartments from the users' viewpoint, and some of his insights resonated with Bloch's philosophy. Životić argued that the process of enacting a value system—for housing in this case—was based on constant opposition between normative and emancipatory values. He described the former as a conventional set of socially accepted standards in a given environment and time, usually related to the value system of the ruling groups (or marginal groups in the case of social stratification). The emancipatory value, on the other hand, is a projection of what could be—an anticipation, as Bloch would call it. It transcends the existing local setting and questions of identity and national framework to address humanization in general. It is based on a critical approach to existing patterns and the creation of new ones by monitoring changes in social relations. When working with architects, Životić asked how work on housing could prioritize emancipatory over normative values. The answer suggested that the involvement of emancipatory value meant re-examining the needs of certain residents rather than making assumptions about what they should be. To do so, the Centre's architects developed a diagram to examine the place of residents in the design process, looking at individual cases. The model, which consisted of a series of interactive steps to be taken by various actors in the design, aimed to indicate the optimal layout of services and maximum flexibility. The resulting model was applicable both in the early phase as a design tool and, afterwards, as a means of evaluation using resident questionnaires (▶FIG. 22).[81]

The diagram as a tool to create flexibility was not a novelty that emerged from the Institute's collaboration with *Praxis* philosophers; it might be seen as a detour. Architects reinforced their previous experience of working with diagrams as a common basis for discussion with philosophers. In the architects' opinion, their diagrams had already proved applicable as a reference for philosophy. One from a 1973 series that studied the relation of activities and housing functions was based on Marx and Agnes Heller's analysis of needs, with humans seen as beings of praxis (▶FIG. 23A). The diagram presents the apartment as a dynamic surface on which activities rather than rooms are laid out. The user is a fictional character who, on entering an apartment, connects to the space in various ways according to needs, wishes and activities. These are listed on the right of the diagram, from biological to intellectual and social performances, imagining what a person might do in an apartment. The activities on the list relate to each other according to the principles of exclusion and proximity in space and time. On the basis of the matrix, a critically tolerable combination of activities was identified, and they were assigned a minimal tolerable amount of space. According to these amounts, areas were formed in the apartment that were not limited to a single function or isolated in time. In this way, for example, the dining room included an extended hallway between the bedroom and the living area, and the living room could be adapted as a children's room, etc. Thanks to a fairly extensive analysis of possibilities, the minimum space covered the maximum number of options. Activities that were initially brought together in mutual relationships are used as an organizational device rather than fixed residential areas. Rather than a living room, dining room or bedroom, they were attached to points that were compatible with the position of the column in the IMS system. Following this gradation from human need to specific spatial layout, the apartment was seen as a dynamic surface set in a time framework with the maximum number of occupants in the minimum possible surface area.[82]

The diagram is very similar to the Generator, the diagram that Cedric Price developed in 1977 to study the same thing: compatibility of activities to attain flexibility (▶FIG. 23B). Price's diagram was far better known than that of the Centre for Housing, but their shared interest was the product of an era concerned with engaging sociological means, emerging data science and language tools to address architecture as a social consciousness capable of adapting to users' needs and desires. As Sylvia Lavin pointed out, Price's Generator project was an attempt to come up with a way of building that promoted feelings conducive to creative impulses. These would be taken from surveys and questionaries designed to gather data from people with the aim of supporting needs and desires by a series of infinitely changeable architectural components. »The creative building was not an outcome, but an inventory of specific options.« At the same time, the material produced offered no evidence as to what the building would look like, instead being a fairly ambiguous state of affairs that invited projection and myth-making.[83] Before the architectural drawing, the diagram was a tool for generating a design not exclusively conceived by architects. It also empowered users to be the architects of their own space.[84]

The difference between Cedric Price's studies and those of the Centre for Housing was that the latter applied its results to concrete building on a far broader scale. The rapid modernization of Yugoslav society provided the framework for translating these

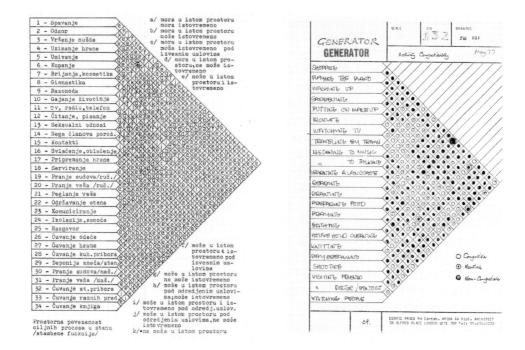

▶23a Left: Spatial relations of housing functions. Čanak Mihailo, scientific work »Ljudske potrebe i stambene funkcije«, 1973, IMS Centre for Housing.

▶23b Right: Cedric Price, Generator: Activity Compatibility Chart, May 1977. Ink and ink stamp over electrostatic print on paper, 29.69 × 20.64 cm. DR1995:0280:651:004:008, Cedric Price Fonds © CCA Collection.

theories and diagrams into buildings according to a range of patterns. Commenting on obstacles to this process, one of the founding members of the Centre for Housing, architect Mihailo Čanak, wrote that the method of determining critical states based on theoretical analysis was not always applicable, because it required more space than the socially and economically justified quality level. The quest for flexibility was also, obviously, due to the need for the fairly restricted number of square metres required by the policy of a right to housing. In an attempt to answer the question of how else to approach the concept of flexible housing, bearing in mind size limit, the author refers to Arnold Gehlen's thesis on the lack of specificity. Human needs can only be met by an entirely indefinite (neutral) space. This remains an ideal, as the apartment is a technical creation. Nonetheless, the search calls for an increase in neutrality of the space. In this way, the maximum possible uncertainty was considered central to the fulfilment of human needs in the Yugoslav context, and the apartments were fairly neutral.[85]

Creating an ideal apartment within the IMS prefabrication system was a constant aim of the Centre for Housing until its dissolution in 1986. Its research has been incorporated into numerous housing projects at home and abroad, and instituted as a handbook that is still in use of official numeric standards for sizes and relations of apartment spaces. Reflecting the Yugoslav position in the Cold War, the diagrams helped to mediate discrepancies between the rise of industrialization and the drive to host migration. Moreover, influenced by philosophical debate, architects developed a variety of flexible solutions by incorporating these diagrams. Among other reasons, this was possible due to the promotion of international research as a means to relate to practice. On this subject, Čanak wrote:

»Incomes at the Institute were miserable, at the existential edge, but there were a lot of foreign scholarships, many congresses in the country and abroad, and apartments were shared. Associates brought projects individually won at competitions to be developed at the Centre. Contrary to practice, research was subsidized. So each year we organized trips to European countries. We completed specializations in France and the Netherlands, and I collaborated for 15 years with the UN Committee for Building, Housing and Urbanism in Geneva.«[86]

As well as engineers, technologists, philosophers and sociologists, numerous semi-skilled and unskilled builders passed through the Institute on short-term contracts. The group involved was very heterogeneous in terms of background and ambitions, while sharing the same imagination. Some were more interested in pursuing the social construct of participation, others in direct profit. In terms of socialization they were aligned with Castoriadis's view on autonomy in that they were concerned with their work as the task of constructing society. The aura of collective production was, then, accepted, raising the profile of the process. Autonomy in this sense meant the possibility of public visibility of their achievements and the freedom to make decisions about all aspects of construction and planning.

What was not in line with Castoriadis' vision was that the Institute was not a short-term union that fell apart when the group ceased to be consistent, leaving the work open to risk. The participants were not all inquirers interested in contemplating and doing at the same time, but rather average people of ordinary decisions caught up by a particular imaginary. As Raphaël Gély recalled in writing about imagination, affection and rationality in Castoriadis: »It is wrong to think that by dint of insisting on the imaginary, Castoriadis would abandon the horizon of critical reason. Simply, critical reason is not on its own capable of generating the emotional adhesion of individuals to the very ideal of an autonomous individual and collective life.«[87] Without the rhetoric of participation, though representing it in the building, members were also driven by emotion and imagination, and this is what pushed cooperation further.

That autonomy existed as a form of emancipatory development is perhaps the strongest parallel that can be drawn with Castoriadis's view of it. This development was due both to interaction with the philosophical debate and the international exchange that had been ongoing since the mid-sixties. In building in different geographies through work with the local population, the initial core of the structural system changed and the level of participation increased. In the application of the system in Cuba, building was done with a significantly higher percentage of local laymen organized into micro-brigades. In its further application in Yugoslavia, the system was not only designed and built by the Institute, but also by architects in general, some of whom used the principle to promote other forms of participation. This was the case in the late seventies of a housing project for the Cerak neighbourhood of Belgrade, where the IMS system was used as part of a solution to negotiate with residents. Housing was built while adopting solutions for individual users. The flexibility was reinforced

▶24
Darko Marušić, Milenija Marušić, Nedeljko
Borovnica, Cerak Vinogradi Housing, Belgrade,
1977–1987, and »Flexible-plan« apartment diagrams,
1981, both ink on paper, 45 × 45 cm. The Museum of
Modern Art, New York.

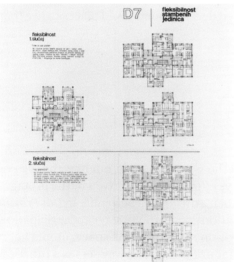

not just in the apartments themselves, but also through the layout of buildings on the site, which, in the spirit of Team 10, abandoned rectangular forms in favour of more circular outlines. Negotiation did not stop in the construction phase; decades-long cooperation between architects and residents has won national and international recognition (▶FIG. 24).[88] In this way, the initial ambition to create an open system, an open diagram, an open flat, and, finally, an open urban layout also gained a degree of autonomy.

What social models were present throughout the process? Engineers in the role of inventors on site gained recognition. The employment of women was promoted, though a lot more could have been done. Women were occasional members of the *Praxis* circle (Agnes Heller, Zagorka Pešić Golubović), were active in youth actions, and worked as architects and sociologists at the Centre for Housing. The attempt to establish self-governance also helped to promote feminism, as apparent in the ency-clopaedia of self-governance that explains the social instruments to enable parents to take part in planning housing to create an urban solution that would reinforce gender equality.[89] This was mostly explicit in day-care centres and public restaurants around the housing development, and in the allocation of laundries on the top floors of buildings so that the home could be partially separated from household work. Despite all this, women mostly ran the domestic space in the new homes and also in Experimental Housing, especially among the first generation of residents. This form of life was an experiment, too, and they liked the facilities, the proximity of schools and shops, and the sense of novelty in general. To modern housing they brought some of their habits, usually from the countryside where they had grown up. They shared things and gathered in the courtyards. With a loose framework of collective owner-ship, they spontaneously appropriated their surroundings. In all of these iterations, housing built as a result of wanting to be modern seemed open enough to accumulate a plural reality without ghettoization. Despite their poor maintenance, mirroring the decline of self-governance, the housing schemes created as a result of the search for an open system were permanently considered decent, much-loved places to live that preserve some qualities of the initial ideals.

Conclusion

Finally, the main focus of this chapter is not the system in itself, but how the system was produced and tested as part of a collective effort. This was driven by the protago-nists' imagination, which corresponds to Bloch's dream of a better life in *Das Prinzip Hoffnung*. This dream in the process of realization goes through stages of anticipation and attempts to build utopia. While anticipation relies on blank space, utopia has a concrete goal to be realized. The utopian that unfolds in this way serves a function as a working tool. Bloch writes that the utopian function appears in accordance with the fields of technical, architectural or geographical utopias. Each plan or object that comes into contact with utopia has a surplus value because it reaches beyond its sta-tionary ideology and represents a substratum of a particular cultural heritage. This means that objects made with a utopian intent affect individuals on an everyday level.[90]

The utopian doing in this case was the search for an open system that would engage social production and construct imagined housing that had previously been anticipated. The concrete attempt to build the imaginary is, then, the first lesson to be learned from this narrative. The same message pervades Castoriadis's quote that opens this chapter: imagination is the power to make be that which *realiter* is not. Although the statement sounds obvious, it is precisely the effort to make the non-ex-isting appear that is the active, difficult and, ultimately, new component of the process. The main challenge in expressing imagination and its best chance for failure is to pursue its concrete construction. However, this is also the most revolutionary task of imagination, as, without the possibility of material construction, we cannot speak of praxis as a form of active doing. Bloch further helped to understand this attempt as a continuous process, a form of accepted material culture of transformation on many levels. In this sense, it might be concluded that insofar as the open system proved to be the ongoing means to transformation, it fulfilled its utopian function.

Another important point is the relevance of the social contract as a means of production of imagination. Although in the Yugoslav case this construct was hugely ambitious and partly rhetorical at the zoomed-out scale of politics, on a closer-to-individual level it tabled the issue of cooperation within the institution. Here, Castoriadis's analysis of the social imaginary and the institution helped to strengthen the knowledge that institutions exist as a non-exclusive higher phenomenon that belongs to the superstructure. Conversely, and ideally, the institution strives to be self-created, based on the nature and content of social life in a given history. Achieved in this way, institutions serve as a necessary precondition for social production where the relation between humans and things, objects and buildings, seems unique because it is instituted in a particular way. In the process, society takes the material from what is already there—in this case, the project of modernization—but also extends towards new possibilities by drawing on imagination. Rooted in imagination, institutions are created by means of social representation: saying (*legein*) and making (*teukhein*) of individuals. *Teukhein* includes praxis, but it also means technology. As such, technology is not left out of the means of social production, but is bound up with language as a social contract. When both saying and making are present, the new institution is a common world, *kosmos koinos*: the positing of individuals, their types, relations and activities, but also the positing of things, their types, relations and signification—all in a framework of reference that is instituted as common.[91]

Castoriadis's interpretation of the interdependence between social imagination, its institutions, and making and saying seems fitting and critical to the work of the Institute for Materials Testing. How were these terms aligned? Insofar as the Institute succeeded in being an institution that provided technological means in the context of the site and the actors in a cooperative-based production chain. In this sense, even controversial topics of architectural modernism such as mass prefabrication had the capacity to be crafted and to mediate collective production.

▶25 Clips from the series of documentary films about the construction of New Belgrade, I. *Kad ratni doboši umuknu*, III. *Biće to novi grad*, IV. *Prepreke su mnogobrojne*, and V. *Život na pesku*, directed by Miloš Bukumirović (Belgrade: Slavija film I, 1959–1962) © Yugoslav Film Archives.

Praxis and *Lebenswelt*: The Construction Site as Lifeworld

In the previous chapters I have argued that housing as part of societal modernisation was actually crafted in Yugoslavia by employing imagination in material production. This was possible due to the historical set-up that merged the active philosophical scene, the post-war need for reconstruction and the shift of means of production towards a self-governed economy. Among the material outcomes of the existing imaginary was the open system, intended to be followed by social participation in its production. The trial of setting it up was led by one of Yugoslavia's self-governed enterprises, the Institute for Materials Testing (IMS). The social engagement in construction that the Institute promoted was part of the same tendency as discussions about participative production that were going on in politics and philosophy. A philosophical interpretation of participation was based on a reinvention of the Marxian concept of praxis, a topic that was for a while present in philosophy worldwide, and which reached its focal point in the gathering of philosophers in Yugoslavia.[1] The overlap between ongoing construction and debates about philosophy in the public realm led to the thesis that, with collective building in Yugoslavia, we can associate the idea of praxis, as discussed by philosophers from and visiting the country. To continue this analogy, the construction site emerged as a place where collective production engaged the everyday life of its protagonists. This life on site took the form either of praxis seen as action or based on imagination. Aspects of the actions and imagination existed both in theoretical discussions and in everyday life, and finally succeeded as categories that brought collective production to life. The work actions generated a movement to build a new city that rose to prominence in a situation of post-war destruction and the need to recuperate and continue life. The Institute for Materials Testing was successful in understanding the collective imaginary of what housing and work should represent for citizens in order to organize the production as a collective effort. In this sense, both concepts proved their importance as mediums for praxis in the collective production of architecture. Insofar as austerity (action) and paradigm shift (imagination) were able to mobilize participants, what happened when the framework seemed to be established and the potential builders found themselves on apparently stable ground? From that moment on, was the further development of technology able to continue address building as a form of praxis without losing focus on individual protagonist? These questions serve as a guideline for exploring the further development of the building practice of the Institute for Materials Testing and the development of the theory of praxis echoing around Yugoslavia.

A Critique: What is Praxis about in Scientific Civilization?

Once the construction site was established as a place of social engagement in New Belgrade, as of the mid-sixties the Institute started to export this invention worldwide. Although some exports were to developed countries such as Austria, Italy, Hungary or

▶1   Non-Aligned Conference, Belgrade, 1961 © Museum of Yugoslavia.

the United States, most involved the newly liberated Global South, with destinations such as Egypt, Angola, Philippines, Ethiopia, Cuba, Iraq or Iran. They were largely the result of Yugoslavia's international politics, the most explicit characteristic of which was the establishment of the Non-Aligned Movement. In order to place the Institute's further production efforts into broader perspective, it seems useful to digress for a moment and explain how this event affected the process of modernization as the Institute's central concern.

The Non-Aligned Movement (NAM) was officially established at the Belgrade conference in 1961. Representatives of the liberated nations of Africa and Asia gathered in Belgrade Parliament, where the amphitheatre slope was refurbished with a double floor to be able to accommodate an oval table to seat speakers at the same level (▶FIG. 1).[2]

The meeting brought the country in the eyes of world media, transforming a rather peripheral geography into the focus of non-global politics. The conference was the culmination of events of the fifties. This was, above all, Yugoslavia's active engagement with the United Nations since the early fifties, when country gained a seat on the UN Security Council. Faced with the blockade from the Eastern bloc, Yugoslavia benefited from activities in the UN to strengthen its position, and this was explicit in the establishment of contact with African and Asian countries that had just gained independence. They had a favourable view of the Yugoslav case, with its colonial heritage and a strong resistance movement. Accordingly, in the fifties, Yugoslavian representatives worked on UN programs and declarations on self-determination of smaller countries. An example of this collaboration was the country's involvement in the UN Special Fund, set up on the initiative of developing countries that could not benefit from the Marshall plan.[3] The country's role as a mediator in UN politics was perhaps best represented by a large-scale sculpture called *Peace* that was commissioned to the established Yugoslav sculptor Antun Augustinčić and placed in front of the UN headquarters in New York (▶FIG. 2). The typical arrangement of a male figure astride a powerful horse, either returning from the victory or going to war, is replaced by a female figure holding a globe in her hand. The power in the stance

▶2
The sculpture *Peace* in front of the UN Headquarters in New York by Antun Augustinčić, 1954. »Antun Augustinčić«, *Alchetron Free Social Encyclopedia for the World*, 14 April 2022. URL: https://alchetron.com/ Antun-Augustinčić (last accessed: 23 September 2022).

of the horse, combined with the nervous expression in its eyes, represented the urge towards progressive movement in the divided world.[4]

In addition to the active decade in the UN, two meetings in the fifties contributed to the formation of the Non-Aligned Movement, one in Belgrade in 1956 and another in New York in 1960. At the first meeting, Yugoslav President Josip Broz Tito met the Presidents of India and Egypt, Jawaharlal Nehru and Gamal Abdel Nasser. At the second, the membership was extended to the representatives of Indonesia and Ghana, Ahmed Sukarno and Kwame Nkrumah. Afro-Asian meetings began to take place, such as the one in Bandung, Indonesia, hosted by Sukarno in 1955, where the concept of the Third World was outlined. As Vijay Prashad argued in his influential book, *The Darker Nations*, the third world that emerged was not an actual place, but a project in which people of Africa, Asia and Latin America dreamed of a better world. For this dream, the institution of the Third World served as an imaginary table that enabled the powerless to engage in dialog with the powerful and to try to hold them accountable.[5] This concept was inseparable from the NAM, which, after the first conference in 1961, continued to grow despite superpower subversions and internal frictions. The next conferences in Cairo (1964) involved 47 member countries and 10 observers, in Lusaka (1970), 54 members and 9 observers, in Algeria (1973), 75 members and 9 observers, in Colombo, Sri Lanka (1976), 86 members and 10 observers, and in Havana (1979), 94 members and 12 observers (▶FIG. 3).

From the moment it originated, non-alignment represented a multidecade phenomenon that was inseparable from life in Yugoslavia. It was one of its constitutional factors and a major cohesive force in unifying extremely diverse citizen profiles made up of multiple identities, religions and backgrounds. The role the country played at geopolitical level gave it an importance that went far beyond its size on the world map. The exchange taking place expanded beyond politics to colour culture and everyday life. The country opened up to tourism in the fifties, its cinema became popular the world over, Pablo Picasso worked on posters for Yugoslavian films, Hollywood stars acted in the country and astronauts came on official visits. Writer Ivo Andrić won the Nobel Prize for Literature, books on colonialism stared to be written and gained a public, and the Museum of African Art opened in Belgrade. A long list of yearly

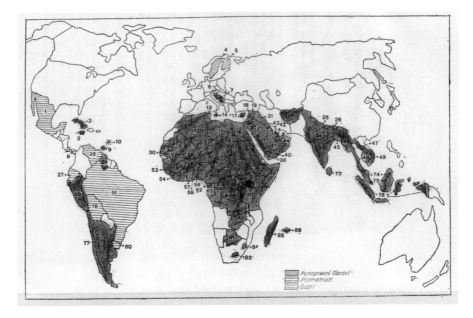

▶3 Maps showing Non-Aligned Movement member countries in 1973 © Ranko Petković, *Teorijski pojmovi nesvrstanosti* (Belgrade: Rad, 1974), available at: Bojana Piškur, »Solidarity in Arts and Culture. Some Cases from the Non-Aligned Movement«, *L'Internationale Online*, 1 October 2016. URL: https://www. internationaleonline.org/research/alter_institutionality/78_solidarity_in_arts_and_culture_some_cases_from_the_non_aligned_movement/ (last accessed: 23 September 2022).

1. Mexico	31. Senegal	60. Nigeria
2. Cuba	32. Mauritania	61. Cameroon
3. Jamaica	33. Mali	62. Equatorial Guinea
4. Sweden	34. Niger	63. Gabon
5. Finland	35. Chad	64. Kongo
6. Austria	36. Sudan	65. The Central African
7. Yugoslavia	37. Ethiopia	Republic
8. Panama	38. Saudi Arabia	66. Zaire
9. Trinidad and Tobago	39. Yemen / Arab Republic	67. Uganda
10. Barbados	40. Yemen / People's	68. Ruanda
11. Morocco	Democratic Republic	69. Burundi
12. Algeria	41. United Arab Emirates	70. Tanzania
13. Tunisia	42. Qatar	71. Kenia
14. Malta	43. Bahrain	72. Somalia
15. Libya	44. Oman	73. Sri Lanka
16. Egypt	45. Bangladesh	74. Malesia
17. Cyprus	46. Burma	75. Singapore
18. Lebanon	47. Laos	76. Indonesia
19. Syria	48. Cambodia	77. Chile
20. Jordan	49. South Vietnam	78. Bolivia
21. Iraq	50. Peru	79. Argentina
22. Kuwait	51. Brazil	80. Uruguay
23. Afghanistan	52. Guinea	81. Botswana
24. India	53. Sierra Leone	82. Zambia
25. Nepal	54. Liberia	83. Lesotho
26. Bhutan	55. Ivory Cost	84. Swaziland
27. Ecuador	56. Upper Volta	85. Madagascar
28. Venezuela	57. Ghana	86. Mauritius
29. Guyana	58. Togo	
30. The Gambia	59. Dahomey	

cultural festivals such as the International Biennial of Graphic Arts in Ljubljana had already gained international recognition as a manifestation that exhibited »basically everything, the whole world«. The country's image of neutrality was explicit when it came to selecting the host for the 1984 Winter Olympics, which were organized in Yugoslavia so that no-one would boycott them. Probably the most famous relic of that time was the famous red passport, which enabled citizens to travel almost anywhere in the world without a visa for decades.[6]

The Yugoslav case was a prototype of how a periphery could obtain significance and become a kind of microcosms. Seen from a broader perspective, the history of the non-aligned movement was a power game in which weaker players sought to establish grounds for survival with their views, always aware of the centres of power (which for a while shifted between East and West). In addition, the NAM was also an ideological project in which the Global South started to construct its own global imaginary. As Bojana Piškur pointed out, its aim was to provincialize world history, as this was the only way it could enter the world forum on an equal footing. To achieve this, the movement made a strong push towards internationalism. Last but certainly not least, the NAM was also a very tangible project that created a new network of economic exchange via alternative routes along which industries, people and knowledge circulated. One important reason for their creation was to strengthen economic collaboration between developing countries in order to avoid dependence on superpowers during the future process of accelerated modernization. In this sense, Yugoslavia supported resistance movements in Africa, Asia and Latin America. This ranged from direct financial donations to technical assistance and offering education to overseas students at schools and universities (40,000 came to Belgrade University alone during the NAM period). Although Yugoslavia never displayed a preference for influencing the development of newly established countries, it also benefited economically from this collaboration. This particularly developed in the seventies and eighties, when Yugoslav enterprises were building throughout Africa, Asia and Latin America. The presence of architects, planners and construction companies settled there offered an alternative source for modern culture and technology.[7]

In this political context, starting in the mid-sixties, one of the new destinations for Institute of Materials Testing was Cuba, just emerging from a revolution and embarking on housing reform. What was the historical set-up in the bigger picture? The well-known British historian Eric Hobsbawm described Cuba at the beginning of sixties as befitting the notion of the Third World, which »became the central pillar of the hope of those who still put their faith in social revolution.«[8] Described as a world revolution area—recently achieved, pending or possible—it had a common denominator of constant social and political instability. Its revolutionary potential was equally evident to both East and West. The latter, though faced with the decline of ideology in stabilized welfare states, still had the entire left wing, humanitarian liberals and moderate social democrats with the »need for something more than social security legislation and rising real wages«.[9] To them, the Third World appeared a fitting scenario to preserve the ideals of the Enlightenment as well as its practical politics. As for the East, the ideology of socialism officially propagated through projects of emancipation, progress and modernization was inevitably compatible with colonial liberation.[10] Although this state of hope did not live up to its promise, the predominate quality of the notion of Third World was its readiness to experiment due to its general instability.

January 1, 1959 served as the official date of the Cuban revolution, which, though small in scale, had the effect of popularizing the guerrilla movement far and wide. For those in Cuba, »the revolution was experienced as a collective honeymoon«,[11] while leftists overseas identified with the image of tropical socialism. The events were a result of certain contingencies leading Cuba to enter communism »by chance« in 1961, driven by the forces of the Cold War. Originally, as Hobsbawm pointed out, the grassroots movement around Fidel Castro never claimed to have Marxist sympathies of any kind. Yet both the social-revolutionary ideology they supported and the passionate anti-communism of the USA »automatically inclined the anti-imperialist Latin rebels to look more kindly on Marx.«[12] The USSR took the Cuba under its wing, increasing its dependence in decades to come.

The historical setting described was turbulent enough to foresee some of the difficulties that the process of social modernization would bring to emerging materiality. In addition, when the Yugoslav Institute completed its open system and started exporting it to Cuba, the moment for this kind of invention was not perfect globally. The theme of prefabrication started to attract criticism and reached its limits at international level. This was far from being directly linked to collective production. The legacy of modern town planning began to leave a rather sour taste due to the loss of urban space in the large monofunctional estates that emerged with the reconstruction of (European) cities after World War II. These were associated either with the bureaucratization of states or with the rise in the periphery driven by the market. From the mid-fifties up until the present day, the well-known debate emerged between the *Siedlungsbau* as a suburban housing estate based on rationalization, standardization, prefabrication and typification most explicit in the paradigm example of New Frankfurt, and the *Städtebau* as cultural model based on historical living conventions. Reactions to modern town planning came from positions of Italian magazine *Casabella-Continuità* (under the direction of Ernesto Nathan Rogers from 1953 to 1965), and later from new generation of architects and historians (Lewis Mumford, *The City in History*, 1962; Aldo Rossi, *L'Architettura della città*, 1966; Colin Rowe, *Collage City*, 1978).[13]

Ernst Bloch himself, who was part of *Praxis* circle, was critical of the lack of ornament in modern architecture, writing that: »The abstract engineer style will not, under any circumstances, become qualitative, despite the phrases that its literati add to it, despite the deceptive freshness of ›modernity‹... Today's technology, which is itself still so abstract, does lead out of the hollow space, even as it is fashioned as an aesthetic one.«[14] The relationship between architecture, industrial production and societal modernization seemed to be a slippery slope that challenged the initial goals of the modern movement. The reaction came in the late fifties with the search for new means of collective production and cohabitation in the field of political theory, too. In 1958, Hannah Arendt published *The Human Condition*, in which she advocated the separation of the concept of work from the repetitive cyclical activities of reproductive labour which she identified with consumer culture and automation processes in production, becoming explicit in the human material environment. In philosophical

►4
Jürgen Habermas's article in the international issue
of *Praxis* journal no. 1/2: »Qu'est que l'histoire« (1966)
© Korčula City Library Ivan Vidali.

terms, the focus on the individual also appeared in works of existentialism, such as those by Jean-Paul Sartre. New voices in the main representative body for modern architecture, the CIAM, were not silent, either, shifting the discourse towards participation. CIAM 1959, then, promoted concepts such as everyday culture and user-based architecture, the emergence of which followed the withdrawal of the older generation of modern movement architects at CIAM X, held in 1956 in Dubrovnik.[15]

In the *Praxis* circle in Yugoslavia, new voices began to talk about the relation between production and the individual. One was Jürgen Habermas, a member of the third generation of German philosophers to take the stage at the Korčula Summer School of Philosophy, following Ernst Bloch, Herbert Marcuse and Hans-Georg Gadamer. After Lefebvre, who brought up Marxian sociology by suggesting that the social engagement of anonymous citizens could take the form of making (*poiesis* as part of praxis), and Bloch, who saw praxis as active imagination and the construction of utopia in reality, Habermas was initially more sceptical and less encouraging. His appearances at Korčula centred on the question of whether there was any possibility at all of praxis in a scientific civilization and modern means of production. This concern was apparent in his article published in *Praxis* journal with the title »Technischer Fortschritt und soziale Lebenswelt« (Technical Progress and the World of Social Life, see ►FIG. 4).

The text was published as part of the debate about how to deal with the notion of history (*Qu'est que l'histoire*). In it, Habermas announced his argument that the relation between technological progress and social life can no longer be seen as naturally given and developed by stochastics of history, and instead needs to be treated and regulated. To achieve this, it is necessary to solve the problem of translation, establishing a link between technology and the world of social life. According to Habermas, this translation is driven not by art, but by social production, which can be both constructive and destructive. The poet does not write a poem after recognising the laws of nuclear physics, but when he sees Hiroshima. By prioritizing the praxis of everyday life as a medium for translation between different fields, Habermas also pointed out the importance of this practical place, and asked how technology could be returned to the

▶5   Left: Jürgen Habermas lecturing at the Summer School of Philosophy, Korčula, 1968, on Marx and Revolution. Right: Habermas's article in the international issue of *Praxis* no. 1/2: »Marx and Revolution« (1969) © Korčula City Library Ivan Vidali.

consensus of democratically united citizens. According to the philosopher, this was not happening in either the East or the West in the sixties. In the former, planning bureaucracy was not a sufficient precondition for the creation of a material project of emancipated society. In the latter, Max Weber's model of strong leadership that guided scientific development reached its limits with the rise of technocracy and scientists in charge of running the machines, accompanied by the weakened political will. This situation called for a third way, which Habermas described as a pragmatic model that relies on translation, so that individuals can acknowledge both political will and technological progress to empower themselves in both ends.[16] Not long after he announced the problem of translation, he expanded his argument with a lecture and article in 1968, when the theme of the summer school was Marx and Revolution. Habermas talked under the topic of the conditions for revolutionizing late capitalist social systems, and his stance was an extension of the argument of his book published in 1963, *Theorie und Praxis* (▶FIG. 5).[17]

The book, an extensive interpretation of the historical development of the concept of praxis and its ultimate decline, was presented in *Praxis* circles before the philosopher. It was reviewed by a local philosopher, Milan Kangrga, in the 1965 issue of *Praxis*. In this review, in Habermas's lecture and also in *Theorie und Praxis*, the basic theme centred on the same issue: critique of the relationship between technology, social labour and the individual in modern means of production. In summary, the argument described the following:

Praxis historically appears as an activity that leads to the emancipation of citizens and relates to the materiality of life in cities. In the classical tradition of philosophy, the relationship between theory and praxis referred to the aspects of good, righteous, truthful behaviour in the life—be it private or collective—of individuals and citizens. In the eighteenth century, this practice was extended. Practice-oriented theory no longer embraced nature as a given, but dealt with the development of humanity as autonomous. After Freud's discoveries in psychoanalysis, the experience of emancipation also included critical insight into relationships of power. This meant that a person should take a critical approach to each dogmatic situation around them and, by engaging practical reason, adopt a position. At different scales, »each new stage of emancipation wins a further victory«.[18] A higher level of reflection is a step towards the autonomy of the individual, and this sequence of emancipatory circles represents the best legacy of the development of Western philosophy. Habermas recognizes this kind of reason as practical (related to praxis) and associates it with an individual who takes action.

The primary means for this kind of action is communication. Habermas writes that »in the time when« theory was still related to the praxis«, society was a system of action of human beings who communicated through speech and »realize[d] social intercourse within the context of conscious communication«. By means of communication, members took their place in a collective subject as a whole, capable of action.[19] In this way, the idea of praxis appears as a process of continual emancipation, self-reflection and the interaction of individuals, who, in various spheres of political, productive and social settings, negotiate their actions.

After explaining what praxis is in terms of citizenship, Habermas focused on its decline due to the rise of positivism—that is, the relationship between science, politics and the public in advanced capitalism.[20] His main criticism was of the consequences of the rise of science as a technological force—the theme present in *Theorie und Praxis* as well as in his lectures at Korčula. Accordingly, he wrote that, in any industrially advanced society »research, technology, production and administration have coalesced into a system which cannot be surveyed as a whole«, that lost its centre while at the same time becoming the basis of our lives.[21] By organizing knowledge as the prime productive force in institutions that advance research and technology, a space is created in which developed societies are able to ensure economic growth and the loyalty of their citizens. Instead of individual advancement, institutionalized progress by means of knowledge and technology has become a source of value in itself. This same apparatus creates a technocratic consciousness that fetishizes knowledge and, according to the argument posited by another praxis philosopher, Herbert Marcuse, becomes the new ideology. What is lost is the position of praxis, as what is practical (related to praxis) is colonized by what is technical (technology).

Further critique addressed the spread of the phenomenon worldwide due to the material production going in the triangle of advanced capitalist states, the East and Third World countries. The tendency towards technocracy was becoming stabilized due to an alliance between the economic stability of the West and the former colonial countries, freed from political imperialism. Another reason was the internal pressure to retain the loyalty of the masses by means of economic growth, due to the external presence of possible alternatives in the form of state socialism, though it did not seem to be long lasting.[22] Later, Habermas was to find this practice obvious in the way cities started to look. The alienation of praxis by industrial production was explicit in all the applications of modern architecture driven by the extremes of either the market or bureaucratic state administration. Habermas reinforced this point, writing: »While the Modern Movement recognized and responded correctly to the challenges [...] of new needs and new technical design possibilities, it was essentially helpless in the face of dependences on the imperatives of the market and administrative planning.«[23]

Much of the problematic that Habermas explained was part of the reality surrounding the Institute for Materials Testing's entry into Cuba, at the same time as the philosopher was lecturing at Korčula. In the first instance, this was the fact that Cuba, regarded as one of the developing countries, was aiming to import internationally developed technological equipment to address an urgency created by internal changes. The urgency in question was the housing issue, which, in the wake of revolution in 1959, seemed to mirror the larger picture: the revolutionary shift in production, pre-revolutionary agrarian heritage, and the fast-track connection to the chain of global industrial production. Havana, which prior to 1959 developed as a city of entertainment, casinos and pleasure dominated by American capital, had by far the greater distribution of services.[24] With underdeveloped countryside and a semi-colonial history, the 1960s brought a huge deficit in housing and social buildings. The figures showed that, in the sixties, 700 000 apartments were needed, with the average annual production focused on the still insufficient 32000 flats.[25] Existing housing made the problem worse: only 30% were described as acceptable, while 45% of housing was slums, and 25% was described as being of abnormal size. A goal of more even distribution was promoted, and the means to this end was prefabrication, a technology which, although unfamiliar, was seen to offer a solution. Furthermore, guided by state politics, Cuba was implementing top-down housing reform. This meant that construction methods were to be applied at the large scale, with all problems of administrative planning addressed by the newly created institutions.

This chain was set up by the Revolutionary Government with the aim of solving living conditions in rural areas and unhealthy neighbourhoods in provincial capitals.[26] The all shared the feature of combining housing and agriculture. So, in 1959 the Institute of Savings and Housing (Instituto de Ahorro y Vivienda, INAV) was created, followed by the Directorate of Peasant Dwellings (Viviendas Campesinas) in 1960. The two were later unified in the Ministry of Construction (Ministerio de Construcciones) that was to mediate the country's biggest building push in the seventies. The final incarnation of this body was the Housing and Urban Planning Group (Grupo Nacional de Viviendas y Urbanismo) of the DESA (Ministry of Development of Social and Agricultural Buildings).[27] The transformation of Cuban agriculture that started in the revolutionary year therefore went hand in hand with housing prospect in an institutional partnership that was active until the fall of the Berlin Wall.

The domestic Cuban Sandino system of traditional load-bearing walls was insufficient for the envisioned scale of housing reform, and in 1962 the search for a suitable construction method began. Prefabrication began to gain ground, but the practice was completely unknown. To acknowledge the system, trials sites for construction using globally available prefabricated systems opened all over the country. From 1965 to 1974, 22 sites, to build 500 apartments a year, were tested in order to provide the government with a compatible partner for the reform.[28] Prior to building, delegations were sent to various countries in order to learn about the technology, visit local construction sites and discuss possible projects in Cuba. Yugoslavia was one of the destinations, as in June 1966 Cuban Vice-Minister of Housing (Ministry of Construction), Alberto

▶6   Cuban magazine *Bohemia*, »Edificios Altos«, image of the IMS open site for prefabrication next to a list of international tested systems (1974, number unavailable): 17, 19 © IMS Archive.

Arrinda Pinero, wrote to the Cuban Ambassador in Yugoslavia, José Luis Pérez, that: »Our Ministry wishes to experiment as soon as we have sufficient technical data with the system of prestressed concrete[29] developed by professor Branko Žeželj.« Floor slabs were of particular interest as it was said that they could be easily made.[30] Not long after, New Belgrade became one of the worldwide construction sites visited by Cuban delegations.[31]

Once the Cubans had completed their reviews, the process ended with the selection of six well-known prefabricated systems: three with large-scale panels, two with movable moulds and one structural framework system from the IMS as shown in the economic section of Cuba's oldest consumer magazine, *Bohemia* (▶FIG. 6).

The six systems were further compared based on the results of the experimental buildings that were assigned to each, to be built in Cuba between 1968 and 1969.[32] The testing process was completed by catalogues of the urban and architectural fit of the system, the number of prefabricated elements needed, and the way in which the element would be produced. The trial, which began with a single building, aimed to address the entire housing reform in Havana and the surrounding province. The IMS delivered its 48-apartment model in the old town of Havana in 1968 and stepped out of the competition, getting the green light to apply its technology in the overall housing reform, beginning in 1971.

With this rather peculiar start, the IMS introduced its work into Cuba with the aim of the country's technological advancement. Seen through the lens of Habermas's critique, there were many preconditions that actually went against production being seen as praxis: top-down planning, centralized resources, the large scale of construction and a non-existent tradition of a technological package imported from abroad. In this light, Habermas seems relevant firstly to address the difficulty of the moment by recognizing the danger of defamiliarized means of production that could ultimately create distance in the participation process. His critique of praxis in the production chain of Cold War politics thereby helps to raise the question of whether collective building was even possible at this intersection of transfer, modernisation and industry. In addition, Habermas's argument contributes to an understanding of the commonality of this situation on a global level and to the relevance of finding the means to understand it to this day. His focus is not unrelated to the anonymous residential landscape that spread in one way or another in the mid-twentieth century at global level, its existence not without justification. By articulating the problem, Habermas, too, was searching for answers; if industrial production faced an obvious problem in relation to the possibility of collective making, what were the possible ways out? Although the framework in which the Institute was operating suffered from a possible deficit of praxis, when the focus turns on a specific microhistory, differences and peculiarities emerge in the way technology was transformed.[33] More precisely, this can be seen in the way the IMS brought its knowledge from Yugoslavia and negotiated with the prevailing social moment in Cuba. To understanding this process, Habermas's further search for a means of praxis within the lines of modernization appears to be relevant as it is to describe close history of transfer in order to learn from its particularities.

How did transformation take place at the level of microhistory?

The answer to this question is a departure from the main reason why IMS was chosen to support housing reform in Cuba. The reason lay in the simplicity of its technology, that seemed intuitive enough for laypeople to build.[34] This capacity had already been developed by the IMS in Yugoslavia, but the concept was further promoted in Cuba. This meant that the production of elements was based on internationally obtained technology, local material and the involvement of *microbrigades*, or microbrigades. Microbrigades were a Cuban invention to enable collective building by laypeople, associated with a plan of economic development to solve the housing shortage. The usual scenario was that workers in particular enterprises who had no housing joined together in groups of thirty-three participants. Instead of an enterprise, a brigade would work on the construction site. The workload was divided between those working regularly in enterprises and groups on leave, both of whom would have a mutual share in the apartments. According to the contract, the microbrigade would construct the building from the foundation up, with project, technical assistance, material and mechanization provided by the Ministry of Construction. The brigade could take three forms. Most conventionally, participants in construction were paid the regular salary they would be earning in their original enterprise. Alternatively, they could either volunteer or work in their free time (pure microbrigades), or the brigade could be made up of members of the surrounding neighbourhood instead of a work unit (social microbrigades).[35] In a recent record of this practice, *Microbrigades—Variations of a Story*, the filmmakers filmed the oral histories of microbrigade members next to the buildings constructed. They explain that the motive for taking part was not always to get an apartment, as fairly frequently those who took part in building were not given a home. They had no say in the design, either; rather, the predominant motivation for taking part was solidarity, along with the model of a social contract. As well as their voices, the film also presents images of materiality of the setting. This materiality appears as a makeshift collage of fragments of imported modernism and the existing surrounding that conveyed a sense of disparity and decay (▶FIG. 7).[36]

The fact that the microbrigade movement started to reach a significant proportions in building throughout Cuba[37] influenced the IMS to further adapt its work

▶7

Stills from the film *Microbrigades—Variations of a Story*, Florian Zeyfang, Lisa Schmidt-Colinet, Alexander Schmoeger (2013) HD, 31 min.

to semi-skilled participation as an integral part of prefabrication. With the aim of technology becoming the work of everyone, people became familiarized with the concept of open construction. This differed from Habermas's critical scenario as, for a while, it provided an opportunity for alternative knowledge arising from the process of industrialization. The advancement of participation on the construction site could be seen as in line with another point that Habermas promoted after his critique of positivism. Namely, although Habermas was critical when arguing that praxis was facing decline, he offered no alternatives to the spheres of scientific development. On the contrary, he directed his arguments to searching for the place of praxis in the only known historical moment as a form of praxis concerned with modern development.[38] He therefore argued that the continuous chain of emancipation needed to advance further in the sphere of knowledge, as it was »prior to positivism (when) critical knowledge referred to scientific orientation in action.«[39] His critique led to the final conclusion that the function of knowledge (and production) needs to be understood in terms of social labour.[40]

In architectural terms, this resonated with the initial social goals of modern architecture and the foundational myth of Bauhaus, where the production of materials was collectively addressed.[41] This was approved by Habermas himself, who, in his writings on architecture, pointed to moments when modern architecture failed, but also to other, successful ones, »when the aesthetic logic of constructivism encountered the use orientation of a strict functionalism«.[42] Here, the social power seen in

»the inherent aesthetic logic of functionalism« managed to merge the processes of societal modernization with cultural modernism.[43] This argument could point to the conclusion that societal modernization is not outside the scope of authentic production and also that a certain marginality of the ordinary residential landscape may be relevant to social activism. K. Michael Hays recognized Habermas's preference as both »pro-modern/anti modern« and explained that, for Habermas, the wholesale rejection of modernism constituted a regression.[44] How, then, could praxis be understood in the context of modernization?

The answer can be found in Habermas's words:

»As artisans were formerly guided, in working on their materials, by rules of experience which had been proven in the tradition of their trade, so in the same way engineers in all sectors can rely on such scientifically tested predictions in the choice of the means they employ, of their instruments and operations.«

Construction based on scientific methods can be practical in the same way as craftsmanship. Still, the reliability of the rules is what distinguishes technique (*techne*) from the technology of today, as the latter has a tendency to extend and rationalize our powers of technical control over objects.[45]

In this rather illustrative passage, there is a hint of an architectural vision pointing to both the new possibilities and the danger of the alienation of the construction site from the idea of praxis—and from the prospect of the collective production of material in the domain of technology. Habermas is, then, returning to us the idea of construction as a place of active engagement, one that was foreshadowed by the IMS open system in the microbrigade context. For its promise to be fulfilled, how could the construction site work as place of praxis? Staying with Habermas's view of it, the process of building would need to be based primarily on communication between the participants. This way of building would need to involve the participants' *Lebenswelt*.

Construction Site and *Lebenswelt*

To explore the analogy of the construction site as connected to the lifeworld of participants, let us briefly examine the notion of *Lebenswelt*.

Lifeworld, or *Lebenswelt*, is the concept introduced by Edmund Husserl and reintroduced by Habermas with the aim of further advancing the Marxist theory of praxis. As we have seen, for Habermas the only possible way to overcome the alienation of production in industrial society was to return to communication as means of practical behaviour. To advocate this point, Habermas built his theory of communicative action, calling it another version of the philosophy of praxis.[46] The essence of this theory is interaction between participants. This was new compared both to Marxian readings, where praxis was based on labour, and Castoriadis and Bloch's argument that praxis revolved around imagination, institution and utopia. To get as close as possible to participants, Habermas introduced the notion of lifeworld, which he explained as a

Reproduction processes \ Structural components	Culture	Society	Person
Cultural reproduction	Transmission, critique, acquisition of cultural knowledge	Renewal of knowledge effective for legitimation	Reproduction of knowledge relevant to child rearing, education
Social integration	Immunization of a central stock of value orientations	Coordination of actions via intersubjectively recognized validity claims	Reproduction of patterns of social membership
Socialization	Enculturation	Internalization of values	Formation of identity

►8
Reproductive functions of action oriented to mutual understanding. From Jürgen Habermas's The *Theory of Communicative Action 2. The Critique of Functionalist Reason* (Cambridge: Polity Press, 1987), 144.

transcendental place where speaker and hearer meet and reciprocally make claims. Serving as a background for communication, the lifeworld is a metaphorical place where they can criticize and confirm the validity of their claims, settle disagreements and come to agreements.[47] When speakers and listeners come to a mutual understanding about something in the world, they are moving within a common lifeworld.[48] The lifeworld is, then, a stage on which common action takes place as related not to the individual participant but to the tacit interconnected sphere of the inner worlds of all. In this way it is not a fixed condition, as participants need to negotiate by arguing on principles, norms and techniques. With the focus on lifeworld, Habermas underscored the ever-present possibility of transition from an unquestionable system and rigid surrounding framework (also political) to the condition of constant change by negotiating from within (present, for example, in pop-up realities).

With his explanation of how the lifeworld is reproduced through communication, Habermas wrote lines that can be easily imagined in the scenario of the building actions:

In communicative action, participants work cooperatively based on a shared definition of the situation (a certain state of the construction site). A leading theme emerges, followed by the plans that participants draw up based on their understanding of the situation (what they would like to build). The participants carry out the plans together by means of action defined as common (an agreement how to build). The consensus regarding the description of the situation is an *a priori* condition. Participants seek to avoid two risks: not coming to an understanding, and the action plan miscarrying.[49] When a consensus is reached, communicative action reproduces the lifeworld in three possible ways: through cultures, through society and through personalities (►FIG. 8).

Here, culture is the stock on which the participants draw for interpretations of the world (such as familiar material culture, conventional tastes, an inherited culture of work, etc.). Society is the legitimate structure such as law, by means of which participants regulate membership of a group and ensure solidarity (as, in construction, the process of testing produces norms for building). Personality refers to the competences that make participant able to speak and act in the process and assert their own identity (hence the possibility for layperson to choose to join).[50] »While participants in interaction turned towards the world« reproduce mutual understanding, they simultaneously reproduce their membership in collectives and their identities.[51] If they succeed, the communicative action reproduces a new culture that emerges from the process. It brings social integration and establishes solidarity. It leads via the process of socialization to the formation of personal identities. This reproduction is accompanied by memorized learning as a form of progress. These Habermas finds in the continuation of valid knowledge, the integration of group solidarity with adopted norms and values, and the socialization of responsible actors and successive generations.[52]

Themes such as situation, plan, consensus, cultural background, solidarity, coordination, socialization, collectives, assertion of identity and continuation of knowledge all point to the good will in undertaking a common task. Explicitly, Habermas's argument on praxis based on the notion of lifeworld has to do with the further emancipation of subjects. Seen in the light of the construction site, this emancipation would mean that the integration of the group by norms goes hand in hand with the testing process in a kind of emerging construction law that entails agreeing how to build by keeping the construction process open. The integration of a group by means of cultural exchange would mean consensus regarding the use of materials and different working cultures. Finally, integration by inserting personal identities involves questioning the oral histories of those involved in the construction process.

To what extent was this present on the IMS's experimental housing construction site in Havana?

Integration by norm: Negotiating how to test

The attempt to integrate a group of builders by means of the material testing process was officially supported from the beginning. Work on the IMS's Experimental Building in Havana began by promoting builders and field engineers as protagonists for whole process. The aim was explicit in the illustration of the project by a drawing that shows construction and occupation of the building as two simultaneous activities, as if the state of construction was a normal everyday practice (▶FIG. 9). The process started in Yugoslavia, where Cubans began their process of education. Those who came had different backgrounds, as can be seen from the documentation of their visits in the Institute's archives. In 1966, Orlei, Ruis and Campos made up the Cuban delegation that came to learn about the technology at first hand and visit New Belgrade construction

▶9
Perspective drawing of the IMS's Experimental Building in Havana by architects from the Cuba Ministry of Construction (MICONS), Institute of Housing, 1968 © The IMS Archive, Belgrade. Also published in Jelica Jovanović, »From Yugoslavia to Angola: Housing as Postcolonial Technical Assistance. City Building through IMS Žeželj Housing Technology«, *Architektúra & Urbanizmus* no. 3–4 (2019): 170–181.

▶10
Testing a model for the IMS Experimental Building in Havana © IMS Archive.

site.[53] Soon after, this group was followed by two more, the first of which was made up of a technologist, an engineer and an architect. They toured Yugoslav construction sites, gaining access to all sources, and began to correspond about the experimental building in Havana.[54] The other group brought Cuban craftspeople and students for a ten-week stay to attend a field practice program to learn how to work with prestressing, produce concrete, organize the construction site and, finally, how to test.[55] After the first field experiences, work continued on planning the experimental building, with the construction of large-scale models as shown in ▶FIG. 10.

This process extended the stay of the Cubans at the Institute, and the initially short visits turned into months-long specializations, with the visitors changing their work profiles and attending programs for working with different materials.[56] In return, people from the Institute started to travel overseas, with some staying in Cuba for years to set up the education process. This was not only the case of the principal Branko Žeželj, who travelled to Havana to lecture, set up research and discuss the building's location in Havana, eventually assigned to the central quarter, bounded by Bellavista, Colon, Reform and Lombillo streets.[57] In addition to his short-terms

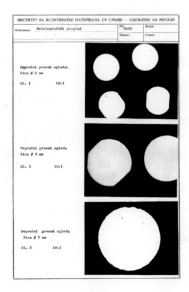

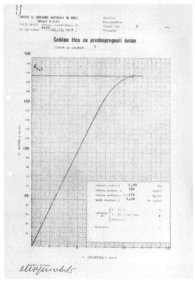

►11 Agreement between the IMS and the Cuban Ministry of Construction, 1967 © IMS Archive.

►12 Top: Cross sections for wires; Bottom: Curve for the introduced force in steel wire for prestressed concrete. Both sent for approval from Havana to IMS Department V: Metals, September 1967 © IMS Archive.

visits, people from the Institute spent a two-year stay in Cuba on a kind of mission to set up the educational process.[58] The fact that the solving of construction site was the main issue to be agreed was evident in the agreements drawn up around how the IMS was to export technology, construction and assembly of experimental building. According to them, the transfer was to be accompanied by constant visit to Belgrade and the on-site education of Cubans in building the experimental house in Havana (►FIG. 11). That the attempt was taking an unforeseeable direction was evident in the right that the Institute requested: to use any improvements that the work in Cuba might bring, free of charge.[59] As well as people, materials started to be exchanged too, as test pieces of steel wire for prestressing were flown back and forth across the Atlantic for approval (►FIG. 12).[60]

▶13
Construction site of IMS Experimental Building in Havana, 1966 © Branimir Grujić personal archive.

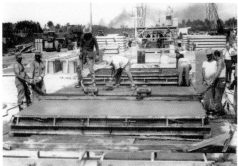

Along with the test samples, whole bundles of bulky items such as moulds for the floor slabs, columns and staircases, devices to lift and assemble elements, prestressing platforms and presses, vats to mix emulsions and IMS fittings were all packed and shipped overseas. The despatch was followed by a telegram from the IMS to the Cuban Institute of Housing, informing that the ship, the *New Moore*, had set sail from Rijeka with all the equipment for the IMS system.[61] The IMS engineer Branimir Grujić became one of the main protagonists in the collaboration project and spent years on Cuban construction sites, working with the local people. He explained how the work of laypeople contributed to construction on the experimental site. The builders, apart from two qualified craftspeople, had never worked in construction, and, though very young, they completed their trainings and earned qualifications. Then those who had passed the training course built the primary structure, and microbrigades worked on other aspects.[62] At this point, the social prospect of promoting microbrigades as construction operatives started to gain ground, and, in this new way, IMS construction gained benefits. In this set up, Grujić explained, the construction parts for the Experimental Building were made on an open site in Wajay, near Havana (▶FIG. 13). Once manufactured, the elements were assembled on the Experimental Building site, where reinforcement was carried out.

This part of the work was mainly done by microbrigades and suffered from local contingencies, as written in the letter from an IMS engineer in Cuba to Grujić and the Institute in Yugoslavia about the prolongation of his stay:

»I need to prolong my stay in Cuba for another month. The exact date of return, as you know yourself, cannot be predicted until the last day. Work is going on regularly, but progress, compared to what I am used to, is very slow. Now it is the time for the sugar cane harvest, and the work groups are much reduced. Of

▶14　The IMS engineer's letter to Branimir Grujić on the state of work on the Experimental Building in Havana, 21 December 1969. IMS Archive.

the 9 people making up the brigade in charge of prestressing at the construction site, there are usually 3 or 4. The same is true at the Ministry, where my work place is. More people are needed to draw the project. Still, *eppur si muove*, in that it will happen, but not with everything we had planned. The final assembly of the first experimental building will not be complete, but we will resolve the basic elements for designing a tall building, and the project for the school will be completed. With the tall building, I had huge problems with the walls, as the wind is twice strong as in Yugoslavia, and the Cubans did not want to do the reinforcement on the site. In addition, the presses for prestressing got damaged and no-one knew how to fix them, so we had to do this manually... You will get the film about the construction, but I don't know when (▶FIG. 14).«[63]
This letter highlights the provisional nature of the site and the somewhat missionary status of the visiting engineer, but also the overall concern for construction as a public concern. People learned to produce and assemble the elements as part of their everyday life experience, and seemed to be familiarized with the construction process, though not many knew how to do the prestressing from the start. In this sense, the coming together of the Institute and the Cuban experiment in construction was based on a degree of improvisation involving the former's experience and active Cuban citizenship. The construction site was domesticized rather than alienated, often with the contradictory consequences that this could bring. In line with Habermas's view of socialization of the group by establishing common norms, it might be said that the technology testing process aimed to establish a consensus for building by means of management of the construction site. This was not determined in advance, nor was the pattern known, but it was a consequence of shared material, knowledge, and contingencies of personal and social life. A similar purpose was recognized and explicit in the further development of the construction site around the Experimental Building. Grujić explained how this evolved:

»After finalising the first experimental building, the Wajay production plant was moved from the suburbs of Havana to the city centre in order to continue production. It was further equipped and continued to produce elements and flats. It served as a school for future builders in construction and for experiments in the production of IMS elements. The open plant in the centre of Havana continued to work, even after the construction of residential buildings ended. Many buildings in the centre of Havana were erected from it. As for the microbrigades, it seems that large numbers of workers eventually changed their existing jobs for ones in construction. Apart from solving the housing issue, there was an increase in the number of people working in construction. This was the case in Havana, with this first IMS plant for construction in Wajay. Another well-known example is one of the newspaper companies, GRANMA, which set up its own microbrigade and built housing in the centre of Havana.«[64]

Integration by culture: Material and work aesthetics

Following Habermas's argument that the lifeworld is reproduced in an open cultural exchange, it is necessary to explain how the events surrounding the experimental building created an intersection of material and work cultures. On the one hand, Cubans were learning how to produce a modern building with Yugoslavian prefabrication principles that were an absolute novelty in terms of materials and techniques. Yugoslavia's leading newspaper, *Politika*, reported how housing construction in Cuba adopted Yugoslavian experiences and was ultimately carried out by sixty-five workers, who built a protype five-storey building in a period of four months.[65] The novelty lay primarily in working with prestressed concrete and building with prefabricated floor slabs. On the other hand, the prefabricated elements started to adopt aspects of the local building tradition, particularly from the specific political moment. As

▶16
In January 1969, one of the six members of the Cuban group that was trained at the IMS (October 1967–January 1968), José A. Cordero, sent a letter to the group in the Institute in Belgrade enclosing a series of photographs from the construction site © IMS Archive.

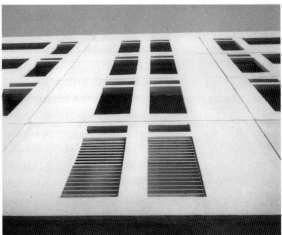

Cuba started exporting sugar extensively to the Soviet Union in 1962, there was an excess of sugar derivatives, and the prefabrication process offered easy solutions for internal walls made from a pressed sugar-cane derivative. Apart from using sugar cane, traditional terrazzo tiles floors were tested for integration into the prefabricated floor slabs in an attempt to adapt to the local housing culture (▶FIG. 15). Even the building scaffolding was made of cane, with palm trees providing supporting elements. One of IMS architects who worked at the centre for housing described how the architectural choices differed from Yugoslavian practice, as the buildings had small openings due to the hot climate and the need for a shade. The design was carried out by Cuban architects at the Ministry of Construction, and a specially produced prefabricated element was used to shade the dining room and at the same time serve as part of a wardrobe.[66]

Modernism was gradually accepted in this overlap of different working cultures, both willing to undertake field trips for years. This was evident in another letter, this time from the Cuban side to members of the Institute. It was written by José Cordero, a member of one of the groups of craftspeople trained in Belgrade.

▶17

From left to right: Individual learning about the system © IMS Archive. First experimental building. From *Istraživanja, projekti i realizacije u graditeljstvu* (Beograd: IMS, 2010). Second experimental building as part of the Microdistrict estate near the Plaza de la Revolución. From Josefina Rebellón, *Arquitectura y desarrollo nacional*. Cuba 1978 (La Habana: Editorial CEDITEC, 1978).

»Do not think that the delay in writing to you is because I have forgotten you. It would be ungrateful if it were so. It is because I left writing for when we finished the first building so that you could see that your effort in teaching us the IMS system has been crowned with total success. Soon we will start a building of 126 m long that, with the experience obtained from the first, will without a doubt be much better. Many thanks to Grujić, Andrić, Ilijan, Mira and all those who collaborated on our course. I am sending you the first photos, and more will come. Greetings from Luis, Melquiades, Carlos, Pedro and Domingo.«[67] (▶FIG. 16).

Enclosing a series of photographs of the Experimental Building construction site, the letter highlights the established dialogue for acceptance of prefabrication. Although the building may seem conventional to Western eyes, the process behind its construction was highly particular, creating a certain intimacy that was established during the trial. The aim of the long building referred to in Cordero's letter was to test joints that, if successful, would make it possible to vary the lengths and shapes of housing. Finally, with the third experimental housing block referred to in letters as the »tall building« (eighteen floors, and very much a novelty in Cuba), options for the high-rise were also resolved.[68] As a result, testing of features of the modern movement, such as concrete prefabrication, the long- slab building, the tall building and the open block, went on until 1971, when the Cuban administration adopted the IMS system as being more competitive than other prefabrication systems.[69] The collage (▶FIG. 17) shows the transition from the individual learning process about the structural system, identified with a layperson's work, to a rather modest sample of one building, to a whole district or *Microdistricto* built near the Plaza de la Revolución. Just how much prefabrication was a novelty can be seen in the gesture of using prefabricated elements as highlights and the main ornamental motive in the façade.

This unique process was marked by a certain naiveté in which Cuba adopted the idea of modern housing by first visiting and testing it as an unknown phenomenon. Once it was finally accepted as a foreign material culture, it absorbed local manners, thereby becoming a new hybrid. The fact that the testing of experimental building combined the Yugoslavian open system and the idea of modernism by means of the engagement of the local population is in line with Habermas's concept of the reproduction of the lifeworld through open cultural exchange. Here, material was a means of transformation by social interaction. As well as being a tool for establishing norms. This corroborates an analogy with Habermas, with the construction process seen as the coming together of different parties that communicate and negotiate familiarization with a new object. When seen from the perspective of a meeting point, the documents describing what the Cubans wanted from the system (fast construction by laypeople) and how they modified it (with new materials, new architectures and new work cultures) point to the presence of dialogue as a means to bring about the end result.

Introducing personal identities into construction

In addition to the prospects of establishing norms by testing and cultural encounter in terms of material exchange, the emergence of the IMS system in Cuba affected the everyday lives of those who were doing the building. When the story takes a closer look at the perspective of the microbrigades, new ways emerge to understand how the construction system entered the lifeworld of the builders.

Cuban journalist Reinaldo Escobar worked for five years on the construction of the IMS building where he has lived since it was built. Before joining the construction project, he had an established career as a journalist for the well-known magazine *Cuba Internacional*, a monthly *publication on quality* paper, with magnificent photos and carefully edited texts to reflect the successes of the revolutionary project internationally. The building he was constructing was—and still is—located in Factor Street, in the centre of Havana. It is a Yugoslavian model called IMS-14, with fourteen floors and 144 apartments, constructed as part of extended work around the experimental site, between 1980 and 1985. There were another three identical buildings in the same quarter (▶FIG. 18). These three buildings succeeded three experimental constructions (the first prefabricated, long and tall) and formed the skyline of the Microdistrict, which had great political significance. Buildings that were the outcome of experiments using different systems of prefabrication (not just Yugoslavian) occupied a central position in the city next to the huge Plaza de la Revolución. The district was intended as a showcase for the further development of housing. In the brochure announcing its importance, the area was described as a generator of collective social values, both through collective labour involved in its building and later, by the envisioned collective

▶18
Satellite view of IMS buildings
built as part of the *Microdistrito
Plaza de la Revolucion* project.

use of its courtyards by inhabitants. The area was meant to be a mix of housing and work, and was to provide flats for some 32700 inhabitants, laid out in predominantly tall buildings. In addition to the IMS process, all the buildings were constructed by microbrigades using another two prefabricated systems (semi-prefabricated SP-72 and *moldes deslizantes*, or sliding moulds). The working process took place in the same place, on the construction site in the city centre, which was the extension of the Yugoslavian experimental one.[70]

Escobar begins his inspiring story of the connection he developed with his building by explaining the general conditions. His microbrigade, shown in ▶FIG. 19, came from various centres of the Cuban Institute of Radio and Television (ICRT). It was founded in 1978 and moved around for a couple of years, working on various construction sites until it began to work on its own housing in 1980. After lengthy discussions, it was possible to reverse the decision taken by the leadership of the Microbrigade Movement to relocate their collective in the eastern Havana province of Alamar in order to build three five-storey buildings there instead of a single tall one, IMS-14 at Plaza de la Revolución. Escobar's participation was driven by his desire to obtain a home, one: »... where he could walk as he wanted, invite whoever he wanted, organize a party, a banquet or a meeting. A place where he could put pictures on the walls, from whose ceilings he could hang a lamp he had made himself, a glass rattle, or one of those rag witches who sway on a broom in the wind. A house where he would grow plants, raise a dog and listen to music, and where he would have a very special corner with his dictionaries and his typewriter to devote himself to writing not just journalistic articles, but above all writing for himself. Make that notebook of love poems that he had never dared to finish, those vignettes about unforgettable scenes from the cinema and perhaps, one day, write a novel, just one, in which he could tell of his life and his reflections on the epoch and the country.«[71]

His group was made up of 120 members from the ICRT, thirteen volunteers and an additional permanent staff of engineers who supported the construction process.

While working at the site, they continued to receive the same salary they had earned in their regular jobs, regardless of what they did as builders. Precast parts were made at a plant and transported to the construction site, where a small group of professional builders assembled the pieces, together with microbrigade members. Although the building was supposed to be completed in two years, this was prolonged to five due to interruptions to carry out other social work, or because of the lack of material. As well as working on the IMS building, Escobar's brigade also participated in missions to various countries connected with the non-aligned movement: Angola, Ethiopia, Grenada and Libya. They also went to harvest sugar cane, care for crops or to help at other construction sites.

The IMS building was assembled by first placing three floor-height columns, after which the floor slabs were added and interwoven with steel wires introduced through holes left in the columns. The wires were tensioned at the ends with hydraulic jacks, and the gap between the slabs was subsequently cast with concrete. While on the construction site, Escobar recounts that he assembled prefabricated structures, operated the concrete, laid bricks, painted ceilings and helped install lifts. He described himself as »for the first time, a worker, whose hands would produce useful things«.[72] Concrete walls were added to separate apartments and to strengthen the structure, while the remainder of the inside walls were built of brick to create two-, three- or four-bedroom apartments. In the end, over a million working hours were invested in their construction. During that time, the workers received support from their work organization (ICRT) in the form of equipment and financing. There were also other institutions on the scene. The Provincial Union of Culture (*Sindicato Provincial de la Cultura*) contributed to the workforce and supported the handover of the apartments by means of the Microbrigade Housing Commission, and there was also the solidarity of other microbrigades.

Escobar recalls how, in a simple ceremony, the keys were handed over in 1985. When the work was completed, the apartments were distributed among the workers of each centre according to a regulation that took into account »the social and working merits of the applicants requesting housing«. In practice, those who had worked directly in their construction turned out to be the most favoured in the distribution process. The beneficiaries of the apartments in the IMS building were all 120 members of the microbrigade, plus the thirteen volunteer workers. Six apartments were handed over to the state, two to the Provincial Union of Culture, and three to the Directorate of Radio and Television, completing the 144 apartments that the building had at that time.[73]

On his return to work when the construction was completed, Escobar (▶FIG. 20) decided to write the novel that he called *La Grieta* (*The Crack*). He narrates the novel in the third person, becoming Antonio Martínez, a young man eager to be »a man of the cause« who ends up being considered an enemy of the revolution. In this excerpt from the novel, Escobar recounts his experiences in the construction of a Yugoslavian model building, IMS-14.

> »His first job, after returning to work as an editor, was an extensive report on housing construction. His experiences as a member of the microbrigade were still fresh in his mind, as was the excitement of opening the door of his flat for the first time.

▶19a
Reinaldo Escobar's microbrigade from the Cuban Institute of Radio and Television © Courtesy of Reinaldo Escobar.

▶19b
Las micras © Courtesy of Reinaldo Escobar.

▶19c
Water tank on the top of the IMS building as the final phase of construction. Courtesy of Reinaldo Escobar.

▶20
Reinaldo Escobar, Photograph:
Sebastian Erb © Sebastian Erb,
»Gegen alle Blockaden«, *Taz
Magazine*, 21 May 2015. URL:
https://taz.de/Unabhaengiges-
Onlinemagazin-aus-Kuba/
!5200459/ (last accessed: 23 October
2022).

As he drafted the text, he discovered that he had enough material to write a
novel. He would not be satisfied with a purely autobiographical narrative, but
could attempt a parallel between the construction of the building and the
task of building a new society. The same anxieties, hopes, internal struggles,
partial successes, contradictions, defeats and risks that appeared in the highly
complex process of bringing the general program of the socialist revolution
to fruition were repeated on a smaller scale in any of the particular tasks of a
microbrigade.

The construction of a building provided him with a magnificent occasion to
refer metaphorically to the program of the revolution, because for both the
building, in the literal sense, and the program, in the figurative sense, the same
remarks could be made as interchangeable subjects for the same predicates.
Of both it could be said, for example:

›It is not easy to do‹ or ›in the effort to complete it, not only is the landscape
transformed, but so too its protagonists‹; or again, ›one day when it is finished,
it will have to be further improved, and another day, much further away still, it
will have to be modernized or demolished to be replaced by a new one‹.

His novel would expose the contradictions that, in his opinion, were essential
to the establishment of socialism, but they would be masked, like the petty
quarrels that arise in the construction of a building.

For example, to refer to those who were convinced of the rightness of the revolution, but had neither the discipline nor the will to endure the rigour of the
process, he would use the case of those who, being possessed of an infinite desire
to finish the building in order to live in it, were overpowered by the temptation to
stay in bed and sleep, prayed for rain so that the day would end early, or wasted
materials in order to stop work and sit down to rest.

To capture the readers' interest and to prevent the novel from turning into a
cryptographic treatise on sociology, he would elaborate a plot, which he called
›catching the criminal‹ of the novel.

His protagonist, whom he would call Reinaldo, would discover that the building,
whose structure was already fourteen storeys high, was sinking imperceptibly
at one end. He would not get bogged down in the technical details, because
any building can begin to sink for a hundred reasons, and the fact would be
accepted by any reader. The important thing would be to establish the dramatic

scope of the event, which functioned as an allusion to the eventual collapse of the revolutionary project, to the fading of utopia.

As proof of the collapse, Reinaldo would show a crack repeated on each floor in the same wall, at an angle of forty-five degrees in relation to the ceiling, deeper on the lower floors and less pronounced on the higher ones. This detail gave him an eloquent title for his novel: *La grieta* (*The Crack*), rich in tragic and con-flictive premonitions that left open the possibility of an eventual solution or an irremediable disaster.

At no time did Antonio calculate such a catastrophe as possible, but it seemed important to him to convey the idea of the vulnerability of the project, because only in this way would critical observations of the mistakes made be heard.

When Reinaldo went public with his concern, when he exposed the technical details that would make his assumption of the collapse practically undeniable, he would have to face those who would reproach him for sowing the discourag-ing suspicion that all the effort he had made had been in vain.

A strong controversy would arise around the issue, with some claiming that even in the rubble of a possible collapse they would still believe that the effort had been worthwhile. Others took the position that they would not stir up the issue, not even take it into account: they would continue raising the building at all costs, masking as far as possible the warnings of the collapse, each getting their own home and then managing to exchange it, or resigning themselves to living in ruins forever. From this group would come the strongest criticism of the protagonist's naïve honesty, accusing him of committing the gravest irresponsibility in bringing something so tremendous and demoralizing to the attention of the masses, without first consulting the specialists »through the corresponding channels« in a disciplined manner.

Among the possible causes of the collapse, those who laid the foundations would be blamed, in a clear reference to the founders of the revolution, who would have made the mistake of rushing, moved by the voluntarism of wanting to jump stages, or would have made the wrong choice of the land on which to build, the time to start or the methods to apply.

Those who had laid the foundations, who until that moment had pointed out the impossibility of sinking, would have merely evoked the moments when they were in the deepest water and no wise man appeared to tell them how to do things.

Throughout a labyrinth of intrigues, Antonio would suggest to the readers the external and internal factors, the objective and subjective causes, to the point that they would be surprised how it had been possible that the building had not collapsed earlier, when the first floor had gone up.

The day that a commission of specialists, equipped with sophisticated instru-ments and presided over by a university professor, assured that the building would not collapse, but was merely going through ›a natural process of structural accommodation‹, Nelson Flores, the union's general secretary in the microbri-gade, would improvise a memorable speech affirming that if the collapse had been true, they would always have been left with the internal satisfaction of having made the mistake of doing, rather than the mistake of not doing. ›That satisfaction,‹ he would say, ›would have given us enough courage to raise the building again.‹

One of the irresistible temptations for Antonio in writing his novel would be to mention each, or most, of his fellow microbrigade members. To achieve this without overwhelming the readers, he came up with the device of an assembly in which, when the list of those attending was passed around, each one's nickname was mentioned. In this way, he would also bring to light the incredible proliferation of nicknames, where there was a whole zoo: the camel, the chicken, the hare, the mule, the crocodile, the ant, the bull, the bear, the donkey, the rat, the monkey, the condor, and others, descriptive or inexplicable, such as hose, medallion, *masarreal*, the little one, *el bolo*, Arafat, bell button, coconut bug, *porcelana*, *macho rico*, *el guajiro*, *ferrocemento*, *silencioso*, *San Lázaro*, *taladro trayectoria*, *pedruzco*, *el muerto*, *mamito*, *Rocinante*, *bombón*, *madera de oriente*, *mikito*, *el loco*, Kruschov, Ferdinando, *el flaco*, *el comemierda*, *el lírico*, *el sargento*, *cuatro cuarenta*, Dundún, *el mago*, *el gordo*, Malú, *compota*, and others, more common, such as Pepe, Chicho, Kique, Pancho or Migue.

To make the metaphor more approximate, his novel could not end with the usual scene of the handover of the houses, sweetened with happy faces at a jubilant party. And it could not end that way because in the other element of his parallelism, in the world of his political allusions, the lofty aims of the socialist revolution were still too far away. Of the luminous future for all, the mirage of a pale glow was barely perceptible.

That is why, in the final scene of what was to be the last chapter, Reinaldo would appear coming down the stairs at the end of the day, stop on a landing on the first floor, exhausted from the hard work of the day, and begin this monologue: ›This is the most advanced floor, and things are missing. The ceiling has no finish or paint. That hole is for a metal box that we haven't put in yet. From there, one day, the ends of two wires will come out; the wires will be out of sight when we put in the lamp; the lamp will be switched on over there, where the switch has not yet been put in. The electricity will come from a transformer not yet installed, on a pole not yet brought in, which we will place in the car park, and these are the hours when the earth of the future car park has not even been moved.‹

After this reflection, Reinaldo sits down on a step to look at his boots with their worn heels and semi-detached soles. The laces, long since rotten, have been replaced with pieces of wire. He takes off his boots to remove the dirt. The socks are damp, muddy, torn, stinking. He lies down and lays his head back, using his boots as a pillow. He looks up through the gap between the steps and continues: ›The hole where the window frame goes needs to be finished off. We'll have to put a pane of glass in it. Those panes of glass have to be brought in, cut, distributed, fitted ...‹ He closes his eyes and pronounces the final words of the novel: ›How much is still missing, damn it, how much is still missing!‹

Clearly Antonio had the material for a novel. He had the characters, a striking anecdote, an inner message and several subplots in which he would narrate the romances, the struggles and the minor intrigues. He had the title and even the ending, but he never finished it.«[74]

▶21
Reinaldo Escobar's novel *La Grieta*, 2018, narrates the building of IMS system housing in the early eighties.

This excerpt was part of the novel which Reinaldo Escobar wrote on his typewriter. The one existing manuscript was confiscated by State Security at Havana airport when Escobar tried to get it out of the country. In 2018, twenty-five years later, he rewrote the novel from memory and got it published in the Spanish edition, which soon started to win prizes (▶FIG. 21). When interviewed about the book, he replied: »I spent almost 20 years working on that novel. It is a book that summarizes my life since I started studying journalism at university, until I was expelled from the profession... It is testimony that I aspire to transcend myself as a person and reach thousands of Cubans who lived similar experiences.«[75]

Escobar's appealing story about the identification of social prospects and construction process takes the Yugoslav system as material for critical reflection in the course of its application. The site appears as a place of dialogue not just among participants in construction, but also among the multiple identities of the person who is reflecting. Decades after the system was originally established in Yugoslavia through on-site tests to support a vision of socialism, and after it was taken over by channels on non-aligned movement, the same system emerged as a means of challenging the idea of socialism by individuals in new circumstances. Pillars, stairs, slabs, windows, pipes and electricity all play the role of allies to the builder who rethinks the framework. This is happening for all 144 participants involved in construction, who, according to their consciousness, shift and change identities and daily masks. Antonio sometimes becomes Reinaldo in the text, leaving him unsure of his own identity while construction is in progress. In this context of role play, Habermas's argument, that identities are affirmed in the successful reproduction of the lifeworld, becomes more self-evident, though it does seems difficult to confirm them. Escobar explains that in their use of IMS floor slabs, some decide to reproduce their identities and some decide not to, or at least decide to reproduce them at different levels. Despite his harsh criticism, the housing project ultimately seems to belong to Antonio, as he shows concern, care and commitment to its completion. »Will it ever be done?« and »How much is still missing?« are questions that can obviously refer both to the building and to socialism. In this case, the building process achieves its own autonomy, becoming a reality for itself, because only Escobar's group moves its lifeworld according to their understanding of the framework. Habermas used this preoccupation with the process of making as a reference when he described the idea of lifeworld as background for communication. To do so, the philosopher introduces a scene at a fictional construction site, in which an older construction worker sends a younger one to fetch some beer, telling him to hurry. The theme is the approaching midmorning snack; taking care of drinks is a goal; the older worker comes up with a plan; the informal hierarchy of workers on site is the normative framework. And still there are shifting bounders: the architect could appear, the homeowner could bring his own beer, someone could fall off the ladder. Situations can change at any time because the horizon of communication can expand and shrink in the same way as a person is moving through rough countryside. What remains fixed for those involved is the existence of action as centre of their lifeworld, despite and together with the moving horizon of the framework.[76] In this sense, Escobar's devotion to action is what brings to the process of making additional qualities as a source of new readings and reproductions.

Continuing the story of the IMS building, in his role as chronicler in 2020, Escobar compared its development to *The Odyssey*. He wrote about numbers to indicate social status:

»One is rarely lucky enough to have an experience like this. This May 9th marked the 35th anniversary of our occupation of this Yugoslav model IMS-14 building. Figures can be boring, but in this case they speak volumes. We were 144 new owners. Of these, 132 had participated in the construction of the building through the microbrigade system. Of those original owners, 48 still live in the building today, 48 have died, and another 48 have moved. In 1985, the average age of those occupying the apartments was 38 years old. Today it is 73. Of the 48 who relocated, 10 emigrated, not counting those who live abroad but retain their apartment in Cuba. We brought our children here. Others were born here. At least 50 of them have decided to live in another country.«[77] (▶FIG. 22).

As for Escobar, in 1986 he resigned from his job at *Cuba International* in order to write more critical articles for another Cuban newspaper, *Juventud Rebelde*. Due to the freely expressed content of his writing, two years later he was expelled from official journalism. Afterwards, with his partner and activist, Yoani Sánchez, he set up the first independent Cuban news platform, which they eventually called 14yMedio. The newspaper met with censorship and discrediting propaganda, and was blocked by the regime. Their commitment to open speech brought them into daily conflict in their role of dissidents in Cuban society.[78] Escobar's participation in construction is, therefore, particularly relevant, as it highlights the position of the individual in relation to the framework and goals of housing reform. It also shows that personal histories are not told in the big picture, and that the microbrigade phenomenon has sufficient autonomy of its own.

From Construction Site to Social Contract

Once established next to the La Plaza de la Revolución, the IMS construction site became the link connecting the microscale of the experimental housing and the district,
and the macro-perspective of housing reform. The fact that the site merged making
with social contract was most clearly indicated by the shift of its initial position in
the periphery (Wajay) to the centre of Havana, where it served as an open test site
for construction. The expansion of the scale affected the further work of the IMS in
Cuba. Once the first buildings successfully passed the trial, Cuba asked the Institute
to set up three prefabricated housing plants for the construction of apartments in
Havana, Cienfuegos and Santiago de Cuba (1974–1979). They were known as *Plantas
de Vivienda Yugoslavia-Cuba* (PVYC) and aimed to be open sites for the production of
housing elements, each capable of guaranteeing the assembly of 1500 apartments
annually (►FIG. 23).[79] This led to a change in intensity of IMS construction work as
of 1971. The Institute started to produce housing on a larger scale, with construction
sites appearing across the country. The stories of these sites are not only relevant in
the context of individual actions. They also have to be seen from the viewpoint of the
construction movement driven by a social and political contract. Habermas's view
of what happens with lifeworld when the scale changes is useful here: how is the
lifeworld as »the horizon within which communicative actions are always moving in
turn limited and changed by the structural transformation of society as a whole?«[80]
With this question, Habermas raises the issue of how a prospect that works at the
individual level and reaches its participants relatively easily can work if expanded at
a higher level. For Habermas, this point is relevant, as society should at least be able
to lead towards some common prospects. Translated into this case, the concerns de-

scribed address the following: whether we can still talk about negotiation in building when the construction experience extends beyond the boundaries of singular sites and personal histories. How did things go for the IMS when it engaged on building at a larger scale?

The first public promotion of experiences on the experimental site began in 1968, when protagonists of the transfer were invited to lecture at universities. Branimir Grujić, whose stay in Cuba was constantly prolonged due to the intention of expanding the system throughout the province, talked at Havana University about the progress of construction (▶FIG. 24).[81] On this occasion, the applicability of the system to various forms of urban development was explicitly promoted. Announcements included statements such as the following: »The system offers architects countless possibilities, both in the design of a single house or building, and for the urban planning of housing developments.« The latter went hand in hand with the possibility of quickly organizing life at construction sites, where the lack of complexity illustrated the system's ability to adapt to anyone's level of knowledge and different budgets. »The installation of these plants does not require large investments and can be calculated at approximately $600 per home (66 m2).«[82]

This positive reception was reflected in a report on the successful work that reached Yugoslavia on Grujić's return to the country. Armando Galguera, representing the Cuban Institute for Housing, wrote that »in the field of assembly and pre-stressing, IMS engineers showed their constant concern with the smooth running and correctness of the work, and the best use by our craftspeople at all levels of the trial ... For all of which we repeat, we are fully satisfied with the work they have carried out«.[83] By offering education to laypeople, the system adapted to the on-site pragmatics of manufacture. The change in scale was accompanied by a new contract, under which Yugoslav exports for construction sites became far more ambitious. The Institute designed schemes for sites with equipment for workshops, administrative buildings, laboratories and canteens. These were imported to Cuba along with the basic materials lacking there, with the overall cost reaching 3 060 000 US dollars (▶FIG. 25).[84]

Cubans continued to visit the IMS to take part in educational workshops. The novelty was that they now included urbanism, connecting it with on-site construction processes. Courses on housing and urbanism were followed by workshops about how to organize production on site, technological equipment and final assemblage. The ultimate aim was to allow participants to understand urbanism and technology on the same level.[85] This practice showed how much the level of planning was dependent on the pragmatics of material production. The leading Cuban publication, *Granma*, featured an interview with Branko Žeželj in front of the IMS, talking about the construction of the Microdistrict and the three prefabrication plants for housing in Havana, Cienfuegos and Santiago de Cuba (▶FIG. 26).[86] In the case of the latter two, construction was extended to the province, where microbrigades continued to be involved on sites in an attempt to merge the practice of collective building with the image of modernism. This was in keeping with the settlement policy in Cuba, which attempted to end Havana's urban dominance of resource use. In the second half of the sixties, the emphasis on agriculture—particularly on the production target of one million tons of sugar for 1970, increased the revolutionary commit-

▶23
The Yugoslavia-Cuba Prefabricated Housing Plant (PVYC) © IMS Archive.

▶24
Invitation flyer to a lecture on the application of the IMS system in Havana, University of Havana © IMS Archive.

ment to end the capital's »exploitative« hold. Old Havana became associated with tourism, while rural development was seen as a powerful means of development, fostering redistribution. Decentralization and the urbanization of the countryside by means of the new towns program were seen as social and economic means compatible with socialism.[87] Prefabrication became important in the development of the countryside, too, though up until that time the best-known housing typology was the vernacular *bohío*.

Following the tendency of rural development, the Cuban newspaper *Juventuo Rebelde* wrote about Yugoslav interventions in the prefabrication plant in Cienfuegos, where »forty workers from Brigade 13 of Industrial Construction are currently working on raising the production buildings and workshops, and constructing the underground network. Completion is planned for the second quarter of 1978, which is fundamental to solving the housing problem in the city...«[88] A similar project was taking place in Camagüey in 1976, where »the brigade is working to finish the first stage of the Yugoslavian IMS system housing plant in the town. After setting up the site,

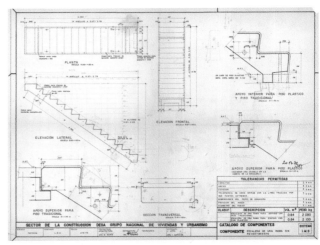

▶25   The IMS' expanded contract with the Cuban Ministry for Construction, 1970. Drawings of executive details of IMS staircases © IMS Archive.

▶26   Left: Branko Žeželj's interview for the Cuban newspaper *Granma*, 6 April 1976. Archive of the IMS, Belgrade. Right: The IMS plant for the production of flats in Cuba, PVYC (*Plantas de Vivienda Yugoslavia-Cuba*) construction site, Havana, 20 April 1977. IMS Archive.

the IMS will leave two plots for tall buildings. This first cycle involves 130 builders«.[89] Among other places, the Institute continued to work in Havana province, in Alamar. The urban outline of this eastern district was planned under the pre-revolution government and designed by one of the leading modern architects of the time, Josep Lluís Sert (Havana Plan Piloto). Sert's plan suited the Americanization process, as it envisioned luxury modern villas of the Los Angeles-type along winding streets close to the beaches, with low-density wealthy suburban settlements. Though few of the buildings in the plan were ever built, the windy street layout remained, giving rise to housing for 130,000 inhabitants to resolve the housing shortage. Within the process, Sert's plan was taken as a given, and »the brigades built around and between the villas that existed here and there«. Following migration from countryside, the plan

▶27
Newspaper article, Marta Jimenez Almira, »La Vivienda en Cuba«, Granma, 1976, page and date not available.

was appropriated by the microbrigade movement, which started building homes even before the action was institutionalized by the government. Eventually, Alamar became a site for the use of prefabricated systems (not just the IMS) by semi-skilled workers around the public green belt.[90]

To describe the process, *Granma* printed the article »La Vivienda en Cuba« (Housing in Cuba) and looked back at the first results of solving the housing crisis, including photographs of previously existing slums and the new living conditions in Alamar (▶FIG. 27). The image was used to announce the forthcoming United Nations' conference on housing in Vancouver in 1976, where the Cuban approach to collective building was to be presented. The scale of intervention was fitting to a context where two-thirds of the population lived in extremely precarious circumstances, with »their ears cocked to hear any news announcing inclement weather, because a lot of water or wind could be the cause, overnight, of the stars becoming the ceiling«. Seen from this point of view, twelve-storey IMS buildings using new technologies looked attractive to those who had never picked up a shovel or worked with cement, sand and concrete. Moreover, the whole district with its promised educational, health and housing facilities sounded not like aesthetic disillusion, but a far better reality than the existing one.[91]

Although Alamar prompted the highest percentage of microbrigade participation, it eventually showed the weakness of the movement. The area did not succeed in offering the envisioned public facilities and, regardless of the rather original manufacturing process, it had to face the problems of lack of human planning. The leading Cuban architect and historian, Mario Coyula, explained that the urban project, conceived by the Ministry of Construction (MICONS) in Havana, was directive in applying »the reductionist model of equal blocks, repeated ad infinitum, [...] so that each work centre had its own«. Alamar therefore represented monotony, in its *déjà-vu* experience in which all roads lead to boredom. Unlike the nearby area of East Havana, where the builders were still working coherently, Alamar, according to Coyula, was regarded as a place where collective production did not give enough credit to emerging architecture. Humberto Ramírez, who was a 28-year-old architect lecturer when he joined the microbrigade at the Alamar site in 1972, later described the builders' disappointment. »In the beginning, there was the desire to do things well, which in many places has been lost... One problem we've always had is that we start out well, but we don't stick with it... We lived under the rule of figures.« The Ministry of Construction did not have enough manpower for all the projects running in the country, and moved microbrigade members from one site to another. »Sometimes three, four, five months passed and the building did not advance« because people were working elsewhere.[92] The buildings stood open for a long time, with their materials accumulating moisture, to the point that they were immediately damaged once built. According to Cuban architecture historian Dania González Couret, there were no compelling arguments to disregard aesthetics. Speed should not have been the justification for doing things wrong and for the scant importance that was given to architecture. Obliged by figures, the house became four walls and a roof with minimum importance attached to the project, with intangible costs cut to lessen expenses.[93]

Amid these developments, the IMS system started to be overtaken by Cuban housing policy. With the development of the transfer, the University of Havana entered into correspondence and, based on the experimental housing project, decided to set up an institute similar to the IMS in Cuba.[94] As a result, Cuba became increasingly autonomous from external knowledge and technical resources to implement its housing reform. In the new circumstances, the IMS system adopted significant changes. Further collaboration agreements included the results of these processes and acknowledged the Cuban right to further transfer experience. In 1976, in Havana, the full independence of the IMS in Cuba was concluded with contractual clauses such as: »Cuban side can transfer knowledge to developing countries and members of the Non-Aligned Movement with which contracts have been signed. Cuba has the right to negotiate, export IMS elements produced in Cuba, as well as its own equipment, and to build in any of the abovementioned countries.«[95] This was the case with the example of Angola, where, in accordance with the transnational solidarity of the non-aligned world, Cuba donated an IMS factory for the production of housing on open sites. When the Yugoslav Institute started its transfer to Luanda in the following years, independently of its Cuban excursion, it found its facilities already installed on the site.[96] The transformability of the initial premises of a system envisioned as open seemed to be demonstrable through its ongoing transfer to the international scene of the non-aligned market. On the other hand, this also meant that influences coming from Yugoslavia began to fade and were eventually replaced.

How did the process evolve? Grujić explained:

»After the construction of the power plants, the collaboration between the Ministry of Construction and the IMS continued, but the Cubans also pursued their own research to improve the system. With the transfer of three factories from the IMS, assistance in production was foreseen until the handover of factories and during the construction of the first buildings. The laypeople, unemployed or construction workers, joined to a larger extent in Cienfuegos and Santiago than in Havana. Over time, construction operations in Cuba gained strength, and the concept of the microbrigade gradually vanished, giving way to specialized construction enterprises. Alongside the plant in Havana and the three transferred from the IMS, Cuba went on to independently build new plants in smaller cities.«[97]

Action and System, Yes or No?

It is hopeful to think that the building process could serve the ground for development of bottom-up initiatives in construction employing social labour. With its idea of an open system, the Institute for Materials Testing promoted this possibility. Participants negotiated the standards applied in the testing processes in construction, and it is here that the level of autonomy was most explicit. It could be said that the practice of test sites, serving as a school and mediating the narrative of collective production towards the formation of participants' personal histories, was perhaps the most significant contribution made through IMS relations with Cuba. With building components that can be replaced, the system generally remained open and sought to adjust to the mainstream, between the skills of the builders and the demographical and political demands of urban development. What could be critically addressed is the fact that the final appearance of IMS housing in Cuba did not really convey the collective production process behind it. The newly built settlements had an aesthetic that marked the division between the fields of production and design. In some cases, this had to do with the fact that the material concerned participants in a very arbitrary way, conveying only very big-picture reasons for participation. These included questions such as: where do we build (position in the city), what do we build (with regard to housing reform), why do we build (to obtain an apartment or join a group), and who is our company? Form was relevant above all in its very provisional configuration, according to whether it was capable of attracting participation. Or, to put it in Habermas's terms, to the extent to which form explicitly represented the motivation for an action to take place. As a rule, anonymous users were not interested in speculating about architecture, but in changing their housing status. At the same time, the engagement of architects did not seem to grasp the possibilities of the open system and collective building as part of the architectural narrative. When asked about their role in whole process, Grujić replied that: »all the buildings using the IMS system were designed by Cuban architects. At the beginning of the collaboration, the architects were informed in detail about the system's characteristics. They further spread this knowledge in Ministry of Construction studios in Havana, Cienfuegos and Santiago.«[98] Unlike the Centre of Housing in Yugoslavia, here architects did not seek to institutionalize the practice or benefit from it. This raises the question of how the norms linking actions at the sites could have been exploited more proactively by the architects, too, as equal participants. Despite the obvious reproduction of lifeworld through the creation of stories like Escobar's, and the history of memory inscribed in all these buildings, a lack of negotiation in the administrative processes could be sensed.

With negotiation missing, the door opens to the familiar argument that this means of modern architecture failed in its initial social preoccupation with offering material for collective production.[99] This argument to some extent overlooks the fact that it is not the form that causes social stratification, but that there is a sphere of mutual influences of different groups in societies. Austerity and lack of care and maintenance tend to contribute to a ghettoized image, whether the property is large or small, modern or pastoral, and this is not far from the reality that affected modern housing in Cuba, including the apartments built using the Yugoslav open system. What can be said in defence of the modern means present in this trial, too, is that its columns, floor slabs and staircases were operational in the collective process of production carried out by network of actors. Furthermore, this production was to some extent appropriated as a widespread cultural attitude rather than being left to the grassroots attempts of enthusiasts only. The difficulty of defending such contradictions was present in Habermas, too, at a time when he was asking how lifeworld could develop. He responded by referring to Niklas Luhmann's systems theory. Defending society's right to generate social movement, have a shared idea of emancipation and accumulate knowledge, Habermas wrote that actions cannot be viewed as irreversible processes of a single attempt. Here, he pointed out the limits of the theory of action seen as a supreme, *a priori* and metatheoretical concept that cannot be addressed from a larger perspective. As it is not about the primacy of the actor but the circular process, Habermas approached it from both angles at once: from the individual and lifeworld on the one hand, and from the intersubjective happenings and validation of relations on the other. In the latter case, normative agreement serves as a bridge between solely value-oriented activity (spontaneous ad hoc action) and an order of integrated values with interests (social perspective).[100] Here, Habermas relies on the need to include members' pre-theoretical knowledge, meaning that participants should acknowledge the possible results of action in advance and obtain consensus. This kind of emancipation views participation from both top and bottom perspectives and requests participants to commit in advance to solidarity, patience and negotiation. Being a rather highly constructed form of negotiation (as is Habermas's theory), this position is one of his most critically addressed points by the school of pragmatism.[101] Viewed in the Cuban context, the following can be seen as parallel with Habermas's position: while it might be said that lifeworld had the opportunity to reproduce in the advancement of personal histories connected with construction at the level of individual buildings, when it comes to negotiating the larger scale of housing reform, the place of consensus was not visible or anticipated in advance.

Although this argument about action seen as a social contract was difficult to prove, either in architecture or society, it remains explicit in Habermas's theory. Among other places, this was in the editorial of the *Praxis International* journal, in which he promoted the idea of emancipatory movements as a legacy of *Praxis* to be continued.[102] When the *Praxis* circle of philosophy in Yugoslavia was dissolved as a consequence of a weakened progressive phase of self-governance and the rise of conservative politics, the gatherings of philosophers continued at international level. In the latter half of the 1970s, this took the form of the creation of an international university in Dubrovnik,[103] where Habermas was co-director of the course »Philosophy and Social Science«. A successor to *Praxis* was set up, called *Praxis International*, with Habermas as a leading participant and member of its editorial board. Habermas's friend and philosopher Richard Bernstein wrote: »Habermas epitomizes the ideals of *Praxis International* [and] consequently the journal has served as a vehicle for the expression and critiques of his views.«[104]

The editorial of *Praxis International* drew on the legacy of the *Praxis* group in its concerns with emancipation at the micro- and macroscale, addressing topics such as the prospects for socialism, human freedom, equality, history, creativity, the nature of social revolution, bureaucracy and technology. Themes were taken from the works of Gramsci, Korsch, Lukacs, Bloch, Marcuse, Fromm and Goldmann, many of whom were themselves *Praxis* participants. In addition to philosophy, editors found the same legacy in progressive twentieth century events such as French working-class movements, student movements, the defeat of a military superpower in Vietnam, Prague Spring, workers' demands for participation, the women's liberation movement and recognition of the rights of ethnic minorities. Although dogmatic Marxism was incapable of understanding emancipatory movements, a critical interpretation of Marx emerged as a tool to address them.[105] In response to the question *Why Praxis international?* in the early eighties, the editorial board highlighted the importance of this legacy in reacting to the historical moment: »The epoch of the development of material production based on cheap labour and natural resources is approaching its end.« Society can develop productive forces but the purpose of the accelerated growth of material output becomes questionable. This requires a change—whether revolutionary again—in the purpose of human work and human communities. All require the transformation of social institutions and individual lifestyles. The same is happening in both capitalist and real socialist countries.[106] New topics emerged that were not discussed in *Praxis*, such as the ecological crisis, alternative technologies, the call for the self-determination of work, growing cynicism about the possibilities of revolution and, finally, the necessary analysis of new social movements.

The shift towards the ecological issue has given more credibility to the perspective of emancipatory movement in theory as well as in construction. If the rigidity of large-scale operations was explicit in the aesthetic inability of prefabricated housing to narrate the collective process of production behind it, an alternative history of collective engagement in construction appeared when there was a shift in material from concrete to greenery. In this context, continuing with Habermas, it can be argued that even if taken to the next level of social contract, collective production can maintain the coherence of the action as an event in which solidarity is challenged and verified. The consequences of the Yugoslavian transfer in Cuba serve to illustrate this.

In 1991, use of the IMS system in Cuba suddenly stopped by government decree. Construction was banned, sites were abandoned, and factories were closed and destroyed over time.[107] This break was the result of Cuba's lost geopolitical balance between East and West after the fall of the Berlin Wall in 1989. With the collapse of the Soviet Union and fading political power in the East, Cuba was left without major trade connections to support its economy. The rather problematic food exchange with the USSR, based on the export of sugar from Cuba and the import of 50% of the rest of the food—turned agrarian land into sugar plantations cultivated with imported chemicals. After the collapse of international exchange, it was a country with an agrarian monoculture, that produced no food and had devastated land. With the Western embargo and the lack of imported oil from the East, large-scale food production systems collapsed, leading to extreme crisis bordering on widespread famine.[108]

These conditions gave rise to the recent urban agriculture movement widely known as one of the most significant conversions from conventional to organic production. This led to mosaics of *organopónicos*, or organoponic farms. These vary in size and type, from small ones situated at crossroads for healing and spiritual needs, or medium-sized courtyards tended by a couple of families, to large-scale farms run by the residents of modern blocks. Urban food production has gone from a symbolic connotation to become the most important source of food distribution in the country. For two million people in Havana, urban farms supply over 90% of the food demand to supply citizens, markets and restaurants.[109]

Alamar found itself in a particular situation as its transport link with Havana as a source of commerce and daily life failed due to fuel shortages. The unresolved gap on the site of the settlement's envisioned public axis soon became a territorial potential. Alamar, as the largest public housing project in Cuba, with 100,000 residents in homes built in the 1970s, developed the biggest organic food production system in Havana, with Vivero Alamar producing a total of 400 tonnes of food annually.[110] Food production followed the footsteps of prefabrication. In Havana, Cienfuegos and Trinidad, various organoponics began to appear after the government program began in 1996. Starting as a spontaneous initiative, the movement has been institutionalized by the Ministry of Agriculture by means of instruction in best practices and the initiation of groups willing to get involved. In 2005, Cuba had over 33,000 urban and suburban farms, and by 2015 the number had increased to 380,000. Individual testing samples were arranged into a functional system without limiting the space for action of particular units. Underdeveloped gaps in the modern blocks that failed to offer public facilities to promote the concept of microdistricts proved to be suitable spaces to address the food issue. Prefabricated wardrobe elements from the IMS experimental house built with the involvement of microbrigades offer a framework to the La Sazón organoponic (▶FIG. 28). The IMS housing project in Alamar ended up as the boundary of a field of Vivero Alamar.[111] The prefabrication testing model, driven by the rise of third-world technology and promoted by the controversial narrative of the modern

block, was the place for a new kind of collective production after the fall of the Iron Curtain. At present, it seems to point to environmentalism as a »new prefabrication«.

Bearing in mind this turn in agriculture, the existence of the open block in a way facilitated communal activities. This context seems to corroborate Habermas's argument that the crisis of modern architecture, driven by the belief that »modernized societies with their interrelationships extend beyond the dimensions of a lifeworld that could be measured by planner's imagination [...] derives less from the crisis than from the fact that architecture voluntarily allowed itself to be overburdened«.[112] The yard schemes of Robert Owen and Charles Fourier could not be enacted because the communal facilities remained unused or were eliminated. If anything contributed to the substitution of prefabrication by urban agriculture as a result of the legacy of the morphological characteristics of modern architecture, it was the yard inside an open block. In addition, the shift from concrete to greenery offered the possibility of a gentler view of collective action seen from the broader perspective of the movement.

Conclusion

The focus of this narrative has centred on the peripheral histories of modern architecture, with the capacity for the collective production of material. This practice was remote from cultural institutionalization and the role of the avant-garde. Rather, it was central to the societal modernization that followed demographic increase and present in the grey field of pragmatic engagement with construction offered by the Institute for Materials Testing. These sites reflected the social patterns of production in the microcosms of which they were part, telling of local laws, ideologies, politics, philosophy and everyday life. By promoting the Institute's attempt to tie technology with social labour in the process of making, the narrative argued for these sites as places for a bottom-up and often critical collective production of architecture. Microhistories of sites from Yugoslavia to Cuba, influenced by austerity and inventions arising from the testing processes, have emerged as relevant to this argument.

The first conclusion of this chapter is just how difficult it is to speak about collective production between the lines of transfer of modernisation, technology and prefabrication. They were mainly regarded as sources of the alienation of praxis from material production, both in social theory and architectural culture. Habermas was helpful in discussing this issue as his theory was original in bringing together, in Hays' terms, the pro-modern and anti-modern positions. He did not reject the social capacity of modern architecture because he saw the philosophy of praxis as rooted in the means of modernism, in a belief in progress and the continuity of learning. On the other hand, he was highly critical of the lost place of participants in the accelerated production process, a phenomenon that he called positivism. He tried to fill this void with a renewed focus on lifeworld, which can serve as a means to expand modernism. In the light of this hope, and despite its controversial connotations, we see that the Institute's encounter with builders in Cuba was able to integrate lifeworld into production by means of the hands-on establishment of building norms, by cultural exchange and, above all, by the assertion of the personal identities of the builders. A construction site of this kind was a place where laypeople could learn and modalities be tried out, where people build themselves apartments or be part of an enterprise. It was a place where people could formulate their critique of the framework, and even expand it. Furthermore, the construction site became a place where the idea of praxis could develop, taking into account local circumstances and the Cold War geopolitical context. In this light, Habermas's theory represents a construct that, nonetheless, also had to be tested—by history. Despite his critique of the obedience shown by the Third World to the First in when it came to technological advancement, the former actually showed a degree of autonomy. The case of the experimental project in Havana shows that, along with the frictions and success of geopolitics in developing countries, there was a possibility of inserting the idea of praxis in modernism in a Third World context. The novelty of the experience, austerity and the strong civil response contributed to what architectural historian Kathleen James-Chakraborty called the potential of the periphery, challenging the assumption that innovation moves solely from the centre to the edges rather than emerging on the fringes of political and economic systems. It is increasingly clear, James-Chakraborty argues, that imported modernism was only effective when local demand already existed. »Arguably modernism only survived the aggressive challenges posed to it first in the 1930s, when it went out of fashion in its original European strongholds, and again at the end of the 1970s, because clients from the fringes of Europe to the shores of distant continents found it useful. There, it was often accepted in inverse proportion to the technological modernity of the society that sponsored it, especially when the resources existed to invest in more expensive alternatives.« This was most explicit among the rising middle classes in Africa, Asia and Latin America, who were looking for inexpensive ways to establish economic progress. However, it is not sufficiently known which technologies were imported where and when, or how they affected builders who may never have heard of Le Corbusier.[113] Arguing that worthy buildings are not the only ones trying to change the world by immediate aesthetic innovation, James-Chakraborty highlights the culture of memory and the process behind the attempts of non-Western modernism in Latin America, Africa and Asia. As regards the processes behind it, the centrality of communal, emancipatory work in Habermas's idea of praxis and its relation to the IMS's encounter with the microbrigades' construction of modernism is relevant. The second conclusion, then, appears to be the benefit of understanding technology and production as open to negotiation on the level of public consciousness, despite the difficulties of the framework.

Once put into practice, the construction site had to adapt to the official housing reform. In Habermas's terms, this meant that positing lifeworld as a source of emancipation in the construction process was further to benefit the creation of an emancipatory movement. This required a high level of normative agreement based on negotiation, interest, solidarity and patience, as foreseen in advance. Although the Yugoslav-Cuban encounter provided a community for construction and served to bring some relief to the housing problem, it still suffered from the problem of centralized production. That this consensus, in Habermas's terms, was lacking at the broader level of the social contract, and consequently in the architectural domain, too, was transmitted through the aesthetics of the surrounding housing. The interpretation of this history would, then, be incomplete without including the other side. The well-known contemporary Cuban novelist Leonardo Padura wrote about the disappointment and the aesthetic effect that the political framework had on the individual. Representing this viewpoint, one of Padura's characters, the Cuban frustrated writer Iván Cárdenas Maturell writes about his sentiment as a citizen:

»We were the gullible generation; the one made up of those who romantically accept and justify everything with our sights on the future; the ones who cut sugarcane convinced that we should cut it (and, of course, without charging for that infamous work); [...] we were the generation that suffered and resisted the ravages of sexual, religious, ideological, cultural and even alcoholic intransigence with just a nod of the head and many times without filling up with the resentment or the desperation that leads to flight—that desperation that now opened the eyes of the younger ones and led them to opt for escape...; we had grown up seeing in each Soviet, Bulgarian or Czechoslovakian a sincere friend—as Martí said—a proletarian brother, and we have lived under the motto, repeated so many times on school mornings, that the future of humanity belonged completely to socialism (to that socialism that, if anything, had only seemed to us a little ugly aesthetically—only aesthetically grotesque—and incapable of creating, shall we say, a song half as good as ›Rocket Man,‹ or three times less lovely than ›Dedicated to the One I love‹)... Orwell's futurist and imaginative fable 1984 ended up turning into a starkly realistic novel. And there we were, not knowing anything... or is it that we didn't want to know?«[114]

Certainly, many similar to Iván Cárdenas may also have been among the microbrigade members on the sites. Viewed from their perspectives, it seems important to say that the argument about the quality of the social processes behind the construction does not imply the absence of a critical awareness of the centrality of the framework. On the contrary, this narrative proposes that the practices of making can be seen as subversive, critical and, ultimately, operative for their surroundings. The case of journalist

▶29
Official poster for the United Nations Conference on Human Settlements Habitat, Canada, 1976 © Lindsay Brown personal collection, available at: https://habitat.scarp.ubc.ca/habitat-i-document-archive/ (last accessed: 10 September 2022).

Reinaldo Escobar, who built his apartment while at the same time formulating a critique that was finally dispatched from the building's top floor supports this interpretation. Other cases may be found among those who, after building in concrete, turned their daily activities to food production in modern blocks built by prefabrication. With them at the centre, the hope for social movement by means of making seems more justifiable in the context of a material shift. Here, a place existed to seek modalities of emancipation in the narrative of introducing plants and gardens into the existing setting and the social legacy of modernization. In this sense, environmentalism can be seen as a new form of prefabrication and a cause for collective production, as was suggested by the UN Habitat Conference 1976 (▶FIG. 29), as well as being included in the lines of *Praxis International*.

The method applied, questioning the history of construction with Habermas's interpretation of praxis in modernization, gives rise to the third conclusion of this chapter. This is that learnings about making cannot be categorized and rejected on the basis of the big-picture scenario, and that the overall aesthetics of modernization cannot be labelled according to the associations produced when revolutionary utopias devolve into totalitarian dystopias. Conversely, understanding microhistories serves to learn how bottom-up processes of making expand as they advance higher. Defending those who participated in the building, this thesis argues that the effects of praxis at individual level have an autonomy of their own, and that material making is a subversive act in itself that creates a process-based aesthetics. This would seem to be supported by the following quote from Habermas:

»By no means does this innerworldly praxis owe its world-building effects to a mechanical dependence of the suprastructure upon the basis, but to two simply

▶30
Telegram correspondence between Cuba and Yugoslavia to solve everyday issues at one of the construction sites, 1975 © IMS Archive.

facts.« The first is the world of ideas of members who cooperatively interpret nature and work on it. The second is the learning process set in motion by this social labour.[115] To this end, »background knowledge of the lifeworld is submitted to an ongoing test across its entire breadth« as a tool to review everyday life.[116]

Habermas's critique of positivism, his search for the place of the user and his understanding of the role of the Third World in production served to seek out realities where encounter, dialogue and interaction took place. These were present both at the macrolevel of the Non-Aligned Movement's attempt to gather around one table, and in Escobar's negotiations with the IMS system, filled with both care and critique.

Conclusion: Praxis and Theory

The narratives presented in three chapters were constructed on the intersection of the philosophy of praxis and histories of building sites that emerged in the course of social modernization in the second half of the twentieth century. *Narrative* was a useful word in the process, because it indicated the experiment of applying the philosophy of praxis to the praxis of construction sites. This experiment aimed to address the modalities of collective production and to answer the question of how the collective comes into being by means of the process of making. In this sense, I used philosophy to create a better understanding of collective building processes. These processes did not only involve the collectively shared space of the building site. They also drew on the collective imaginary of a social vision, in the form of the collective development of institutions such as the Institute for Materials Testing and, finally, on collectively shared knowledge, as in the case of its transfer to Cuba.

I did not end up with a single universal theory of the collective and cannot offer just one answer of how the collective came into being. Instead, I found it relevant to explore this question by means of particular views, by studying different notions of praxis and combining them with episodes from construction history. The combination of these narratives offered a slightly better understanding of theories of praxis, which I partially illustrated with one possible interpretation while applying them to building. The act of narration also provided a better understanding of this history of construction and the social environment in Yugoslavia. In this sense, there is a mutual highlighting of theory by practice, and practice by theory. Philosophy, political decisions, economic schemes and everyday culture are organized not hierarchically but as a complex mesh of mutual dynamic influences.

The notion of the collective changes as praxis theories do. It is the accumulation of these stories that produces the plural nature of findings in the conclusion. The **experimental character of the Yugoslav setting** was helpful in this respect, with its experiments in production, geopolitics, development of philosophical discourse and city planning, and in solving housing and living issues. On the one hand, there is a thread that connects all the narratives into a single story set in a given place and time. On the other, the constantly shifting nature of trial and error led to many consequences that can be viewed as pop-up realities in their own right. These experiments did not all give positive answers, as they were conditioned by their scale and ambition. The scope of these ambitions was also very clear to the makers at the construction sites.

This conclusion is a place for a critical assessment of what it means to read Marx, Petrović, Supek, Lefebvre, Castoriadis, Bloch and Habermas alongside architecture. How successful was this as a method? What are its limits? To what extent was the philosophy of praxis helpful in working with architectural theory and history? This is a series of questions to reflect on.

In the first instance, it is necessary once again to highlight the relevance of philosophy and political theory in dealing with the social concerns of architecture, in this case in relation to the question of how collective production developed in the experience of Yugoslavian social modernization and technological growth. The huge ordinary residential landscape that emerged in the second half of the twentieth century, not just in Yugoslavia, remains a topical issue due to its built impact. It is nothing new to say that an approach to the subject should avoid a generalized view of modernism and engage in a closer study of particular cases through the lens of microhistories and with the agency of documentary material. Victor Buchli's *An Archaeology of Socialism* (Routledge, 2000), Lynsey Hanley's *Estates, An Intimate History* (Granta Books, 2008) and *Storie di case* (Filippo De Pieri, Bruno Bonomo, Gaia Caramellino, Federico Zanfi, eds., Donzelli, 2013) are just some examples that study the rise of communal and social housing through field research into material culture with the bottom-up perspective of the actors involved in the USSR, Great Britain and Italy. Viewed in this way, these rather pragmatic histories present a complex overlap of political, cultural, economic, aesthetic and everyday aspects that shaped housing emergence, its existence and its eventual decay. When the material traces of social modernization are seen as a footprint of all of these aspects, and as a knot that needs to be untied to gain understanding, some of these histories offer surprising insights into the primacy of the pragmatism of making. The Yugoslavian case was one such. Understanding them requires the application of knowledge to the interaction of scales, starting with an exploration of the political decisions and economic schemes present in construction company contracts, learning from the literature, the philosophies created, the press and culture of everyday life, and, finally, listening to individual voices. In the case of Yugoslavia, the material supporting these analyses talks about the culture of memory and the process of making as a form of activism. To understand the social concerns that influenced the process of making at construction sites carried out by groups of frequently unskilled actors, I could not remain solely in the realm of architecture and its aesthetic codes, however broad. To understand social concerns and still talk about architecture, it is possible to draw on the fields of philosophy and political theory. These theories, then, needed to be at least equally relevant as sources and tools. This immediately gave rise to the problem of translating from philosophy—in this case, the philosophy of praxis—to microhistories, such as the development of the Yugoslav system of prefabrication to deal with the housing shortage.

What I learned along the way, as someone who needed to carry out this translation, was that this **does not mean identification**, and that fields cannot be forced to correspond—on the contrary, the two remain autonomous in a dialogue that accompanies their proximity and distance. In this sense, the translation is the result of questioning architecture by means of philosophy, and even the other way around (though to a far lesser degree in this narrative). It is quite certain that Habermas would not advocate the repression of the Cuban regime, and that Castoriadis would not recognise some of the achievements of self-governance in Yugoslavia, which he found rhetorical. Nor is Marx's ideal of society embodied in Yugoslavian practices, or, probably, anywhere in the world. But their theoretical insight helped to **break down social processes** and point up the positive side of building practices. Moreover, theory helped to show how these practices need to be read not just in the local context, but also more universally, drawing on local particularities. In this process, it was necessary to **draw constructs**, depicting philosophy by means of building. Once explicit, the comparison serves as a model for dialogue between disciplines and for questioning the consistency of the argument. In this sense, the way of writing is also a testing process, and theory is tasked with becoming an illustrative expression. This is not unlike how Habermas saw philosophy's role in contemporary society; in one of his

Praxis lectures, he situated it in radical self-reflection as opposed to the separation of concepts from the context in which they emerge in everyday praxis and when arguing against the concept of pure theory.[1]

What was also needed was a **simplification of philosophy**, reducing the complexity of its language in order to ensure recognition. In this sense, I read philosophy through an architectural lens, and then I read architecture from the perspective of a philosophy reader in order to detect possible threads and draw constellations. This required an **analytical method** when reading both sources, but it also required an **interpretative method** to combine the threads. What helped give the interpretation greater credibility was a readiness to accept the **negative answer** to whether a certain thought, thesis or theory could fit or be explicit in some of the building practices. Being ready to fail and free of the ambition of proving an argument removed a certain amount of rhetoric that appeared here and there. It also introduced an additional quality and interest during the writing process. This I found in possible new readings that emerged in the cracks of history, and what might have been better or at least slightly different. This potential scenario of **the alternatives offered by a certain history** was reinforced by theoretical investigation, and these conclusions belong to theory only as a part of the material that **theory abstracted from history**. Here, imagination can be considered a scientific tool, in the same sense as laboratory analysis and material testing. Because imagination, viewed not just as illusory or fictitious speculation, but as an **articulation of archival material** based on previous reading, is a starting point at which Roland Barthes' structural man begins to construct and test his work.[2] When viewed in this sense, scientific writing is not necessarily devoid of imagination but can hold on to it and appear both scientifically and culturally credible. Just as in pianism or in drama, there is constant potential for new readings of philosophies and histories, a possibility of new interpretations, the success of which also relies ultimately on a certain **language craft**. This has to do with finding the right conjunction, putting a word in the correct place to enable a smooth transition, where to suggest that the narrative is a trail and where to reinforce it almost as fact, where to step back as the author and where to appear.

The threads of praxis theories and histories of construction sites first appeared in the immediate post-war period, connected to what might be described as the spirit of the era. The alignment with Marx was easier to establish here than in other chapters due to the historical background of a public turn towards Marxism in search of answers about production. The actions came about as a result of this trial; the philosophy of praxis also emerged for this purpose. Approaching the argument from this historical viewpoint, I was interested in how Marx's thought was contextualized, how it was interpreted by local and visiting philosophers, how it entered official doctrines, and, finally, how it influenced brigade-members' work at a construction site. Questioning the act of construction using Marx's theories showed me their huge ambition, which, if applied all at once, led to naive conclusions. This is due to the ultimately utopian nature of Marxist insights which, as I have learned, are difficult to apply or read holistically. Conversely, their application can be **fragmentary**, based on insights that allow **certain spheres of production to be reinforced** or improved. When applied to microsamples, Marxian theories highlight the benefits of socially constructed cultural practices, such as building together through work actions. In such case, Marxism could be applied as a negotiation tool to introduce these practices into life in any political context, but not applied to the functioning of society as a whole as a state doctrine. The need to downscale the application of Marx's theories helped to partly avoid the burden I would otherwise have had in defending the establishment of socialism at large in the culture of youth work actions. Conversely, I have tried to address the quality of beginnings and to apply existing and rather overwhelming social concerns to the scope of the individual. Seen through the eyes of the protagonists of actions and builders on site, Marxian theories had the quality of a message in a bottle, interwoven with material reality and finding ways to penetrate into production, even when transmitted through political challenges. His initial words on creative labour, on production as a form of *Entäußerung*, and on objectification as a self-fulfilling way of making things became true in a reality that encompassed a phenomenon like voluntary building work for decades. What interested me was to reconsider what was achieved in this unusual building experience in regard to everyday reality, rather than the officially announced goal.

Reading Marx in this context served to recognize the idea of **mediation** in the history in question: the extent to which walls, tiles, pipes, buildings and infrastructure were all seen as mediators in the formation of groups, for the learning of a skill, for the development of migration, for the depiction of the city's imaginary, and, finally, for the continuing culture of memory that surrounded the buildings once they were complete. In this context, the idea of mediation by things became a kind of **cultural practice**, a ritual and habitual model that inspired youth travel and communes, and where the level of **publicity** became important not in the sense of ideology, but as an existing social norm that the individual chose to accept, or not. Through the lens of mediation, Henri Lefebvre's interpretation of Marxian praxis was particularly useful. As well as being in touch with a leading Yugoslavian philosopher, Rudi Supek, who recorded histories of work actions, Lefebvre's engagement and influence in the *Praxis* circle involved promoting Marxian sociology. This enabled a public debate on promoting making skills as a means to establish social bonds and interaction. Lefebvre had in mind an anonymous, citizen, and this idea of an anonymous *them* led me to identify the main character in the building process by way of a series of persons who changed throughout the chapters in keeping with the oral histories I was studying. Starting as local and international students at the New Belgrade construction site, and overlapping the voices of makers and inhabitants in experimental housing, such as Mirjana Obradović, this person eventually took on the identity of Reinaldo Escobar in the history of the Yugoslavian transfer to Cuba. Bearing in mind that the beginning of the work actions actually preceded the peak of philosophical discussion of mediation, there is reason to believe that construction also influenced philosophy, not just vice versa. This becomes even more relevant when we discover that Rudi Supek, prior to setting up the Summer School of Philosophy, spent years at construction sites while studying work actions.

With mediation at their core, the actions helped to extend construction to many actors. During this time, field engineers around Branko Žeželj worked side by side with volunteers on testing the new prefabricated system. Photographs of actions involved in building New Belgrade were sent to Zurich to encourage Mirko Roš to bring knowledge about concrete in order to develop the existing construction work into a universal system. As a reflection of the moment in which it emerged, centring on participation, this system was to be flexible, transformative, adjustable, simple to assemble, lightweight, cheap and, finally, open. The way in which the system came into being, through a process of collective making and unspecialized work, was to mark its future. It became a means for social engagement, whether directly at sites with the makers, in the imaginary of residents and architects, or in its role in international transfer. This process, which involved a series of different actors, meant that the idea of praxis had to be upgraded from one of direct investment of labour to a version that also contained an imaginary. Last had to do with the fact that the system existed in order to support a particular idea of housing not just as an urban form but above all as a constitutional and social right of citizens. With an apartment regarded as a basic human need for which people should not need to pay, but be employed as a precondition, the prefabrication system was a precondition for prompt, large-scale interventions to enable this right to housing. In this sense, the idea of self-governance and its relation to housing, as two sides of the same coin, interested me in terms of what this meant for Lefebvre's anonymous citizens. What prospect did it offer them, and how did this prospect activate participation in making their envisioned home and work? Physical construction was a means to articulate and materialize both a housing policy and a participatory economy, and, as such, it was not a one-off transformation by an imaginary, but continued to change as it developed.

Reading Bloch's parallel with the development of construction in Yugoslavia was very helpful and, somehow, natural for a series of reasons. The first was Bloch's general popularity in the country, including his well-received books, and his frequent visits and lectures in the *Praxis* circle. There were even direct connections, as Bloch was in contact with Yugoslavian philosophers (Zagorka Pešić Golubović, Miladin Životić) who eventually collaborated with the Institute for Materials Testing while working on prefabricated housing. In this sense, there was a historical basis for Bloch's theories on active engagement with the material, which he called »the warm breeze of Marxism«, affecting the discussion about creating and developing a construction system by means of which makers could build their utopia. In addition, there was an optimism in Bloch's thinking that was devoid of cynicism. His writing came across not as cautious and calculated in the expression of his arguments, but as outspoken and bold. The theories were expressed openly, and this was welcomed in a culture that required promptness in its production efforts. Seeing construction from Bloch's viewpoint served to extract two important arguments. One was the parallel between the **desire for a material shift** present in his theory and the existence of the same attitude in Yugoslavia. In this need to change the environment, Bloch followed Marx's »dream of the thing« and promoted the agencies of hope, engagement and the impetus to take part. More than any praxis philosopher, Bloch stressed the values of visible transformation of reality by moving things physically, to be literal, for the explicit construction of a new place that he called the *Novum*. In this sense, he was a philosopher of material and its transformation, with constant new experiments in the process of world-making (*Experimentum mundi*, Suhrkamp Verlag, 1975). The strong belief he expressed in the craftsmanship of the era helped to anchor the origins of prefabrication in **two social dreams**: housing rights for all and a participatory economy. Furthermore, his arguments helped to establish that the influence of praxis theories did not need to be phantasmagorical, serving instead as a direct stimulus for the most pragmatic making. Reading Bloch in Yugoslavia certainly helped people to dare to move and experiment with material to build the dream, and this attitude was more than welcome.

Another point promoted by reading Bloch was the subsequent **cultural value of objects produced by the utopian transformation of material**. His argument about transformation as a cultural attitude led me to search for housing designed with an open system evidence that the idea of openness was a source of interpretation, more than can usually be conveyed. This incursion into the domain of **cultural memory** came from Bloch and, in the further narrative, anchored itself as an active feature of the system with its adaptation to other cultures, too. Based on a reading of Bloch, I established the argument that what the IMS learned from the pragmatics of construction based on the mediatory capacity of the building was continually transformed with each new application.

Castoriadis was contextualized in another way, as his historical proximity was not so direct as Bloch's, though he also engaged with the *Praxis* circle and had a reading audience in the country. Castoriadis was more reserved regarding the production trials and often critical of them. In his arguments, he was distant from Bloch, despite the fact that both worked with the concept of imagination. His theory was applicable not so much in terms of visible transformation through the medium of material as in **understanding the initial social constitution of the group** (society), which could later affect the material. He was not optimistic about existing histories and was critical of many social realities in different political contexts, as well as a great deal of philosophy. Although I struggled with contextualizing his critique while still extracting constructive findings from history without distorting his thesis, Castoriadis's assessment was extremely useful in mapping relevant material to study in the history of building. It served to focus on practices that show how **relations between people were imagined** and organized within the existing scheme of a cooperative. Castoriadis's concept of the **institution**, then, not as a higher phenomenon but as a creation made up of socialized individuals, helped to show the Institute for Materials Testing as a place where experiments in construction were the result of the makers' own concerns. In this scenario, **technology was seen as an organic extension** of human agreements, responsible for both making and saying, or for *teukhein* and *legein* as Castoriadis termed it, drawing on Ancient Greek philosophy. Readings of the Institute's constitution, minutes of meetings, and documents and photographs from construction sites all illustrated the idea of technology in the process of creation. The aim of this technology was to create tools for the construction of housing that, rather than promoting the modern movement, responded to a particular **social *eidos***. Castoriadis's theory helped to explore the process of making that surrounded this *eidos*. His praxis theory highlighted the vulnerability and instability of social and material craft, while pointing to the need to cultivate imperfection, include semi-specialization, and adopt learning in the process by means of flexible planning strategies. His praxis was based on provisory, **fragmentary knowledge** that develops by means of the process itself.

In addition to the creative investment of labour based on social mediation (Marx), and a constant transformation of the material environment to construct utopia (Bloch), praxis in Castoriadis also meant a self-reflective process that led to **individual autonomy**. By introducing the question of autonomy, Castoriadis created a bridge between earlier Marxian theories of praxis, like those of Lefebvre and Bloch dealing with the creative mediation of labour through society, and an explicit focus on the capacity of an individual that came centre stage with Habermas. In terms of construction, Castoriadis's critique, arguing that praxis should be performed by individuals and institutions on the path of emancipation, meant that **the construction experience should adopt a level of critical assessment** and be a tool for questioning the group's internal profile in regard to external frameworks, including the very idea of socialism.

Finally, the scope of Castoriadis's theory was useful in arguing for a rather liberated view of social affairs that in any society, according to the philosopher, should not be read as mechanical dependence among elements in the system, such as the well-known division into classes, or the influences that superstructures apparently have on infrastructures. Conversely, Castoriadis's **organic and holistic way of understanding society** as a mixture of affections and energies that penetrate milieus and create institutions anew focussed on the level of freedom in individual gestures. This proved to be the opposite of generalizations and simplified bird-view conclusions, where pop-up realities are always influenced by a higher order. This thesis, arising directly from his critical assessment of various interpretations of Marx, helped me to study the Yugoslavian history of construction as not just freed from dependence on the political constitution, but also as reactive to it. This, extending Lefebvre's focus on anonymous individuals, moved the research focus towards a deeper reading of the **microhistories** contained in oral records or in documents describing the particularities of life and material production. When an autonomous character emerged as someone who, according to Castoriadis, was socialized, aware of the social setting, interested in history and material, and the practice of free inquiry, and, finally, concerned with the environment, then the testing processes were useful not only for production, but also for reflection that ultimately seeks emancipation. This argument prompted me to explore the further history of the prefabricated system for moments when emancipation reached a new level. Bearing in mind the country and the Institute's devotion to the modern idea of progress, emancipation meant, firstly, exposure to the **heterogeneity of international influences** and economies.

When exported internationally, the prefabricated system itself, and the way it continued to function, changed significantly once again. These changes mostly had to do with new ways the system was used and applied by an even higher percentage of semi-skilled citizens in societies in the Global South in search of their own ways of developing the process of modernization. Seen in contemporary terms, there was nothing usual in the way groups came together and built themselves dwellings in these geographies, in long-lasting processes and according to the idea, for them distant, of modern living. However, these scenarios existed in such different places as Angola and Cuba, and they certainly had to do with austerity, as well as with the new geopolitical formations of the nonaligned world and their economic and material routes. The introduction of the IMS system to these channels and to UN operations supporting the creation of the nonaligned market and housing institutes in South East Asia, for example, required the materiality of the system to respond to new construction processes. Although Castoriadis would have taken issue with Habermas, and vice versa, regarding which came first, institution or communication, the institution served as a good link to connect labour-based praxis in the case of work actions with the individuals by means of social imaginary. Castoriadis's argument on autonomy in imagination, then, played a role in transforming the idea of praxis from an initial interest in what the system could be and how to create it (which was successful in Yugoslavia) to how the system could be used by a citizen in changing contexts that call for negotiation (such as the Cuban case). In this sense, Castoriadis offered a connection with Habermas that served to understand **the universal negotiating capacity of materials**, in this case the open prefabrication system, for further engagement at new construction sites.

The story of the prefabricated system in the global context is more than an outdated assessment of bloc struggles, excesses in planning rigidity or unrestrained market dominance. As shown in the research of Pedro Ignacio Alonso and Hugo Palmarola, *Panel* (AA Publications, 2014), and Philipp Meuser, *Die Ästhetik der Platte* (DOM, 2015), to name just some, it traces economies, alliances, hopes, attempts to deal with demography and housing issues, material and memory culture. In this context, material represents a complex network of actors. Contextualizing Habermas, the third chapter on the transfer to Cuba of the Yugoslav prefabrication system showed that the praxis of making was **more than a one-time action**. There, on the contrary, praxis had to do with everyday life coloured by the context of the Cuban Revolution. The gap that appeared between pre-war casino culture and the colonial architecture legacy and the postrevolutionary state raised the question as to how citizens could transform an existing situation by means of revolution, and how material praxis could be rewritten when the old system ceased to exist. This need, largely related to changes in housing policy, gave rise to a new form of praxis by means of the building process, and the microbrigade seemed to offer a positive response. The system imported from Yugoslavia made it possible to create this praxis in the everyday life of the brigade due to the cultural exchange that took place. This exchange established a link between the material praxis that emerged in Yugoslavia to build housing and the new reality in Cuba. The transition was not completely straightforward and seamless. It called for **moderation** which was taken on as a task by the Yugoslavian system and field engineers who engaged in the process of teaching local craftsmen and citizens. The system had to adjust to provide the answer as to how individuals can be active in newly formed collectives.

As a result, the prefabricated system and the way it was produced had to be reinvented, above all socially, compared to its origins in Yugoslavia. The openness of the Yugoslav system involved, then, not only offering technology, but providing the social means to influence the new post-revolutionary world in Cuba. Its value lay in an attempt to approach laypersons so that they could understand the technology and their new surroundings at the same time. In the act of building, the whole setup of the construction site presented a new way of understanding the postrevolutionary world in which individuals were to play their part. The world of making that appeared in these collective processes could potentially fail, and this reality certainly existed at certain sites. The culture of exchange established at the sites was to complete government action, but it also allowed individuals to speak out. Contrary to the opinions of Habermas, whose worldview while lecturing in Yugoslavia was based on a democratic setup in which individuals could at least speak their minds, in Cuba the ground was not prepared for freedom of speech. Democratic conditions were not a given, which is why everyday culture needed moderation and why, ultimately, the IMS needed to build a process in which **people could negotiate by means of materials**. This was the core element of the cultural exchange that was established. It was a **democratic process inscribed in the building process** and reflected in the learnings of **process aesthetics** arising from this exchange.

Everyday testimonies such as those of Reinaldo Escobar were particularly important in highlighting this aspect of negotiation with material as a universal language, as well as a **subversive constructive means**, in the fields of technology and modernization. The reaction in Cuba, where in the early 1970s the IMS system was announced the most competitive prefabrication system due to its ease of appropriation by microbrigades, holds the key to the success of this act of moderation. Its emphasis on columns and lack of walls or any explicit element that could limit the future life of a building; the fact that it required very little basic material and could be filled with others; and the simplicity of manufacture were some of the neutral formal features that responded to social demand. Its materiality showed that, in the end, Yugoslavia had a different idea of socialism and different political means to establish the system, which ultimately diverged from panel systems such as the Gran Panel Soviético, made in the USSR. The interest in the democratic processes behind the materiality of the system finally became explicit in the concrete.

Habermas's idea of praxis was a happening that was continuous rather than fixed in time, based on a day-by-day process of renegotiation as regards political frameworks, but also material surroundings and the internal lifeworld of the builders. His idea of praxis centred on dismounting certain dominant aesthetic codes and focusing instead on process-based ones in which architecture emerged as a consequence. As Farhan Karim points out in *The Routledge Companion to Architecture and Social Engagement*, this social concern of architecture is nothing new; it has always been part of architectural production. However, society as an essential part of the architecture discourse was not previously a basis of the discipline as it has been in recent studies. The growing tendency to redefine architecture, from the dominance of a market-driven profession to a »complex mix of praxis, altruism, and activism«, tends to counter social exclusion and contributes to a more egalitarian global society based on process-based aesthetics. Equality between design and activism comes to the fore, and social engagement—not new but part of the historical process—reinvents itself in order to include marginal geographical or institutional positions. It has become »important for socially engaged architecture to unveil the concealed production process and also to exhibit the demonstration of the construction process«. By so doing, the role of the avant-garde can be further improved from one that still oscillates between »the architect's role as social agent and the discipline's exclusive aesthetic implementations«.[3]

The construction history that ended with Yugoslav exports to Cuba is an example of a practice where the construction process came to the fore as one that affects architecture and is not just a consequence. To piece it together, I introduced the mutual influence of practices and theories by reinforcing the historical and theoretical links between them. A rather literal comparison can be made figurative by saying that the IMS embedded pieces of praxis theories, present in Yugoslavia as part of the system, and transferred them to Cuba. The possibility of literally bringing theory to the level of the construction system is what theoreticians of praxis, such as Habermas, might find it relevant for. The fact that material was used in an attempt to construct socialism in Yugoslavia and then to negotiate a new framework oversea, ultimately shows that objects may sometimes be even stronger than theory, that they can bear the responsibility and that the IMS system conveyed different readings of praxis. To refer to Bruno Latour (*We Have Never Been Modern*, 1991, *Reassembling the Social*, 2005), we might speak here of things that act together with humans in search of different levels of production. Extending Habermas's thought in the direction of building by means of a metaphorical walk through the construction site with him also shows that there was a gap that he as a philosopher could not bridge by advocating praxis. Ultimately, it was material that gave form to philosophical thought by bringing it directly to the site, where the collective came into being through the praxis of making.

Literature Review

The decision to base my interest in collective production of the construction history of Yugoslavia was partially due to my background and education in Belgrade. During this time, and certainly while growing up in Yugoslavia amid the consequences of its dissolution, I was surrounded by literature and public debate on politics, architecture and philosophy that created a very present body of material. As I refined the focus of my research, this body of material served as a reference that guided it. In this process, I recalled first the sediments laid down over the years, identifying and tracing certain evocations that were to be my basis. I aimed to come up with interpretative lines of the history I was familiar with, in the first instance capturing the influence of material production on everyday life. This influence provided the best material for my interest in the social production of space. In the meantime, as social attempts in the country played out, worlds were built, existed and decayed, leaving little remembrance of secondary realities. This experience sparked my interest in microhistories and peripheries, as often occurs in the wake of imposed forgetting.

This heritage of Yugoslavia, seen as a laboratory of politics, economics and culture, has been covered extensively, particularly in recent times when it came to greater international attention.[1] I wanted to add to this chain by using the condition of *testing* in production to emphasize the process of making, focussing on the pragmatism of building on construction sites by a variety of agents ranging from volunteers and self-governed enterprises to microbrigades. In this sense, I was interested in the histories of construction sites, as I found them to be the most authentic and original contributions of the overall Yugoslavian trial. They represented a huge responsiveness of people to the construction of socialism. I wanted to relate histories of construction in micro stories in order to reveal bottom-up processes of making in everyday life that managed to create pop-up realities. I used these histories to reflect theoretical questions about the collective production of space. And additionally, to highlight the fact that these episodes are, in themselves, footprints of larger concerns, together with their highs and lows, trials and errors. The Yugoslavian case was a testing ground whose fragments I could use to present my argument. To accompany this narrative, and as a starting point for understanding these histories of production, I used the philosophy of praxis. This was part of the given history that managed to capture a plurality of international philosophic positions and, like any theory, to go beyond history. In this overlap, I focused on two main groups of sources: those dealing with the history of construction, and those dealing with the development of the philosophies of praxis.

Philosophies of Praxis

In my study of philosophical aspects, I relied primarily on *Praxis* journal (1964–1974), with its well documented archive and online access. As well as issues published in

German, French, English and Serbo-Croatian, the archive contains numerous documents about the Korčula Summer School of Philosophy (1963–1974) that paralleled the publication of the journal as the main source of its articles. These documents include letters exchanged by praxis philosophers, scans of international press articles of the time about the school's content (*Stuttgarter Zeitung*, TÜTE, *Der Spiegel*, *France Observateur*), timetables, programs of talks, and lists of participants at the school. The archive also includes recent studies on *Praxis* heritage promoted by researchers in social theory and philosophy that helped me to understand the general context (Ante Lešaja, *Praxis Orientation, Journal Praxis and The Korčula Summer School*, Rosa Luxemburg Stiftung, 2014; *Praxis, Kritika i humanistički socijalizam*, ed. Dragomir Olujić and Krunoslav Stojaković, Rosa Luxemburg Stiftung, 2012; *Aspekti praxisa. Refleksije uz 50. Obljetnicu*, ed. Borislav Mikulić, Mislav Žitko, Filozofski fakultet Sveučilišta u Zagrebu, 2015). Visits to the Ivan Vidali local library at Korčula provided relevant additional material such as recorded films of summer schools throughout the years. Talks with *Praxis* philosopher Božidar Jakšić, *Praxis* archivist and chronicler Ante Lešaja, and with my thesis advisor, philosopher Petar Bojanić at the Institute for Philosophy and Social Theory in Belgrade were also very productive.

In the narratives of philosophy and construction in each chapter, I opted for a particular notion of praxis of the many that provided the content of the journal. This plurality was the result of interaction between philosophers lecturing at the school and local debate in search of operative theories. Among the international visits, lectures and articles in the *Praxis* circle, I focused on particular philosophers who offered relevant theoretical frameworks for the episodes of construction in each chapter. Accordingly, in the first chapter, »Praxis and Action«, I study the Marxian notion of praxis based on the involvement of active labour in the context of voluntary youth actions. *Praxis* issues 2/3, »Sinn und Perspektiven des Sozialismus« (1965) and *Praxis* no. 1, »Die Aktualität der Gedanken von Karl Marx« (1967) were important sources when addressing the local interpretation of Marxism. These issues also offered a link between Yugoslavian philosopher Rudi Supek and French philosopher Henri Lefebvre with regard to their views on Marxian praxis. Some of Lefebvre's positions can be found in his *Praxis* writings (such as »Sur quelques critères du développement social et du socialisme«, in issue 2/3, 1965, or »Le socialisme en vacances«, published in *France Observateur,* no. 746, 20. August 1964), as well as in his books *Métaphilosophie* (Éditions de Minuit, 1965) and *Sociologie de Marx* (Presses Universitaires de France, 1966), which were both presented at and relevant to the *Praxis* circle. Supek's books on youth work actions (*Omladina na putu bratstva. Psihologija radne akcije*, Mladost, 1963, articles from the Yugoslavian magazine *Naše teme*) and his arguments on the mediatory capacity of objects (»Henri Lefebvre: Sociologie de Marx«, *Praxis* no. 3, 1967) served to establish links with the same notion of how to make sociology out of things. I further compared these with more general writings on praxis in Marx offered by philosophers close to the topic, or by Marx himself, such as Norman Geras, *Marx and Human Nature: Refutation of a Legend* (Verso, 1983), Erich Fromm, »The Application of Humanist Psychoanalysis to Marx's Theory« in *Socialist Humanism* (Doubleday & Co., Anchor Books, 1965), the well-known *Writings of the Young Marx on Philosophy and Society* (eds. Loyd D. Easton & Kurt H. Guddat, Doubleday & Co., Anchor Books, 1967), and Karl Marx and Frederick Engels' *Collected Works Vol. 3, 1843–1844* (Lawrence & Wishart, 1975). An important theoretical source for the first chapter was the book of the same title, *Praxis and Action* (University of Pennsylvania Press, 1971), by American philosopher Richard J. Bernstein, who was part of the praxis debate in Yugoslavia. As well as describing the heritage of the philosophical movement in Yugoslavia, Bernstein also gave a very comprehensive account of different praxis positions based on Marx's legacy.

Bloch's lectures and articles in *Praxis* served as a reference to formulate the argument of chapter two, »Praxis and Imagination«. For this purpose, I relied on Bloch's opening speech at the Summer School of Philosophy in 1968, which was later published as »Eröffnung der Korčula Sommerschule« in *Praxis* no. 1/2: »Marx and Revolution« (1969). On the same occasion, Bloch gave the lecture titled »Marx als Denker der Revolution«, published in the same issue. In further tracing Bloch's contributions to the debate on praxis, I had recourse to the articles that usually succeeded his lectures: »Geschichtliche Vermittlung und das Novum bei Hegel« (*Praxis* no. 1/2 »Hegel und die Gegenwart. Leninismus – die Neue Linke«, 1971), »Why and For What Purpose A Large Majority of Philosophers Are Not Yet Materialists« (*Praxis* no. 3/4: »Marksizam i društvena svijest«, 1972) and »Die bürgerliche Welt und der Sozialismus« (*Praxis* no. 1/2: »Bourgeois World and Socialism«, 1974). While lecturing at Korčula, Bloch also gave an extensive interview to Michael Landmann in 1968 for the philosophical journal *Telos* (»Talking with Ernst Bloch: Korčula, 1968«, *Telos* no. 25, 1975), which summarized the main arguments of his philosophy and was useful for understanding the broader scope. These sources I further complemented with arguments from his books *Literarische Aufsätze* (Suhrkamp, 1935), *Das Prinzip Hoffnung* (Suhrkamp, 1959) and *Experimentum Mundi. Frage, Kategorien des Herausbringens, Praxis* (Suhrkamp Verlag, 1975). The reception of Bloch's philosophy in the country proved to be relevant. The history of this reception was recalled by one of the leading Yugoslavian philosophers, Gajo Petrović, for the German magazine *TÜTE* (»Ein Gewisser Ernst Bloch«, *TÜTE* special edition *Zum hundertsten Geburtstag von Ernst Bloch*, June-July 1985). It was also present in the issue of *Praxis* devoted to Bloch's philosophy (*Praxis* no. 3: »Misao Lukacs-a i Bloch-a«, 1966). Finally, I consulted articles about Bloch and more recent collections of his writings (*The Utopian Function of Art and Literature*, translated by Jack Zipes and Frank Mecklenberg, The MIT Press, 1988).

Cornelius Castoriadis was another philosopher whose theory I applied in the second chapter. I did this firstly through his articles in the leftist mid-twentieth-century journal of which he was editor, *Socialisme ou Barbarie* (*SouB*). In a couple of issues of *SouB*, the topic of Yugoslavia's geopolitical position and self-governance was present, most notably in Castoriadis's article published under his pseudonym (Pierre Chaulieu and Georges Dupont, »La bureaucratie yougoslave«, *Socialisme ou Barbarie*, no. 5–6, March-April 1950). In addition, in the same journal Castoriadis wrote about the possibility for the positive content of socialism (Pierre Chaulieu, »Sur le contenu du socialisme«, *Socialisme ou Barbarie*, no. 17, 1955). His writings were later collected in *Political and Social Writings* Vol. 1, 1946–1955 (University of Minnesota Press, 1988). Castoriadis's critical re-examination of the social and political applications of Marxism worldwide was a useful resource. Above all, it showed that the actors in building society can relate in a more organic way than the one that is based on mechanical causalities between leaders and followers (»Marxisme et théorie révolutionnaire«, *Socialisme ou Barbarie* no. 36–40, 1964–1965). To explore the trial of material culture in Yugoslavia, I have used the argument he expounds in *L'institution imaginare de la société* (Editions du Seuil, 1975); »Radical Imagination and the Social Instituting Imaginary« (*Rethinking Imagination: Culture and Creativity*, ed. Gillian Robinson and John Rundell, Routledge, 1994); *A Society Adrift. Interviews and Debates 1974–1997* (Fordham University Press, 2010, ed. Enrique Escobar, Myrto Gondicas, and Pascal Vernay), and *The Castoriadis Reader* (Blackwell Publishers, 1997, ed. David Ames Curtis).

When searching for additional historical connections, I studied how Castoriadis's thinking was introduced to Yugoslavia following the dissolution of the *Praxis* circle of philosophy. This occurred as part of the courses at the Inter-University Postgraduate Centre Dubrovnik that was the successor to the *Praxis* gatherings, and where Castoriadis lectured on themes of creativity and theories of modernity. His engagement was recently described in François Dosse's book *Castoriadis une vie* (La Découverte, 2014), in the section on his international connections, »Le rayonnement international«. Regarding his proximity to Yugoslavia, I also studied the writings of German philosopher Jürgen Habermas, who recalled the influence of Castoriadis's philosophy of praxis on the discourse in the country in *Der philosophische Diskurs der Moderne: Zwölf Vorlesungen* (Suhrkamp Verlag, 1985).

It was at the seminars in Dubrovnik that Castoriadis and Habermas met, the latter being the last in the linage of praxis philosophers on whom I focused in chapter three, »Praxis and *Lebenswelt*«. Here, I parallel Habermas's theory with the transfer of the prefabricated system, together with its social vision, from Yugoslavia to Cuba. For this, I drew on Habermas's appearances in the *Praxis* circle that accompanied the development of his argument of praxis based on communication. His book, *Theorie und Praxis* (Hermann, 1963), was the first point of reference, being one of the earliest mentions of this topic in Habermas. This book was introduced into Yugoslavia by the 1965 issue of *Praxis*, in a review by Yugoslav philosopher Milan Kangrga: »Jürgen Habermas: Theorie und Praxis« (*Praxis* no. 4/5, 1965). Once the book was introduced, Habermas himself wrote in *Praxis*, and visited and lectured in Yugoslavia. The first occasion was in the 1965 issue, in which he published his article on the relation between technological progress and social life in cities, »Technischer Fortschritt und soziale Lebenswelt« (*Praxis* no. 6, 1965), which played an important role in addressing the problem of social modernization on a general level. Soon afterwards, in 1968, he lectured at the Summer School, on the same occasion as Bloch, on the reduced capacity of capitalist society to hold onto positive aspects of revolutionary practices, seen as the emancipation process (»Bedingungen für eine Revolutionierung spätkapitalistischer Gesellschaftssysteme«, *Praxis* no. 1/2, »Marx and Revolution«, 1969). In the article, Habermas described market flows between the East, the West, and the Third World. This finding was further relevant to understanding what the development of technology (prefabrication) actually meant in the context of the Global South. Habermas's next lecture then dealt with the topic of the operative role of theories and philosophies in contemporary society (»Role of Philosophy in Marxism«, *Praxis* no. 5/6 »Le Monde Bourgeois et le Socialisme«, 1973). More than being relevant to a single chapter, this influenced the overall argument of this text, addressing the capacity of theories to narrate material production. It therefore appears explicitly in the conclusion.

Habermas remained involved after the dissolution of *Praxis*, with its successor journal *Praxis International* that later became *Constellations*, which still exists today. Richard Bernstein wrote about his role on the editorial board in *Habermas and Modernity* (MIT Press, 1985), which I also used as a reference to track the history of journals and arguments about praxis. The editorial of *Praxis International* showed how the idea of praxis shifted further towards environmental concerns. I found this change fitting to track the substitution of unskilled prefabrication in Cuba by extensive food production by citizens in the courts of modern blocks. I have used other articles from *Praxis International*, such as one by the German sociologist Hans Joas on Habermas, to complement the argument with a new critical position (»The Unhappy Marriage of Hermeneutics and Functionalism«, *Praxis International* 1, 1988). Habermas's argument in *Praxis* was an extension of his theories that I have studied through his major works: *Theorie des kommunikativen Handelns, Band 2: Zur Kritik der funktionalistischen Vernunft* (Suhrkamp Verlag, 1981), *Der philosophische Diskurs der Moderne: Zwölf Vorlesungen* (Suhrkamp Verlag, 1985), *Erkenntnis und Interesse* (Suhrkamp Verlag, 1968), »Modern and Postmodern Architecture«, in *Architecture Theory since 1968* (The MIT Press, 2000, ed. K. Michael Hays).

In addition to research into particular praxis notions of Marx, Petrović, Supek, Bloch, Castoriadis and Habermas, I have also used more general material from the *Praxis* archive, such as articles on the history of the philosophy of praxis by Branko Bošnjak (»Betrachtungen über die Praxis«, *Praxis*, no. 1 »A quoi bon Praxis?«) and by Gajo Petrović (»A quoi bon Praxis?«, *Praxis* no. 1, 1965). The same purpose was served by another insightful article by Petrović, »Praxis«, published in *A Dictionary of Marxist Thought* (Blackwell Publishing, 1983, ed. Tom Bottomore, Laurence Harris, V. G. Kiernan, Ralph Miliband), and his book *Marx in the Mid-Twentieth Century* (Anchor Doubleday, 1967).

In all of the sources mentioned, I have read the philosophies of praxis from an architectural viewpoint, seeking connotations that work in proximity to material culture in general. At the same time, I explored the moments of their historical connections with public life in Yugoslavia and with the protagonists of construction. When correlating philosophy and history of construction, I found useful studies and trials in comparative methods such as Roland Barthes' »The Structuralist Activity« in *Critical Essays* (Northwestern University Press, 1972, trans. Richard Howard, originally published as *Essais critiques*, Editions du Seuil, 1964). Another example is the recent research of Heike Delitz on the comparison of sociology and architecture (e.g. »Architectural Modes of Collective Existence. Architectural Sociology as a Comparative Social Theory«, *Cultural Sociology* 12, 2018). Also beneficial in this respect was an appealing collection in *Rethinking Imagination. Culture and Creativity* (Routledge, 1994, ed. Gillian Robinson and John Rundell), which argued for modalities of interaction of the various spheres of cultural production.

The preoccupation with interactions between society and architecture were certainly relevant, with works such as Adrian Forty's analysis of modern architecture's concern with society (»Dead or Alive – Describing the Social«, *Words and Buildings. A Vocabulary of Modern Architecture*, Thames & Hudson, 2000), a broader look at CIAM meetings (Eric Mumford, *The CIAM Discourse on Urbanism 1928–1960*, MIT Press, 2000) and more recent studies in *The Routledge Companion to Architecture of Social Engagement* (Routledge, 2018, ed. Farhan Karim) and *The Social (Re)Production of Architecture* (Routledge, 2017, ed. Doina Petrescu and Kim Trogal).

Field Research

In addition to the philosophical thread, I have documented histories of construction sites, primarily by means of archive work, followed by analysis of the material. Archives of Yugoslavia and the Historical Archives of Belgrade were places where I found documentation about the building of New Belgrade by voluntary youth work actions. At Archives of Yugoslavia I consulted primary documents that explain the daily life of brigade members, constitutions, the youth membership structure and correspondence between the actors involved. I also found data about the amount of material produced, international visits referred to in collections of letters and telegrams, and newspaper articles from the period about the progress of construction. Documents on relations with the newly established United Nations, as part of archive fonds, were helpful to understanding the phenomenon of voluntary building as not strictly related to Yugoslavia. At the Historical Archives of Belgrade, I found photographs that depicted the atmosphere at sites; the *Novi Beograd* journal that followed the construction process and issued reports about everyday life and building achievements; and interviews and books documenting the voices of brigade-members. Here, too, I found original drawings and data about the first buildings constructed by actions, such as Hotel Yugoslavia, Student City, the future Federal Executive Council building and the first housing districts. To study the work actions, I also consulted literature from the period, such as *ORA—Mladost naše zemlje 1942–1982* (ed. Toma Dragosavac, Belgrade, 1983); Belgrade's yearbooks (various volumes of *Godisnjak grada Beograda*); relevant historical literature (Branko Petranović, *Socijalistička Jugoslavija 1955–1988*, Nolit, 1988), and more recent anthropological studies (e.g. Reana Senjković, *Svaki dan pobjeda. Kultura omladinskih radnih akcija*, Srednja Europa, 2016).

At the Historical Archives of Belgrade, I studied plans for the Experimental Housing in New Belgrade, presented in the second chapter, while tracing the further history of construction once the main push of the youth actions was over. Bearing in mind that this housing scheme was the trial for a new system of prefabrication developed by the Institute for Materials Testing (IMS), its archive became an important place for further research. At the IMS archive I collected data on constitutions from different periods, foundational documents, letters between researchers and principals, lists of Amsler equipment that was transferred from Switzerland, and early Institute plans to promote the specific idea of participative work. There, too, I found scientific studies on concrete that led to the idea of a flexible, open prefabricated system, drawings, calculations, descriptions of the system's characteristics and technical data. These were accompanied by photographs depicting the role of semiskilled makers in the construction process, and extensive data on the international export of the prefabricated system. Folders on Iran, Iraq, Cuba, the Philippines and Egypt were just some containing relatively unknown data on the transfer of technology, full of different kinds of material from official letters, contracts, newspaper articles and lists of equipment to photographs and private correspondence. There I found extensive data on the export of the Yugoslavian system to Cuba, and many documents from Cuba that were filed in the IMS archive (such as newspapers, photographs and letters). In the library of the Institute for Materials Testing, along with a wide selection of international architecture journals, I found bulletins and books issued by the Institute itself, such as the IMS Bulletin (*Bilten IMS*) and a bulletin of one of its departments, the Centre for Housing (*Bilten centra za stanovanje*), which dealt with the adaptation of the system to the idea of flexible living.

In Belgrade City Museum, I worked mainly with the photographic material of Belgrade photographer Branko Turin, who, in his images of the newly built Experimental Housing in New Belgrade, depicted inhabitants' emerging social imaginary of modern living. In addition, the museum also offered insight into old maps of Belgrade and the state of the construction site prior to the building process. In the National Library of Serbia and Belgrade City Library, I studied journals and newspapers that dealt with the process of constructing a new city, and with the culture of everyday life (*Beograd, Arhitektura, Arhitektura Urbanizam* and *Jugoslavija* journals, and the *Politika* daily newspaper). In the library of the Institute of Technical Sciences of the SASA there were additional journals on the work of the IMS and the Centre of Housing (*Sveske CS*). I consulted scientific studies documenting the search for flexibility in new housing built using the IMS prefabricated system. In the Museum of Technology and Science, I studied early plans for New Belgrade drawn by architects such as Nikola Dobrović and Stanko Mandić, which were useful to complement the main argument. At the same museum, I found a well-documented journal that followed the development of construction in Yugoslavia (*Izgradnja*).

In the Urban Planning Department, I researched the planning history of New Belgrade. Thanks to ongoing work there at the time of my visits (*70 godina Urbanističkog zavoda Beograda*, ed. Žaklina Gligorijević, Ana Graovac, Urbaistički zavod Beograda, 2018), I was able to study great storyboards that simplified the larger picture: the main phases of New Belgrade development, degrees of political autonomy, the main institutions and individuals involved, and the achievements of each phase. Large-scale drawings of different areas of New Belgrade also offered me an insight into the idea of communal housing with all the elements developed to support it. This part did not directly influence making on the site, but connections between this planning institution and the Institute for Materials Testing illustrated the fact that the making processes also affected planning.

At the Yugoslav Film Archive, I gained access to the series of films documenting the process of construction of New Belgrade (*Kad ratni doboši umuknu*, 1960; *Biće to novi grad*, 1960; *Prepreke su mnogobrojne*, 1959–1962, and *Život na pesku*, 1963, all directed by Miloš Bukumirović, Slavija film). These were valuable for their visual documentation of the radical nature of the building effort that guided the argument on process aesthetics. At the Museum of Yugoslavia, as well as viewing the collection of photographs of work cooperatives and the establishment of non-alignment, I was able to view exhibitions and catalogues dealing with different aspects of Yugoslavian history (such as causalities between different modalities of production and consumer culture).

My archive work included many discussions, talks and interviews that I conducted to include an oral history. In this respect, I recorded interviews with retired IMS members such as:

- Branimir Grujić, the main person responsible for the construction and export of the IMS system, who spent many years at Cuban construction sites, engaging with builders;
- Ksenija Petovar, a sociologist at the Centre for Housing IMS, who was able to recall the work environment, the process of devising flexible housing based on a universal system, and the Institute's collaborations with *Praxis* philosophers (Zagorka Pešić Golubović and Miladin Zivotić);
- Branislav Vojinović, who explained the foundational process of the Institute and importing the equipment and knowledge on concrete from Switzerland thanks to the commitment of Mirko Roš;
- Milan Pajević, who started out testing materials at the Institute, and moved on to the UN to support housing development in the Middle and Far East;
- Živojin Kara-Pešić, who was engaged in IMS projects in Angola, and explained the role of architects in the process.

The careful documentation of IMS practice shown by the architect Mihailo Čanak in many journals and books, including his own monographs, provided proof that the group at the IMS Centre for Housing managed to transmit the concern with flexibility from the construction site to the apartment estates produced. Oral histories of the first inhabitants of Experimental Housing in New Belgrade, like that of Mirjana Obradović, enabled me to understand how culture-making further developed in the use of space once housing was complete. Correspondence with Reinaldo Escobar, the Cuban journalist and builder of one of the IMS buildings in Havana, offered me the perspective of the makers on reception of the system overseas. Throughout all of these iterations, archive work and conversations allowed me to see the small scale and combine it with the broader view.

As well as archive documents and oral histories, I referred to books and journals dealing with architecture, construction and housing in the Yugoslav context, such as the publications of the Directorate for the Construction of New Belgrade (*Novi Beograd 1961; Beograd. Novi Beograd*, 1967); others documenting construction achievements (*Almanah 1961*, Savez gradjevinskih inžinjera i tehničara Jugoslavije, 1961; *20 godina rada 1948–1968*, ed. Milutin Maksimović, Institut za ispitivanje materijala, 1968; *Savetovanje o industrijalizaciji stambene izgradnje*, ed. Milan Mole, Savezna gradjevinska komora, 1960); general urban planning brochures (1950); press articles and books about the international perception of construction in Yugoslavia (Edward Palmer Thompson, *The Railway: An Adventure in Construction*, The British Yugoslav Association, 1948, and Arthur Gillette, *One Million Volunteers. The Story of Volunteer Youth Service*, Penguin

Books, 1968); UN reports (United Nations, *European Housing Situation*, 1956); housing laws (Branislav Krtić, Dušan Pajović, *Zakonodavstvo urbanizma, baštine, čovjekove sredine, prostornog uredjenja*, Naučna knjiga, 1987), and journals (*Urbanizam Beograda*).

Literature from the field of political theory dealing with self-governance and non-alignment was also important, and I have tried to capture causalities with the building sites. Recent studies by Gal Kirn offer a relevant study of attempts at self-governance that is not without critical argumentation, while also rooted in historical analysis. A degree of sharpness and clarity of language without an excess of particularities make his books relevant internationally and useful for thinking about modalities of participation in general. The literature on self-governance is extensive in its own right. There are books that offer a kind of primary source, such as those written by one of the leading theorists, Edvard Kardelj (*Samoupravljanje u Jugoslaviji 1950–1976*, Privredni Pregled, 1977; *O Komuni*, Radnička štampa, 1981, etc.). As Kardelj was highly influential in state politics as well as being relevant to an understanding of economic schemes and preoccupations, these books are also coloured by his involvement. There are many others who study self-governance from a similar perspective of involvement, which does not rule them out as a source of research material despite a tendency to emphasise peculiarities. Branko Horvat wrote the well-known books *The Political Economy of Socialism* (New York: M. E. Sharpe, Inc., Armonk, 1982) and *ABC jugoslovenskog socijalizma* (Globus, 1989) that are often referred to. In addition to these examples, there is the literature that dealt with a critique of self-governance while the trial was taking place. This group includes books and articles written by *Praxis* philosophers in Yugoslavia, such as Rudi Supek (»Some Contradictions and Insufficiencies of Yugoslav Self-Managing Socialism«, *Praxis* no. 3/4, »Un moment du socialisme Yougoslave«, 1971). Another example is *Self-Governing Socialism. A Reader*, vol. 1 and 2, edited by Branko Horvat, Mihailo Marković and Rudi Supek (International Arts and Sciences Press, 1975, M.E. Sharpe, 1975), addressing practice internationally with contributions from philosophers and economists. A critical review cannot overlook books by exposed dissident Milovan Đilas (e.g. *The Unperfect Society. Beyond the New Class*, Harcourt, Brace & World, 1969).

From a broader perspective, many international philosophers addressed the topic in their reflections on the Yugoslavian case (Bloch, Castoriadis, Lefevre, etc.). There are also books on self-governance by historians, such as Alvin Rubinstein's *Yugoslavia and Nonaligned World* (Princeton University Press, 1970), and recent examples of more operative advocates such as Michael A. Lebowitz's *Build It Now: Socialism for the Twenty-First Century* (NYU Press, 2006). Certainly worth mentioning is Frank Georgi *L'Autogestion en chantier. Les gauches françaises et le ›modèle‹ yougoslave, 1948–1981* (Arbre bleu, 2018).

Additionally, as a valuable source of information about bottom-up protagonists and microhistories, there are minutes of the meetings of self-managed enterprises, such as those of the Institute for Materials Testing. Analysis of the themes that appear in these minutes shows that sometimes practice worked better and sometimes worse. Also, the legal framework created and affected the working environment, which is not usually pointed out clearly enough (it tends to be assumed in the local context and very unknown further afield). In addition, I have used official documents such as laws, gazettes, encyclopaedias and indexes in which these terms and explanations are given in precise forms.

And, finally, I used books about the history and theory of architecture, and history in general, referring not to the Yugoslavian case but to international experiences of society, modernization and the Cold War context. This literature includes the heritage of the CIAM movement (Gregor Harbusch, Muriel Pérez, Kees Somer, Daniel Weiss, Evelin van Es, *Atlas of the Functional City: CIAM 4 and Comparative Urban Analysis*, gta Verlag, 2014; Silvia Malcovati, »Das alte Frankfurt: Urban Neighborhood versus Housing Estate, the Rebirth of Urban Architecture«, *Urban Planning* vol. 4, no. 3, edited by Luca Ortelli, Chiara Monterumisi and Alessandro Porotto, 2019); books affecting the international discourse of modern architecture, such as Le Corbusier's *Charte d'Athènes* (Plon, 1943); studies on modernism in the Third World (*Team 10 in Search of a Utopia of the Present 1953–81*, ed. Max Risselada and Dirk van den Heuvel, NAi Publishers, 2006; *Casablanca. Colonial Myths and Architectural Ventures*, Jean-Louis Cohen and Monique Eleb, The Monacelli Press, 2002; Darke, Roy, »Housing and Spatial Policies in the Socialist Third-World«, *Netherlands Journal of Housing and Environmental Research*, Vol. 4, no. 1, 1989; Kathleen James-Chakraborty, »Beyond Postcolonialism: New Directions for the History of Nonwestern Architecture«, *Frontiers of Architectural Research* no. 3, 2014); those describing the historical Third World context (Vijay Prashad, *The Darker Nations*, The New Press, 2007; Eric Hobsbawm, *The Age of Extremes 1914–1991*, Abacus, 1995); studies on memory and the material culture of social modernization in different geographies (Victor Buchli's *An Archaeology of Socialism*, Routledge, 2000; Lynsey Hanley's Estates, An Intimate History, Granta Books, 2008, and Filippo De Pieri, Bruno Bonomo, Gaia Caramellino, Federico Zanfi, eds., *Storie di case*, Donzelli, 2013); reviews on the heritage of prefabrication (Pedro Ignacio Alonso and Hugo Palmarola *Panel*, AA Publications, 2014; Philipp Meuser *Die Ästhetik der Platte*, DOM, 2015), etc.

I found relevant insights into the capacity of microhistories to reflect larger questions when tackled from different perspectives. Some examples were the work of Italian historian Giovanni Levi on microhistory (»On Microhistory«, in *New Perspectives in Historical Writing*, edited by Peter Burke, Polity Press, 1992), Carlo Ginzburg (*Il formaggio e i vermi*, Einaudi, 1976), and more recent studies such as Jan de Vries's »Playing with Scales: The Global and the Micro, the Macro and the Nano« (*Past & Present*, vol. 242, no. 14, 2019) and Georg G. Iggers' *Historiography in the Twentieth Century: From Scientific Objectivity to the Postmodern Challenge* (Wesleyan University Press, 2005). It was important to me to combine sources that were as diverse as possible and to find materials in archives as well as in talks, books or on the internet, allowing a broad plurality of voices to penetrate these histories of construction from different angles in order to understand their social and material scope.

Endnotes

INTRODUCTION: TOWARDS MUTUAL
HIGHLIGHT OF PRAXIS PHILOSOPHY AND
CONSTRUCTION

1   Charles Joyner, *Shared Traditions. Southern History and Folk Culture* (Chicago: University of Illinois Press, 1999), Introduction.
2   Richard D. Brown, »Microhistory and Postmodernism«, *Journal of the Early Republic* Vol. 23, No. 1 (Spring, 2003): 11.
3   Giovanni Levi, »On Microhistory«, in *New Perspectives of Historical Writing*, ed. Peter Bruke (Cambridge: Polity Press, 1991), 97, 98, quoted in Richard D. Brown, »Microhistory and Postmodernism«, 13, 14.
4   Richard D. Brown, »Microhistory and Postmodernism«, 14.
5   Carlo Ginzburg, »Microhistory and world history«, *The Cambridge World History* Vol. VI, ed. Jerry H. Bentley, Sanjay Subrahmanyam and Merry E. Wiesner-Hanks (Cambridge University Press: 2015), 446–473.
6   Richard D. Brown, »Microhistory and Postmodernism«, 18, 20.
7   Roland Barthes, »The Structuralist Activity«, (1963) in *Critical Essays*, trans. Richard Howard (Evanston: Northwestern University Press, 1972), 214, 215. Originally published as Roland Barthes, *Essais critiques* (Paris: Editions du Seuil, 1964).
8   György Márkus, »A Society of Culture: The Constitution of Modernity«, in *Rethinking Imagination. Culture and Creativity*, ed. Gillian Robinson and John Rundell (New York: Routledge, 1994), 15.
9   John Rundell, Introduction in *Rethinking Imagination. Culture and Creativity*, ed. Gillian Robinson and John Rundell (New York: Routledge, 1994), 11.
10   Adrian Forty, »Dead or Alive—Describing the Social«, *Words and Buildings. A Vocabulary of Modern Architecture* (London: Thames & Hudson, 2000), 102–117.
11   Heike Delitz, »Architectural Modes of Collective Existence. Architectural Sociology as a Comparative Social Theory«, *Cultural Sociology* 12 (2018): 37–57. https://doi.org/10.1177/1749975517718435.
12   Ernesto Laclau, Chantal Mouffe, *Hegemony and Socialist Strategy: Towards a Radical Democratic Politics* (London: Verso, 1985), 112.
13   Cornelius Castoriadis, *L'institution imaginare de la société* (Paris: Editions du Seuil, 1975), English translation *The Imaginary Institution of Society* (Cambridge, Malden: Polity Press, 1987), 204.
14   Jeremy Till, »Foreword« in *The Routledge Companion to Architecture and Social Engagement*, ed. Farhan Karim (New York: Routledge, 2018).
15   Peter Sloterdijk, *Critique of Cynical Reason* (Minnesota: University of Minnesota Press, 1987), 3. Originally published as *Kritik der zynischen Vernunft* (Frankfurt am Main: Suhrkamp Verlag, 1983).
16   Castoriadis, *The Imaginary Institution of Society*, 20.
17   See also *Histories of Postwar Architecture* no. 6, »Thick Descriptions: Socialist Yugoslavia in Construction« (October 2020), ed. Vladimir Kulić, Bojana Videkanić, https://doi.org/10.6092/issn.2611-0075/v3-n6-2020.
18   Edvard Kardelj, *Samoupravljanje u Jugoslaviji 1950–1976* (Belgrade: Privredni Pregled, 1977).
19   For an early critique of the Yugoslav attempt, see: Cornelius Castoriadis, »The Yugoslavian Bureaucracy«, in *Political and Social Writings Vol. 1, 1946–1955* (Minneapolis: University of Minnesota Press, 1988), 179–198. The article was first published under Castoriadis's pseudonym Pierre Chaulieu, Georges Dupont, »La bureaucratie yougoslave« (October 2020), Socialisme ou Barbarie no. 5–6 (March, April 1950): 1–76. For the critique offered by Yugoslavian philosophers see: Rudi Supek, »Some Contradictions and Insufficiencies of Yugoslav Self-managing Socialism«, *Praxis* No. 3/4: »Un moment du socialisme Yougoslave« (1971): 375–399.
20   These restaurants were part of the milk kitchens that UNICEF opened in Yugoslavia in 1947. Milk kitchens were important institutions in Europe after World War II, set up to provide children with milk, which was hard to find due to the death of animals during the war. After the period of austerity, milk restaurants in Yugoslavia became social places offering bread and milk specialties. In the early sixties, they were accompanied by more luxurious express restaurants. See Sanja Petrović Todosijević, *Za bezimene: Delatnost UNICEF-a u Federativnoj Narodnoj Republici Jugoslaviji 1947–1954* (Belgrade: Institut za noviju istoriju Srbije, 2008).
21   On some positive aspects of the Yugoslavian trial see: Michael A. Lebowitz, »Seven Difficult Questions«, in *Build It Now: Socialism for the Twenty-First Century* (New York: NYU Press, 2006), 73–84. Another comprehensive recent study is offered by Gal Kirn, *Partisan Ruptures. Self-Management, Market Reform and the Spectre of Socialist Yugoslavia* (London: Pluto Press, 2019).
22   Published by the Croatian Philosophical Society and the Yugoslavian Society for Philosophy from 1964 until 1974.
23   Gajo Petrović, »A quoi bon Praxis?«, *Praxis* no. 1: »A quoi bon praxis?« (1965): 3–7. https://www.marxists.org/subject/praxis/praxis-international/Praxis%2C%20international%20edition%2C%201965%2C%20no.%201.pdf (last accessed: 10 August 2022).
24   »Macht zersetzen«, *Der Spiegel* no. 36, 1.9.1968, https://www.spiegel.de/kultur/macht-zersetzen-a-de7da828-0002-0001-0000-000045950125?context=issue (last accessed: 6 May 2021].

25 Dragomir Olujić, Krunoslav Stojaković, ed., *Praxis, Kritika i humanistički socijalizam* (Belgrade: Rosa Luxemburg Stiftung, 2012); Ante Lešaja, *Praxis Orientation, Journal Praxis and The Korčula Summer School* (Belgrade: Rosa Luxemburg Stiftung, 2014).

26 For a contemporary anthropological analysis of the phenomenon of youth work actions, see: Andrea Matošević, »Više od zbroja infrastrukturnih postignuća: omladinske radne akcije i fenomenologija moralne ekonomije dara«, *Narodna umjetnost* no. 53/2 (2016): 71.

27 Gajo Petrović, »Praxis«, in *A Dictionary of Marxist Thought*, ed. Tom Bottomore, Laurence Harris, V. G. Kiernan, Ralph Miliband (Blackwell Publishing, 1983), 437.

28 Karl Marx, »Theses on Feuerbach«, *Writings of the Young Marx on Philosophy and Society*, ed. Loyd D. Easton and Kurt H. Guddat (New York: Doubleday & Co., Anchor Books, 1967), 400–402. Quoted in: Richard J. Bernstein, *Praxis and Action* (Philadelphia: University of Pennsylvania Press, 1971), 11.

29 Bernstein, *Praxis and Action*, 39, 42.

30 Jürgen Habermas, *The Philosophical Discourse of Modernity. Twelve Lectures* (Cambridge, Massachusetts: The MIT Press, 1987), 62. Originally published as *Der philosophische Diskurs der Moderne: Zwölf Vorlesungen* (Frankfurt am Main: Suhrkamp Verlag, 1985).

31 Gajo Petrović, »Praxis«, in *A Dictionary of Marxist Thought*, 435–440.
See also: Branko Bošnjak, »Betrachtungen über die Praxis«, *Praxis* no. 1: »A quoi bon praxis?« (1965): 17. Available at: https://www.marxists.org/subject/praxis/praxis-international/Praxis%2C%20international%20edition%2C%201965%2C%20no.%201.pdf (last accessed: 24 Februar 2021).

32 Srećko Mihailović, »Ciljevi ORA i njihovo ostvarenje«, *ORA—Mladost naše zemlje 1942–1982* (Mladost: Belgrade, 1983), 90–91.

33 On the development of concrete, see: Peter Collins, *Concrete. The Vision of a New Architecture* (London: Faber and Faber, 1959).

34 For a critique of the modern architecture movement see Ernst Bloch, »Die Bebauung des Hohlraums«, in *Das Prinzip Hoffnung* (Frankfurt am Main: Suhrkamp, 1959), Eng. Ernst Bloch, »Building in Empty Spaces«, *The Utopian Function of Art and Literature*, trans. Jack Zipes and Frank Mecklenburg (Cambridge, Massachusetts, London, England: The MIT Press, 1988), 186–200. See also: Lewis Mumford, *The City in History: Its Origins, Its Transformations, and Its Prospects* (New York: Harcourt, Brace & World, 1961). Also noteworthy here is Kenneth Frampton's search for a third way between »the reductive functionalism of late modern architecture and the superficial aesthetics of the newly acclaimed postmodern architecture«. See: Léa-Catherine Szacka, Véronique

Patteeuw, »Critical Regionalism For Our Time«, *The Architectural Review* no. 1466 (November 2019).

35 Jürgen Habermas, *Theorie des kommunikativen Handelns, Band 2: Zur Kritik der funktionalistischen Vernunft* (Frankfurt: Suhrkamp Verlag, 1981), Eng. *The Theory of Communicative Action 2. The Critique of Functionalist Reason* (Cambridge: Polity Press, 1987). Habermas writes about the social theory of communicative action as »just another version of praxis philosophy« from the origins of Marx's social praxis and Western Marxism. See: Jürgen Habermas, *Der philosophische Diskurs der Moderne: Zwölf Vorlesungen* (Frankfurt: Suhrkamp Verlag, 1985), Eng. *The Philosophical Discourse of Modernity. Twelve Lectures* (Cambridge, Massachusetts: The MIT Press, 1987), 316, 317.

36 Habermas, *The Theory of Communicative Action 2. The Critique of Functionalist Reason*, 126.

37 Raymond Williams, *Keywords. A Vocabulary of Culture and Society* (New York: Oxford University Press, 1976), 316–318.

PRAXIS AND ACTION: TOWARDS BUILDING AS A COLLECTIVE PRACTICE

1 Shorter version of this chapter will be published as the article in *Grey Room* no. 90 (Winter, 2023).

2 Henri Lefebvre, *The Sociology of Marx*, »The Marxian Concept of Praxis«. Kindle. Originally published as: Henri Lefebvre, *Sociologie de Marx* (Paris: Presses Universitaires de France, 1966).

3 Gajo Petrović, *Marx in the mid-twentieth century* (New York: Anchor Books, 1967).

4 Gajo Petrović, »Praxis«, in *A Dictionary of Marxist Thought*, ed. Tom Bottomore, Laurence Harris, V. G. Kiernan, Ralph Miliband (Blackwell Publishing, 1983), 435–440.

5 Published by the Croatian Philosophical Society and the Yugoslavian Society for Philosophy from 1964 until 1974. See Introduction«.

6 Richard J. Bernstein, »Introduction«, in *Habermas and Modernity*, ed. Richard J. Bernstein (Cambridge, Massachusetts: The MIT Press, 1985), 31, 32.

7 Srećko Mihailović, »Ciljevi ORA i njihovo ostvarenje«, in *ORA—Mladost naše zemlje 1942–1982* ed. Toma Dragosavac (Mladost: Belgrade, 1983), 90–91.

8 For a recent study of the youth action as a cultural phenomenon see: Reana Senjković, *Svaki dan pobjeda. Kultura omladinskih radnih akcija* (Zagreb: Srednja Europa, 2016).

9 In his 1951 article on Yugoslavia, Greek-French philosopher Cornelius Castoriadis pointed to the Five-Year Plan as one of the roots of the conflict due to its goal of increasing the country's industrial potential. As Moscow tended to conserve Yugoslavia's pre-war economic structure based on agricultural production, the country developing its own industry to support the process of modern-

ization was seen as rather problematic. Cornelius Castoriadis, »The Yugoslavian Bureaucracy«, in *Political and Social Writings Vol. 1, 1946—1955* (Minneapolis: University of Minnesota Press, 1988), 179–198. The article was first published under Castoriadis's pseudonym, Pierre Chaulieu, Georges Dupont, »La bureaucratie yougoslave«, *Socialisme ou Barbarie* no. 5-6 (March, April 1950): 1–76.

10 Richard J. Bernstein, *Praxis and Action* (Philadelphia: University of Pennsylvania Press, 1971), 76–78.

11 Ludvik Vrtačič, »Marxist-Leninist literature in Jugoslavia (1945–1959)«, *Studies in East European Thought* 1 (1961): 111–119.

12 Luka Bogdanić, »Čemu *praxis*? Ili o historijskom porijeklu i mjestu Praxisa«, in *Aspekti praxisa. Refleksije uz 50. obljetnicu*, ed. Borislav Mikulić, Mislav Žitko (Zagreb: Filozofski fakultet Sveučilišta u Zagrebu, 2015), 25–45.

See also: Dragoljub Nešić, »Ideja asocijacije proizvođača kod socijaliste-utopiste Charlesa Fouriera«, *Pogledi* no. 2 (December 1952): 66–78. Gajo Petrović, »Filozofija u SSSR-u od Oktobarske revolucije do 1938«, *Pogledi* no. 2 (December 1952): 79–86.

13 See: Edvard Kardelj, *Samoupravljanje u Jugoslaviji 1950–1976* (Belgrade: Privredni Pregled, 1977).

14 Ana Panić, Jovo Bakić, Srđan Cvetković, Ivana Dobrivojević, Hrvoje Klasić, Vladimir Petrović, *Yugoslavia 1918–1991* (Belgrade: Museum of Yugoslavia, 2014), 40. Published following the exhibition *Jugoslavija: od početka do kraja* at the Museum of Yugoslavia, Belgrade, 1 Dec 2012–17 March 2013.

15 See: Vladimir Kulić, Maroje Mrduljaš, Wolfgang Thaler ed., *Modernism In-between. The Mediatory Architectures of Socialist Yugoslavia* (Berlin: jovis, 2012).

Mrduljaš and Kulić also edited the book that accompanied the exhibition *Unfinished Modernisations—Between Utopia and Pragmatism* (Zagreb: Udruženje hrvatskih arhitekata, 2012), which pointed to modernization as a precondition for the creation of a democratic, emancipatory society.

The most recent is the exhibition catalogue *Toward a Concrete Utopia: Architecture in Yugoslavia 1948–1980*, ed. Martino Stierli, Vladimir Kulić (New York: The Museum of Modern Art, 2018). See also *Histories of Postwar Architecture* no. 6, »Thick Descriptions: Socialist Yugoslavia in Construction« (October 2020), ed. Vladimir Kulić, Bojana Videkanić, https://doi.org/10.6092/issn.2611-0075/v3-n6-2020.

For the studies analysing developments in architecture in the East and West during the Iron Curtain era, including the Yugoslav case, see the three-volume publication *East West Central. Re-Building Europe 1950–1990*, ed. Ákos Moravánszky, Judith Hopfengärther (Basel: Birkhäuser, 2016, 2017).

For some aspects of the export of Yugoslavian material practice to the Global South, see: Łukasz Stanek, *Architecture in Global Socialism: Eastern Europe, West Africa, and the Middle East in the Cold War* (Princeton: Princeton University Press, 2020).

16 For material development and changes in demography in general, see: Branko Petranović, »Materijalni razvoj i demografsko-socijalne promene«, *Istorija Jugoslavije*, knjiga III *Socijalistička Jugoslavija 1955–1988* (Belgrade: Nolit, 1988), 418–432. For the constitution of work actions as a form of building practice, see: Srećko Mihailović, »Ciljevi i njihovo ostvarenje«, *Omladinske radne akcije—mladost naše zemlje*, ed. Toma Dragosavac (Belgrade: Poslovna Politika i Mladost, 1983), 90.

17 Jovan Golubović, ed., *Beograd grad akcijaša* (Belgrade: Gradska konferencija SSO Beograda Omladinska radna akcija »Beograd«, 1985), 20–22. Available at: https://sites.google.com/site/orabeograd/ (last accessed: 14 October 2021).

18 At the New Belgrade construction site, 49807 participants worked in 1948, of whom 27 949 were rural people, 12947 workers, 7750 students and 1137 highly educated professionals. See: Typescript of the report »Savezna akcija Novi Beograd. Učešće omladine 1948«, unpaged document, Fonds 114: Savez socijalističke omladine Jugoslavije. Radne akcije 1948–1950, Folder 152, Archives of Yugoslavia, Belgrade.

19 The actions were proposed to potential participants through personal connections, local youth centres, posters and the press (there was no television). The actions were organized by a youth movement called SOJ (Socialist Youth of Yugoslavia), which worked at municipal level, usually connected to local cultural institutions known as youth centres (*Dom omladine*). Throughout the history of Yugoslavia, these places have served as motors of cultural life, local meeting and development of international bonds.

20 For the condition of the site before the war, see: Bratislav Stojanović, »Istorija Novog Beograda I«, *Godišnjak grada Beograda* no. XXI (1974): 211–236.

21 See: Predrag J. Marković, *Beograd izmedju istoka i zapada 1948–1965* (Belgrade: Službeni list Beograd, 1996).

22 Gajo Petrović, *Marx in the mid-twentieth century* (New York: Anchor Books, 1967), 23, 57.

23 This is explicit in Marx: »Above all we must avoid postulating ›society‹ again as an abstraction vis-à-vis the individual. The individual is the social being. His manifestations of life—even if they may not appear in the direct form of communal manifestations of life carried out in association with others—are therefore an expression and confirmation of social life.« Karl Marx and Frederick Engels, *Collected Works* Vol. 3 (London: Lawrence & Wishart, 1975 ff.), 299. Quoted in Norman Geras, *Marx and Human Nature: Refutation of a Legend* (London, New York: Verso, 1983), Chap. 3, Kindle.

24 Henri Lefebvre, *Métaphilosophie* (Arguments, 1965). In English: *Metaphilosophy* (London, New York: Verso, 2016), 343, 329, 331, 344. Kindle.

25 At state level, there were ten big cooperatives organized to repair 12900 existing machines, of which 29% were of American or British origin, 15% were German and Italian machines captured as trophies, 25% were inherited from pre-war Yugoslavia, and 31% were obtained from different countries after 1944. See: Jože Valentinčić, »Jugoslovensko gradjevinarstvo u period 1945–1960«, in *Almanah 1961*, ed. Milutin Maksimović, Radmio Živković, Prvoslav Trajković, Ratko Jovčić (Belgrade: Savez gradjevinskih inženjera i tehničara Jugoslavije, 1961), 26.

26 Apart from being an active member of the *Praxis* circle in Yugoslavia, Fromm further promoted it through the book he edited and for which many of contributions were written by Yugoslavian philosophers. In the introduction, he directly greets Gajo Petrović for correspondence. See: Erich Fromm, *Socialist Humanism. An International Symposium* (New York: Doubleday & Company, Inc., 1965).

27 Erich Fromm, »The Application of Humanist Psychoanalysis to Marx's Theory«, in *Socialist Humanism*, ed. Erich Fromm (New York: Doubleday & Co., Anchor Books, 1965), 228, 231.

    This is a point where Marx diverges both from Hegel's idealism and from mechanical materialism by applying philosophy and economy *ad hominem*.

28 Gajo Petrović, *Marx in the mid-twentieth century* (New York: Anchor Books, 1967), 79. Quote from: Erich Fromm, *Marx's Concept of Man* (New York: Frederick Ungar Publishing Company, 1961), 135.

29 See Marek Fritzhand's analysis, »Marx's Ideal of Man«, in *Socialist Humanism*, ed. Erich Fromm (New York: Doubleday & Co., Anchor Books, 1965), 174–177.

30 For the early Marx, see: Karl Marx, *Ökonomisch-philosophische Manuskripte aus dem Jahre 1844* (Berlin: Zenodot Verlagsgesellschaft, 2017). Originally published in Karl Marx, Friedrich Engels, *Werke*, Band 40 (Berlin: Dietz-Verlag, 1968). Available at: http://www.mlwerke.de/me/me40/me40_465.htm (last accessed: 21 Januar 2021). See also: *Praxis* issue devoted to the topic of alienation which, through the work of Georg Lukács, became known as reification *Praxis* no. 1/2: »Créativité et réification« (1968); Gajo Petrović, »Alienation and de-alienation«, in *Marx in the mid-twentieth century* (New York: Anchor Books, 1967), 135–153.

31 Bratislav Stojanović, »Istorija Novog Beograda I«, *Godišnjak grada Beograda* XXI (1974): 226, 227, 230. The Plan was adopted by vote on 27 December 1947, by the People's Committee of Belgrade (Narodni odbor Beograda). See: Ljubica Radojković, »Omladinske radne brigade na izgradnji Beograda 1947–1950 godine«, *Godišnjak grada Beograda* V (1958): 365.

32 A series of institutions emerged alongside the first youth work action in New Belgrade (1947–1950). In 1945, the Urban Institute (Urbanistički institut) was set up as part of the Ministry of Construction, while work to repair war damage was led by the Executive People's Council (Izvršni narodni odbor). People's Councils emerged as a means of governance in Yugoslavia, with citizens electing a union of people, starting at city level and extending to federal level. The Urban Institute, under the leadership of the architect Nikola Dobrović, produced the very first drawing for the regulation of streets in New Belgrade in 1946. The plan was based on a circular scheme. This scheme was presented as the basis for an open competition in 1947 for three public buildings (two political and a hotel), together with an overview of the city. After the competitions and public discussions, the plan was proposed in 1948. Meanwhile, in 1948, the Urban Institute was divided into two branches: the Town Planning Institute (Urbanistički zavod) and the Chief Architect's Department as part of the Executive People's Council (IONO). The latter was to be dissolved at the end of the same year. In its place, the Design Department (Uprava za projektovanje IONO) was founded to bring together urban, architectural and engineering operations in one location. This institution further worked on the General Urban Plan for Belgrade, 1950.

    Bratislav Stojanović, »Posleratna beogradska arhitektonska izgradnja«, *Godišnjak grada Beograda* XVII (1970): 201–235. Bratislav Stojanović, »Istorija Novog Beograda I«, *Godišnjak grada Beograda* XXI (1974): 211–234, and »Istorija Novog Beograda II«, *Godišnjak grada Beograda* XXII (1975): 199–217.

    See also: Miloš Somborski, »Problemi urbanističkog planiranja Beograda«, in *Beograd. Generalni urbanistički plan 1950* (Belgrade: Izdanje IONO, 1951), 5–11.

33 »Omladina Jugoslavije je juče počela svoje veliko delo—izgradnju Novog Beograda«, *Politika*, 12 April 1948, front cover; »Novi Beograd-ponos petoletke«, *Duga* no. 218–219, October 1949, 197, 198. »Novi Beograd. Svedočanstvo socijalističke izgradnje u novoj Jugoslaviji«, *Yugoslavia* no. 14–16 (1948): 180–184.

34 Ljubo Ilić, »Uz izgradnju Novog Beograda«, *Arhitektura* 8–10 (1948): 9.

35 Among others, the enterprise New Belgrade which, in 1956, became the Directorate for the Construction of New Belgrade and led work on building the city in the following decades.

36 Bernstein, *Praxis and Action*, 59, 44.

37 Rudi Supek, *Omladina na putu bratstva. Psihologija radne akcije* (Belgrade: Mladost, 1963), 23.

38 Rudi Supek, »Smisao jedne radne akcije. Iz bilježnice na auto putu«, *Naše teme* no. 4–5 (1958): 534–542, translation by author.

39 Henri Lefebvre, »Socijalizam za vrijeme ljetnjeg odmora«, *Praxis* no. 1: »Suvremeni problemi socijalizma« (1965): 164–167. Originally published as Henri Lefebvre, »Le socialisme en vacances«, *France Observateur*, no. 746, 20. August 1964, 20. (Free translation by the author.)

40 Henri Lefebvre, »Sur quelques critères du développement social et du socialisme«, *Praxis* no. 2/3: »Sinn und Perspektiven des Sozialismus« (1965): 156–168.

41 Lefebvre, *Metaphilosophy*, 6. Also in: Lefebvre, *The Sociology of Marx*, »The Marxian Concept of Praxis«. Kindle.

42 Ibid., 6.

43 Lefebvre, *The Sociology of Marx*, »The Marxian Concept of Praxis«. Kindle.

44 Ibid.

45 Rudi Supek, »Henri Lefebvre: Sociologie de Marx«, *Praxis* no. 3: »Aktuelnost Marksove misli« (1967): 421–423.

46 Marek Fritzhand, »Marx's Ideal of Man«, 174–177.

47 Jürgen Habermas, *The Philosophical Discourse of Modernity. Twelve Lectures* (Cambridge, Massachusetts: The MIT Press, 1987), 64. Originally published as *Der philosophische Diskurs der Moderne: Zwölf Vorlesungen* (Frankfurt am Main: Suhrkamp Verlag, 1985).

48 Ljubica Radojković, »Omladinske radne brigade na izgradnji Beograda 1947–1950 godine«, 367, 368, 377, 378.

49 Typescript of the report »Dnevni raspored života i rada u studentskim brigadama«, Fonds 114: Savez socijalističke omladine Jugoslavije, Radne akcije 1948–1950, Folder 152, Archives of Yugoslavia, Belgrade.

50 There were three state construction firms engaged at the New Belgrade construction site: Novi Beograd, the Construction Department of the People's Committee (IONO) and the Sector of Communal Works in New Belgrade. There were also seven companies directing the construction of the buildings on which the brigades worked. See typescript of the report: »Rad omladinskih radnih brigade na izgradnji Novog Beograda 1949«, Fonds 114: Savez socijalističke omladine Jugoslavije. Radne akcije 1948–1950, Folder 152, Archives of Yugoslavia, Belgrade, 1.

51 »Rad omladinskih radnih brigade na izgradnji Novog Beograda 1949«, 1.

52 In 1949, 6500 youth participants from the site of the action went directly into full-time employment. See: »Rad omladinskih radnih brigade na izgradnji Novog Beograda 1949«, 3.

53 Rudi Supek, »Some Contradictions and Insufficiencies of Yugoslav Self-Managing Socialism«, *Praxis* 3/4: »Un moment du socialisme Yougoslave« (1971): 375–399.

54 Rudi Supek, »The Sociology of Workers' Self-Management«, in *Self-Governing Socialism. Volume 2. A Reader*, ed. Branko Horvat, Mihailo Marković, Rudi Supek (New York: Routledge, 2015), 3–4. The first edition was published by M. E. Sharpe, New York in 1975.

55 Jürgen Habermas, »Tehnički napredak i svijet društvenog života«, *Praxis* no. 6 (1965): 846–865.

56 Habermas, *The Philosophical Discourse of Modernity. Twelve Lectures*, 66. This was also explicit in his writings, maintaining that the reconciliation between man and nature comes through the abstraction of science, technology and culture. Bernstein, *Praxis and Action*, 50. See also: Lefebvre, *Metaphilosophy*, 293.

57 Lefebvre, *The Sociology of Marx*, »The Marxian Concept of Praxis«. Kindle.

58 The history of Marxism tended to imagine a group of producers in various scenarios. On the one hand, there was the image of social labour that was present in the prototype of the craftsman, as in the reform movement of John Ruskin and William Morris. They promoted handmade art, while industrial labour became more remote from the integral process of making. On the other, there were positions that praised technology. Habermas was critical of this ambiguity and found that Marx did not give a clear account of how palpable, purposive activity is related to the rationality of social praxis. According to Habermas, this was only presented through the vague image of an association of free producers. See: Habermas, *The Philosophical Discourse of Modernity. Twelve Lectures*, 66.

59 Habermas, *The Philosophical Discourse of Modernity. Twelve Lectures*, 64.

60 Ibid., 304.

61 Actions were accompanied by a programme of plays, films, books, journals and trips that each participant would attend. See: »Razvijajmo što bolji propagandno-agitacioni rad u brigadama«, *Novi Beograd*, 3 April 1949, front cover.

62 »Rad omladinskih radnih brigade na izgradnji Novog Beograda 1949«, 22.

63 Typescript of the decision »Odluka o programu, planovima i uputstvima u radu CK NOJ«, Glavnom štabu omladinskih radnih brigada na izgradnji Beograda od strane Centralnog komiteta Narodne omladine Jugoslavije, 8 March 1949, Fonds 114: Savez socijalističke omladine Jugoslavije. Radne akcije 1948–1950, Folder 152, Archives of Yugoslavia, Belgrade, 1.

64 Arthur Gillette, *One Million Volunteers. The Story of Volunteer Youth Service* (Harmondsworth, Ringwood: Penguin Books, 1968), 66, 69.

65 Gillette, *One Million Volunteers. The Story of Volunteer Youth Service*, 112.

66 Typescript of the document »Pravilnik izdavaštva za inostrana izdanja pri izdavačkom preduzeću *Novo pokoljenje*«, Fonds: Savez socijalističke omladine Jugoslavije. Međunarodna saradnja 1948–1969, Folder 223, Archives of Yugoslavia, Belgrade.

67 Typescript of the document »Spisak društvenih organizacija, listova i rukovodstava Saveza omladine Jugoslavije kojima treba slati Tanjugov

bilten *Omladina u svetu*«, Fonds: Savez socijalističke omladine Jugoslavije. Međunarodna saradnja 1948–1969, Folder 223, Archives of Yugoslavia, Belgrade.

68 Typescript of documents »Plan izdavačke delatnosti uredništva za inostrana izdanja pri izdavačkom preduzeću *Novo pokoljenje* za 1949. godinu« and »Plan izdavačke delatnosti uredništva za inostrana izdanja pri izdavačkom preduzeću *Novo pokoljenje* za 1950. godinu«, Fonds: Savez socijalističke omladine Jugoslavije. Međunarodna saradnja 1948–1969, Folder 223, Archives of Yugoslavia, Belgrade.

69 *People's Youth of Yugoslavia Open Call* (via World Federation of Democratic Youth) Fonds: Savez socijalističke omladine Jugoslavije. Međunarodna saradnja 1948–1969, Folder 229, Archives of Yugoslavia, Belgrade.

70 *Ujedinjene nacije* brochure (Belgrade: Radio služba odjeljenja za informacije pri Ujedinjenim nacijama New York, October 1951) 2, 9. Fonds: Savez socijalističke omladine Jugoslavije. Međunarodna saradnja 1948–1969, Folder 229, Archives of Yugoslavia, Belgrade.

71 Geneva 1950 was devoted to overcoming the tension between East and West, and transferring knowledge in the form of technical assistance.

See: Typescript of United Nations document »Report on the Fourth Conference of International Non-Governmental Organizations at Geneva«, June 1950, Fonds: Savez socijalističke omladine Jugoslavije. Međunarodna saradnja 1948–1969, Folder 229, Archives of Yugoslavia, Belgrade.

72 Typescript of the decision »Savjet za nauku i kulturu Vlade FNRJ dostavlja brošuru *To Combine Our Efforts* svim savjetima za prosvetu, nauku i kulturu«, 4 October 1951, Fonds: Savez socijalističke omladine Jugoslavije. Međunarodna saradnja 1948–1969, Folder 229, Archives of Yugoslavia, Belgrade.

73 *Clubs de Relations Internationales et groupements analogues* brochure (UNESCO Publications, 1949), Fonds: Savez socijalističke omladine Jugoslavije. Međunarodna saradnja 1948–1969, Folder 229, Archives of Yugoslavia, Belgrade.

74 Yugoslavia was particularly involved in UN conferences about youth organizations, like the one in India dealing with the organization of youth movements and possible programmes for voluntary actions. See typescript of the document: »United Nations Youth Welfare Seminar India«, 1–21 November 1951, Fonds: Savez socijalističke omladine Jugoslavije. Međunarodna saradnja 1948–1969, Folder 229, Archives of Yugoslavia, Belgrade.

75 Manuscript document, »Catalogue of International Work Brigades on the Construction of the Brotherhood and Unity Highway«, Fonds: Savez socijalističke omladine Jugoslavije. Međunarodna saradnja 1948–1969, Folder 229, unpaged. Archives of Yugoslavia, Belgrade.

Part of the international brigades working on the highway visited the New Belgrade construction site, including the French brigade in 1949 (20 August 1949). It was led by a philosophy student and had a mainly student population. The brigade explained its involvement in youth actions as an attempt to help »the construction of socialism«. See: Joža Horvastvi, »Franscuska brigada posjetila Beograd«, *Bratstvo-Jedinstvo*, 20 August 1949, 38.

76 Edward Palmer Thompson, »An Open Letter to Leszek Kołakowski«, *The Socialist Register* (1973): 1–100. Available at: https://www.marxists.org/archive/thompson-ep/1973/kolakowski.htm (last accessed: 12 September 2022). See also: Edward Palmer Thompson, ed., *The Railway: An Adventure in Construction* (London: The British Yugoslav Association, 1948).

In 1947, in addition to Yugoslav participation, the Šamac-Sarajevo railway attracted 56 international youth brigades, representing 47 nations with over 5800 participants. See: *People's Youth of Yugoslavia Open Call.*

77 Quote: »Dear Friends, we have just published a pamphlet on Omladinska pruga. It was written as an account of the experiences of our group, which went there last summer. We enclose a few copies for your foreign department.« From the letter of chairman Fritz Walter Brichacek to the Central Council of the People's Youth, Vienna, 12 February 1948, Fonds: Savez socijalističke omladine Jugoslavije. Međunarodna saradnja 1948–1969, Folder 229, Archives of Yugoslavia, Belgrade.

78 Ivan Hofman, »Susret drugačijih svetova: Strani državljani na omladinskim radnim akcijama u Jugoslaviji 1946–1951. godine«, *Godišnjak za društvenu istoriju* 1 (2012): 55, 56.

79 Prof. Slobodan Ž. Marković on being part of the youth action at the New Belgrade construction site in Slobodan V. Ristanović, *Novi Beograd, Graditeljski poduhvat veka* (Belgrade: IA KSE-NA, 2009) 379–381. (The translation is abridged and paraphrased by the author.)

80 Srećko Mihailović, »Karakteristike omladinskih radnih akcija«, in ed. Toma Dragosavac, *Omladinske radne akcije—mladost naše zemlje* (Belgrade: Poslovna Politika i Mladost, 1983), 56–69.

PRAXIS AND IMAGINATION: TOWARDS
PARTICIPATION IN PREFABRICATION

1 Cornelius Castoriadis, »Radical Imagination and the Social Instituting Imaginary«, in *Rethinking Imagination: Culture and Creativity*, ed. Gillian Robinson and John Rundell (London and New York: Routledge, 1994), later published in *The Castoriadis Reader*, ed. David Ames Curtis (Oxford UK, Malden USA: Blackwell Publishers, 1977), 322.

2 See Chapter 1.

3   Pierre Chaulieu et Georges Dupont, »La bureaucratie yougoslave«, *Socialisme ou Barbarie*, no. 5–6 (March April 1950): 1–77. Latter reprinted in Cornelius Castoriadis, *Political and Social Writings Vol. 1 1946–1955: From the Critique of Bureaucracy to the Positive Content of Socialism* (Minneapolis: University of Minnesota Press, 1988), 179–198.

4   Cornelius Castoriadis, »On the Content of Socialism 1: From the Critique of Bureaucracy to the Idea of Proletariat's Autonomy«, *Political and Social Writings Vol. 1 1946–1955: From the Critique of Bureaucracy to the Positive Content of Socialism* (Minneapolis: University of Minnesota Press, 1988), 297. The article was originally published under the pseudonym Pierre Chaulieu, »Sur le contenu du socialisme«, *Socialisme ou Barbarie*, no. 17 (July 1955): 1–25.

5   See: »Entretien avec un ouvrier yougoslave«, *Socialisme ou Barbarie* no. 26 (November December 1958): 141–144. The article is signed by the editor and is therefore not explicitly Castoriadis's view. The critique of historical readings of Marxism in bureaucratic manner, including in Yugoslav state politics, is also present in Cornelius Castoriadis, *The Imaginary Institution of Society* (Cambridge, Malden: Polity Press, 1987), 11. Originally published as Cornelius Castoriadis, *L'institution imaginare de la société* (Paris: Editions du Seuil, 1975).

6   For the broader context of the *Praxis* circle in Yugoslavia, see the Introduction.

7   For a list of visitors to Korčula, see the text written by Yugoslav writer and member of the *Praxis* circle Predrag Matvejević, »Requiem za jednu lјevicu«, *Praxis: Kritika i humanistički socijalizam*, ed. Dragomir Olujić, Krunoslav Stojaković (Korčula: Rosa Luxemburg Stiftung Souteast Europe, 2011), 7, 8.

8   François Dosse, »Le rayonnement international«, in *Castoriadis une vie* (Paris: La Découverte, 2014), 521–551. URL: https://www.cairn-int.info/castoriadis-9782707198723-page-521.htm (last accessed: 25 November 2021).

9   Richard J. Bernstein, ed., *Habermas and Modernity* (Cambridge, Massachusetts: The MIT Press, 1985), 32.

10   Jürgen Habermas, *Der philosophische Diskurs der Moderne: Zwölf Vorlesungen* (Frankfurt: Suhrkamp Verlag, 1985), English translation *The Philosophical Discourse of Modernity* (Cambridge Massachusetts: MIT Press, 1987), 327.

11   See Habermas's analysis in *The Philosophical Discourse of Modernity*, 330.

12   Ernst Bloch, *Subjekt-Objekt, Erläuterungen zu Hegel* (Berlin: Aufbau-Verlag, 1951).

13   Luka Bogdanić, »Čemu praxis? Ili o historijskom porijeklu i mjestu Praxisa«, in *Aspekti praxisa. Refleksije uz 50. Obljetnicu*, edited by Borislav Mikulić, Mislav Žitko, (Zagreb: Filozofski fakultet Sveučilišta u Zagrebu, 2015), 38–39.

14   Ernst Bloch, »Jugoslawien nagelt die Flagge an den Mast«, SPIEGEL interview with Ernst Bloch about the blow to the *Praxis* circle, *Der Spiegel*, no. 6, 1975, 80.

15   Their difference was underlined by Castoriadis himself. Castoriadis saw Bloch as a Marxist philosopher and considered him influential for the twentieth-century preoccupation with the term utopia. In describing why the institution of society is not utopia but a concrete realistic possibility, Castoriadis recalled that that utopia is a mystifying word that represents what did not and will not ever exist.

      See interview with Cornelius Castoriadis by Jocelyn Wolff and Benjamin Quénelle, »Le projet de l'autonomie n'est pas une utopie«, *Propos*, 10 (March 1993): 34–40. In English published as Cornelius Castoriadis, »The Project of Autonomy is Not Utopia«, in *A Society Adrift. Interviews and Debates 1974–1997*, ed. Enrique Escobar, Myrto Gondicas, and Pascal Vernay (New York: Fordham University Press, 2010), 3.

16   Cornelius Castoriadis, »*Nomos/Phusis* Opposition«, *Bedeutung Magazine* no. 1: Nature&Culture (2008): 14–20.

17   Ernst Bloch, »Marxismus und Dichtung«, *Literarische Aufsätze* (Frankfurt am Main: Suhrkamp, 1935). In English: Ernst Bloch, »Marxism and Poetry«, *The Utopian Function of Art and Literature* (Cambridge Massachusetts, London England: The MIT Press, 1988), 157, 159.

18   Ernst Bloch, »Die bewusste und die gewusste Tätigkeit im Noch-Nicht-Bewussten, utopische Funktion«, *Das Prinzip Hoffnung* (Frankfurt am Main: Suhrkamp, 1959), in English »The Conscious and Known Activity within the Not-Yet-Conscious, the Utopian Function«, *The Utopian Function of Art and Literature*, 136.

19   Patrick Goode, »Cooperative Association«, in *A Dictionary of Marxist Thought*, ed. Tom Bottomore, Laurence Harris, V. G. Kiernan and Ralph Miliband (Malden, Oxford, Carlton: Blackwell Publishing, 1983), 111–112.

20   »Samoupravljanje u radnim organizacijama«, *Pravni leksikon* (Belgrade: Savremena administracija, 1964), 814, 815.

21   Edvard Kardelj, *Samoupravljanje u Jugoslaviji 1950–1976* (Belgrade: Privredni Pregled, 1977), 9–10.

22   Branko Horvat, *The Political Economy of Socialism* (New York: M. E. Sharpe, Inc., Armonk, 1982), Yugoslavian edition *Politička ekonomija socijalizma* (Zagreb: Globus, 1983), 200–208.

23   Michael A. Lebowitz, »Seven Difficult Questions«, in *Build It Now: Socialism for the Twenty-First Century* (New York: NYU Press, 2006), 73–84; Gal Kirn, »Contradiction of Yugoslav Self-Management: Class Struggle after the 1965 Market Reform«, translated part of the book *Partizanski prelomi in protislovja tržnega socializma v Jugoslaviji* (Ljubljana: Zalozba Sophia, 2014); See also: Rudi Supek, »Some Contradictions and Insufficiencies of Yu-

goslav Self-Managing Socialism«, *Praxis* no. 3/4: »Un moment du socialisme Yougoslave« (1971): 375–399.

24   Bloch's first lecture at the Summer School of Philosophy was in 1968 when the topic was Marx and Revolution. On this occasion, Bloch gave an opening speech on self-governance, with a lecture titled »Marx als Denker der Revolution«, and led discussion with Herbert Marcuse. He also gave an extensive interview with Michael Landmann, later published in the international philosophy journal *Telos* (September, 1975) with the title »Talking with Ernst Bloch: Korčula 1968«, 165–185. His second appearance at Korčula was in 1970, when the course was titled »Hegel und die Gegenwart. Leninismus—die Neue Linke«. Bloch gave an introductory lecture titled »Historical Mediation and the *Novum* in Hegel's philosophy«, later published in *Praxis* 1/2, 1971. The third visit was in 1973 under the school title »Le Monde Bourgeois et le Socialisme«, after which the article was published in *Praxis* 1/2, 1974 (Yugoslavian *Praxis* edition no. 5–6: »Gradjanski svijet i socijalizam«, 1973). The opening address was by Ernst Bloch, »Die bürgerliche Welt und der Sozialismus«. Bloch's speech was mainly an extensive critique of Soviet politics as unrecognizable since its progressive period in the 1920s. Here, Bloch traced the damage that this interpretation of socialism had transmitted to the rest of the world, most particularly international leftist movements that he saw as the main emancipatory force.

25   Ernst Bloch, »Eröffnung der Korčula Sommerschule«, *Praxis* no. 1/2: »Marx and Revolution« (1969): 6; Ernst Bloch, »Marx als Denker der Revolution«, *Praxis* no. 1/2: »Marx and Revolution« (1969): 17. See also: Gajo Petrović, »Ein Gewisser Ernst Bloch«, TÜTE special edition *Zum hundertsten Geburtstag von Ernst Bloch* (June, July 1985): 8.

26   Ernst Bloch, »Marx als Denker der Revolution«, 18.

27   Miloš Jarić, »Specijalizacija, kooperacija i udruživanje u gradjevinarstvu«, in *Almanah 1961*, ed. Milutin Maksimović, Radmio Živković, Pravoslav Trajković (Belgrade: Savez gradjevinskih inžinjera i tehničara Jugoslavije), 98. See also: *Almanah 1961*, 21, 68.

28   Mirko Roš Archive, ETH Zurich, Erinnerungsalbum, Hs 359:2; See also: Branislav Vojinović, »Mirko Roš (1879–1962)«, *Lives and Work of the Serbian Scientists*, Book 14 (Belgrade: Serbian Academy of Sciences and Arts, 2014), 41, 48, 53, 85; Branko Žeželj, »Role of the Institute in the Development of Science and Industry«, in *20 godina rada 1948–1968*, ed. Milutin Maksimović (Belgrade: Institut za ispitivanje materijala SR Srbije, 1968), 11, 23.

29   Mirko Roš, Letter to the presidency of the Government of Serbia, »Pismo predsedništvu Vlade NR Srbije od upravnika instituta Mirka Roša na

potraživaju opereme«, 3 July 1952, IMS Archive; Mirko Roš, Report of work on founding the IM-SAN institute to the Serbian Academy of Sciences, »Izveštaj o radu na osnivanju instituta IM-SAN Srpskoj akademiji nauka«, 11–20 January 1952, 6, 7. IMS Archive.

30   Decree on transaction of property from the Directorate for the Construction of Machines to the Serbian Academy of Sciences, »Rešenje o prenosu imovine generalne direkcije na Srpsku akademiju nauka, Sreski sud za grad Beograd«, 7 August 1951, IMS Archive; Mirko Roš, Report of work on founding the IM-SAN Institute to the Serbian Academy of Sciences »Izveštaj o radu na osnivanju instituta IM-SAN Srpskoj akademiji nauka«, July 1952, 5, IMS Archive.

31   Branko Žeželj in the role of deputy to principal Mirko Roš wrote to the Executive Council FRS for authorization to use the whole building, »Pismo Branka Žeželja u svojstvu zamenika upravnika Izvršnom veću NRS povodom prava na korišćenje čitave zgrade«, 10 March 1953, IMS Archive. See also: Decision on registration of Institute for Materials Testing FR Serbia, People's Council Topčidersko brdo, »Rešenje o registraciji ustanove sa samostalnim finansiranjem Instituta za ispitivanje materijala NRS u Beogradu«, no. 499, 6 September 1955; Chapter from Official Gazette FR Serbia »Izvod iz Službenog glasnika NRS no. 89«, 15 October 1955, p. 900, both IMS Archive.

32   Svetozar Pejanović, »Development of the Institute«, *20 godina rada 1948–1968*, 38; Žeželj, Introduction, *20 godina rada 1948–1968*, 4.

33   Rulebook on the Procedure of the Council of the Institute for Materials Testing, *Poslovnik o radu Saveta Instituta za ispitivanje materijala SR Srbija* (Belgrade: Institute for Materials Testing, 1965), IMS Archive.

34   Minutes from the meeting of the Board and Heads of Departments of the Institute for Materials Testing, 10 August 1961, *Zapisnici sa uprave 1959–1961* (Belgrade: Institute for Materials Testing), 1–6, IMS Archive.

35   Minutes from the meeting of the Board and Heads of Departments of the Institute for Materials Testing, 26 June 1961, *Zapisnici sa uprave 1959–1961*, 1–3 (51, 53, 54, 55).

36   Scientific Council. Minutes from meetings (*Naučno veće. Zapisnici sa sednica*) book 2, 1967–1968 (Belgrade: Institute for Materials Testing), IMS Archive.

37   Cornelius Castoriadis, *L'institution imaginare de la société* (Paris: Editions du Seuil, 1975), English translation: Cornelius Castoriadis, *The Imaginary Institution of Society* (Cambridge, Malden: Polity Press, 1987), 260, 261.

38   United Nations, *European Housing Situation* (Geneva: January 1956), 5, 42.
    See also: Miloš Jarić, »Organizacioni i tržišni uslovi za industrijalizaciju stambene izgradnje«, in *Savetovanje o industrijalizaciji stambene*

izgradnje, ed. Milan Mole (Belgrade: Savezna gradjevinska komora, 1960), IV–1. Housing construction reached a peak in the following five-year plan (1961–1965), targeting half a million flats and making the sixties the decade of highest housing production.

39 Jarić, *Savetovanje o industrijalizaciji stambene izgradnje*, IV–3. See also: Opšti izveštaj sa zaključcima, *Savetovanje o industrijalizaciji stambene izgradnje*, 1–8; Leon Skaberne, »Stambena izgradnja«, *Almanah 1961*, 120, 125.

 For housing laws, see: Branislav Krtić, Dušan Pajović, *Zakonodavstvo urbanizma, baštine, čovjekove sredine, prostornog uredjenja* (Belgrade: Naučna knjiga, 1987), 26–27.

40 Branislav Krtić, Dušan Pajović, *Zakonodavstvo urbanizma, baštine, čovjekove sredine, prostornog uredjenja*, 286.

41 Dušica Seferagić, *Kvaliteta života i nova stambena naselja*, Zagreb: Sociološko društvo Hrvatske, 1988), 84.

42 Castoriadis, *The Imaginary Institution of Society*, 262–264.

43 *Belgrade Institute for Materials Testing*, Activities section (Belgrade: Radnička štampa,1968), n.p.

44 Branko Žeželj, »Uslovi i izgledi za punomontažno gradjenje stanova u Jugoslaviji«, in *Savetovanje o industrijalizaciji stambene izgradnje*, ed. Milan Mole (Belgrade: Savezna gradjevinska komora, 1960), i, ii.

 The building of experimental housing was offered to the IMS by the Directorate for the Construction of New Belgrade, the investor and developer on behalf of the Executive People's Council of Belgrade. See Branko Petričić, »Izgradjeni stambeni blokovi 1 i 2 u Novom Beogradu. Eksperimentalni rejon«, *Urbanizam Beograda* no. 2 (1969): 14–19. http://urbel.com/uploads/Urbanizam_Beograda/UB2.pdf (last accessed: 12 April 2021).

45 Branko Petričić, »Prve urbanističke realizacije. Novi Beograd 1955–1975«, *Godišnjak grada Beograda XXII* (Belgrade: Belgrade City Museum, 1975), 223. http://www.mgb.org.rs/images/godisnjaci/GodisnjakXXII/219-234GodisnjakXXII.pdf (last accessed: 18 April 2021).

 See also: Branko Petričić, »Izgradjeni stambeni blokovi 1 i 2 u Novom Beogradu. Eksperimentalni rejon«, 14–19.

46 Mihailo Čanak, »Architectonic Activities«, *20 godina rada 1948–1968*, 295.

 For the collaboration of Petričić and Le Corbusier, see: Ljiljana Blagojević, *Novi Beograd: Osporeni modernizam* (Belgrade: Zavod za užbenike, 2007), 148.

47 Branko Turin, *Novi Beograd*, Belgrade City Museum, 24 × 18 cm, Urban Planning and Architecture Collection (Ur_12170, Ur_12180), 1962.

48 Hans Joas, »Institutionalization as a Creative Process: The Sociological Importance of Cornelius Castoriadis's Political Philosophy«, *Pragmatism*

and Social Theory (Chicago, London: The University of Chicago Press, 1993), 157, 158.

49 Castoriadis, *The Imaginary Institution of Society*, 87. Also: Joas, »Institutionalization as a Creative Process: The Sociological Importance of Cornelius Castoriadis's Political Philosophy«, 158.

50 Cornelius Castoriadis, »Marxisme et théorie révolutionnaire«, originally published in the last five issues of *Socialisme ou Barbarie* no. 36–40 (April 1964–June 1965) and reprinted in *The Imaginary Institution of Society*, 71–77.

51 Žeželj, »Uslovi i izgledi za punomontažno gradjenje stanova u Jugoslaviji«, 3.

52 Department II: Concrete, »Study on the testing of prefabricated floor slabs«, (Belgrade: Institute for Materials Testing FRS, 1960), 5–6. IMS Archive.

53 Boško Petrović, »Evolution of Prestressed Concrete Structures«, in *20 godina rada 1948–1968*, ed. Milutin Maksimović, (Belgrade: Institute for Materials Testing FR Serbia, 1968), 222.

54 These included a prize at 13 Salon International des Inventeurs Bruxelles, 1964; FIP (Fédération Internationale de la Précontrainte) Medal in Prague, 1970, for the development of prestressed concrete; Honorable membership of the American Concrete Institute, 1975, and Honorable membership of the AIPC Zurich (Association international des Ponts et Charpentes), 1979. See: Biography of Branko Žeželj, documents, IMS Archive. Also: *Institute for Materials Testing*. DVD. Directed by Aleksandar Ilić. Belgrade: Institute for Materials Testing FR Serbia.

55 For example, in 1968 the IMS had 450 employees, a hundred of whom were scientists, and 350 unskilled, skilled and qualified staff such as lab technicians. See: Pejanović, »Development of the Institute«, 36, 37.

56 Boško Petrović, »Evolution of Prestressed Concrete Structures«, in *20 godina rada 1948–1968*, ed. Milutin Maksimović, (Belgrade: Institute for Materials Testing FR Serbia, 1968), 222, 207.

57 Petričić, »Prve urbanističke realizacije. Novi Beograd 1955–1975«, 227. The year of the start of construction is often given as 1959. However, according to IMS sources, the first buildings were erected in 1957–1958.

58 Mihailo Čanak, »Funkcionalni aspekti stambenih zgrada u sistemu IMS«, *Izgradnja* no. 4 (April 1970): 68.

59 Mihailo Čanak, »Architectonic Activities«, *20 godina rada 1948–1968*, 295.

60 Cornelius Castoriadis, »Praxis and Project«, *The Imaginary Institution of Society* (Cambridge, Malden: Polity Press, 1987), 77, 78.

61 Ernst Bloch, »Geschichtliche Vermittlung und das Novum bei Hegel«, *Praxis* no. 1/2: »Hegel und die Gegenwart. Leninismus—die Neue Linke« (1971): 13–27. Also printed in the Yugoslavian issue of *Praxis* no. 5/6 (1970): 710, 711.

62 The series of documentary films about the construction of New Belgrade consists of *Kad ratni*

doboši umuknu, Biće to novi grad, Prepreke su mno-gobrojne and *Život na pesku*, directed by Miloš Bukumirović (Belgrade: Slavija film I, 1959–1962), Yugoslav Film Archives.

63 Mirjana Obradović, interview with Andjelka Bad-njar Gojnić, 11 December 2020, Belgrade.

64 Žeželj, »Uslovi i izgledi za punomontažno grad-jenje stanova u Jugoslaviji«, 10.

65 Pejanović, »Development of the Institute«, 36, 37. For the creation of the Centre for Housing, see: Mihailo Čanak, »Architectonic Activities«, *20 godina rada 1948–1968*, 305. See also: Mihailo Čanak, »Funkcionalni aspekti stambenih zgrada u sistemu IMS«, 9.

66 Branimir Grujić, interview with Andjelka Badnjar Gojnić, 28 April–5 May 2019, Belgrade.

67 Ivan Petrović, »Mogućnosti primene IMS sistema u individualnoj stambenoj izgradnji na područji-ma sa tropskom i sub-tropskom klimom«, *Bilten IMS* no. 1–2 (December 1980): 7–14.

68 Ibid. 3.

69 Ernst Bloch, »Causality and Finality as Active, Objectifying Categories (Categories of Trans-mission)«, *Telos* no. 21 (Fall 1974): 96–107. The article in *Telos* journal was part of Bloch's later published book *Experimentum Mundi. Frage, Kat-egorien des Herausbringens, Praxis* (Frankfurt am Main: Suhrkamp Verlag, 1975).

70 Hans Joas, »Institutionalization as a Creative Pro-cess: The Sociological Importance of Cornelius Castoriadis's Political Philosophy«, *Pragmatism and Social Theory* (Chicago, London: The Univer-sity of Chicago Press, 1993), 162.

71 An Introductory Interview: »The Only Way to Find Out If You Can Swim Is to Get into the Water«, in *The Castoriadis Reader*, ed. David Ames Curtis (Oxford UK, Malden USA: Blackwell Publishers, 1997), 30.

72 Cornelius Castoriadis in dialogue with Robert Legros, *Postscript on Insignificance. Dialogues with Cornelius Castoriadis*, ed. Gabriel Rockhill (London, New York: Continuum, 2011), 105.

73 Ibid., 100, 47.

74 Castoriadis, *The Imaginary Institution of Society*, 121.

75 Ksenija Petovar, interview with Andjelka Badnjar Gojnić, 19 May 2017, Belgrade.

76 Branimir Grujić, interview with Andjelka Badnjar Gojnić, 28 April–5 May 2019, Belgrade.

77 Jelena Vesić, Rachel O'Reilly, Vladimir Jerić Vlidi, *On Neutrality*, Volume 6 in the series *Non-aligned Modernisms* (Belgrade: Museum of Contempo-rary Art, 2016), 40.

78 Milan Pajević, interview with Andjelka Badnjar Gojnić, 6 November 2018, Belgrade, followed by a talk in summer 2018 in Sveti Stefan.

79 Ibid.

80 For reactions to the dissolution of *Praxis* see: Noam Chomsky, »The Repression at Belgrade University«, *The New York Review of Books*, 7 Feb-ruary 1974. Url: http://www.chomsky.info/arti-cles/19740207.htm (last accessed: 18 December 2021).

81 Centre for Housing, *Model vrednovanja stanova i stambenih zgrada CS'80—1. Kvalitet stana*, Branka Gavrilović, Ivan Petrović, Ksenija Petovar, Mihai-lo Čanak, Miladin Životić (Belgrade: Institute for Materials Testing, 1979); Also: Centre for Hous-ing, *Model vrednovanja stanova i stambenih zgra-da CS'80—2. Kvalitet stambene zgrade* (Belgrade: Institute for Materials Testing, 1980).

82 Mihailo Čanak, scientific work »Ljudske potrebe i stambene funkcije«, 1973, IMS Centre for Hous-ing. Abstract published in *Informativni bilten. Centar za stanovanje* no. 15 (Belgrade, 1974), 10.

83 Sylvia Lavin, ed., *Architecture Itself and Other Postmodernization Effects* (Montreal: Canadian Centre for Architecture, 2020), 100.

84 Interview with Dominique Cheng, »The Power of Diagram«, 9 March 2020. https://www.koozarch. com/interviews/the-power-of-the-diagram/ (last accessed: 3 June 2021).

85 Mihailo Čanak, »Dinamika stambenih funkcija i njen uticaj na formiranje stambenog prostora«, *Bilten. Centar za stanovanje* no. 29/30 (Belgrade, 1981): 26.

86 Mihailo Čanak, »Centre for Housing IMS«, *ARD Review* 38 (Belgrade, 2011): 19, 39–40.

87 Raphaël Gély, »Imaginaire, affectivité et rational-ité. Pour une relecture du débat entre Habermas et Castoriadis«, *Cahiers Castoriadis* no. 4 (2008): 139–182. Quoted in: Dosse, *Castoriadis une vie*, 543.

88 Aleksandar V. Kušić, »Change of Urban and Ar-chitectural Paradigm Exemplified by Belgrade Housing Estates: The Period of Yugoslav Late Socialism (1965–1991)«, (PhD diss., University of Belgrade, 2014).

89 *Enkciklopedija samoupravljanja* (Belgrade: Savre-mena administracija, 1979).

90 Bloch, »The Conscious and Known Activity within the Not-Yet-Conscious, the Utopian Function«, 118.

91 Castoriadis, *The Imaginary Institution of Society*, 121, 178, 179, 370.

PRAXIS AND *LEBENSWELT*: THE CONSTRUCTION SITE AS LIFEWORLD

1 For the foundation of the *Praxis* circle of phi-losophy in Yugoslavia surrounding the *Praxis* journal and the summer school in Korčula, see Introduction.

2 Dubravka Sekulić, *Constructing Non-Alignment: The Case of Energoprojekt*, Volume 3 of *Non-Aligned Modernisms* (Belgrade, Museum of Contempo-rary Art, 2014–2017), 11.

3 Alvin Rubinstein, *Yugoslavia and Nonaligned World* (Princeton: Princeton University Press, 1970), 20. Also Chapter 5, »Yugoslavia and Inter-national Economic Cooperation«. Referred to in Sekulić, *Constructing Non-Alignment: The Case of Energoprojekt*, 10–11.

4 Ana Videkanović, *Nonaligned Modernism: Socialist Postcolonial Aesthetics in Yugoslavia, 1945–1985* (Montreal: McGill-Queen's University Press, 2020), 1.

5 Vijay Prashad, *The Darker Nations* (New York, London: The New Press, 2007), Introduction.

6 Ana Panić, Jovo Bakić, Srđan Cvetković, Ivana Dobrivojević, Hrvoje Klasić, Vladimir Petrović, *Yugoslavia 1918–1991* (Belgrade: Museum of Yugoslavia, 2014), 30, 33. Published following the exhibition *Jugoslavija: od početka do kraja* at the Museum of Yugoslavia, Belgrade, 1 December 2012–17 March 2013.

See also: Bojana Piškur, »Southern Constellations: Other Histories, Other Modernities«, in the exhibition catalogue *Southern Constellations. The Poetics of Non-Aligned*, curated by Bojana Piškur (Ljubljana: Moderna galerija, 2019), 9–25.

7 Vladimir Kulić, *Building Babylon,* Volume 2 of *Non-aligned Modernisms* (Belgrade: Museum of Contemporary Art, 2014–2017), 25–27; Vladimir Kulić, Maroje Mrduljaš, Wolfgang Thaler ed., *Modernism In-Between. The Mediatory Architectures of Socialist Yugoslavia* (Berlin: jovis, 2012), 49; Piškur, »Southern Constellations: Other Histories, Other Modernities«.

8 Eric Hobsbawm, *The Age of Extremes 1914–1991* (London: Abacus, 1995), 436.

9 Ibid., 437.

10 Ibid., 435.

11 Ibid., 439.

12 Ibid., 439.

13 For the development of debate between the *Siedlungsbau* and *Städtebau* concepts, see the recent study by Silvia Malcovati, »Das alte Frankfurt: Urban Neighborhood versus Housing Estate, the Rebirth of Urban Architecture«, *Urban Planning* vol. 4, no. 3, eds. Luca Ortelli, Chiara Monterumisi and Alessandro Porotto (2019): 117–133. URL: https://www.cogitatiopress.com/urbanplanning/issue/viewIssue/134/PDF134 (last accessed: 23 July 2022).

14 Ernst Bloch, »Building in Empty Spaces«, *The Utopian Function of Art and Literature*, translated by Jack Zipes, Frank Mecklenburg (Cambridge, Massachusetts, London, England: The MIT Press, 1988), 190. The essay was originally published as »Die Bebauung des Hohlraums«, in *Das Prinzip Hoffnung* (Frankfurt am Main: Suhrkamp, 1959).

15 Eric Mumford, *The CIAM Discourse on Urbanism 1928–1960* (Cambridge MA: MIT Press, 2000); *Team 10: In Search of a Utopia of the Present,* eds. Max Risselada, Dirk van den Heuvel (Rotterdam: NAi Publishers, 2006).

16 Jürgen Habermas, »Tehnički napredak i svijet društvenog života«, *Praxis* no. 6: »Što je povijest?« (1965): 846–865.

17 Jürgen Habermas, »Bedingungen für eine Revolutionierung spätkapitalisticher Gessellschaftsysteme«, *Praxis* no. 1/2: »Marx and Revolution« (1969): 212.

18 Jürgen Habermas, *Theorie und Praxis* (Paris: Hermann, 1963), English translation: *Theory and Practice* (Boston: Beacon Press, 1973), 253, 254.

19 Ibid., 255.

20 Ibid., 1, 3.

21 Ibid., 256.

22 Habermas, »Bedingungen für eine Revolutionierung spätkapitalisticher Gessellschaftsysteme«, 212. Habermas's speech, that began as an echo of the critique of Marxism, turned into one of the milestones of his theory, that is the critique of the organization of knowledge in advanced industrial systems. He further formulated this argument in *Erkenntnis und Interesse* (Berlin: Suhrkamp Verlag, 1968), English translation: *Knowledge and Human Interests* (Boston: Beacon Press, 1972).

23 Jürgen Habermas, »Modern and Postmodern Architecture«, in *Architecture Theory since 1968*, ed. K. Michael Hays (Cambridge Massachusetts, London England: The MIT Press, 2000), 422.

24 *Alamar, The New Town Travel Guide* (Rotterdam: International New Town Institute in collaboration with TU Delft, 2017), 5.

25 Branimir Grujić, »The Further Development of the IMS System in Cuba«, *Bilten IMS*, no. 4 (Belgrade 1974): 41 (»Dalji razvoj sistema IMS na Kubi«).

26 Marta Jimenez Almira, »La Vivienda en Cuba«, *Granma*, September 29, 1971, page unknown.

27 Marta Jimenez Almira, »La Vivienda en Cuba.« The full name of DESA was Ministerio de Desarrollo de Edificaciones Sociales y Agropecuarias.

28 Maggie Marin, »Edificios Altos«, *Bohemia económica* no. unavailable (Havana, 1974): 16, 18.

29 The full name of the system was IMS-PCFAC Prestressed Concrete Framework Assembly Construction.

30 Alberto Arrinda Pinero. Letter from the Cuban Vice-Minister of Housing of the Cuban Ministry of Construction, Alberto Arrinda Pinero, to the Cuban Ambassador to Yugoslavia, José Luis Pérez, 9 June 1966, Habana, Cuba. IMS Archive.

31 Svetozar Pejanović, IMS Principle. *Report on negotiations on the application of the IMS system in Cuba* to *The Federal Institute for International Technical Cooperation*, 28 September 1966. IMS Archive.

32 Branimir Grujić, »The Application of the IMS System in Cuba«, *Izgradnja*, no. 4 (Belgrade 1970): 179. The selected systems were: E-14, Gran Panel IV, Gran Panel Soviético, Molde Deslizante, Gran Panel 70 and IMS Žeželj.

33 On microhistory as a research scope see: Giovanni Levi, »On Microhistory«, in *New Perspectives in Historical Writing*, ed. Peter Burke (Cambridge: Polity Press): 1992.

34 See Chapter 2.

35 Branimir Grujić, »Dalji razvoj sistema IMS na Kubi«, *Bilten IMS*, no. 4 (Belgrade 1974): 41. For

https://www.marxists.org/subject/praxis/praxis-international/Praxis%2C%20international%20edition%2C%201969%2C%20no.%201-2.pdf (last accessed: 7 January 2021).

development of concept of microbrigades see: Kosta Mathéy, »Microbrigadas in Cuba: A Collective Form of Self-Help Housing«, *The Netherlands Journal of Housing and Environmental Research* vol. 4, no. 1. Special issue »Housing in the Third World: Self-Help and Governmental Programs« (1989): 67–83.

36   Florian Zeyfang, Lisa Schmidt-Colinet, Alexander Schmoeger, *Microbrigades-Variations of a Story* (2013) HD 31 min.

37   At the beginning of 1969, 11,000 flats had already been built, while during 1971, 1141 microbrigades with 26,562 participants were building 25,748 of flats in different parts of the country (Almira, »La Vivienda en Cuba«). DESA foresaw the production of some 20 thousand homes a year, starting in 1973 in a five-year cycle that aimed to raise standards of living (Maggie Marin, »Edificios Altos«, 16, 18).

38   Addressing the question of the role of philosophy in *Praxis*, he described the operative capacity of philosophy in society as insufficient, as it needed to be bound up with progress in physics and social theory. As for philosophy itself, he wrote: »I see [its] role in bringing strong theoretical strategies to stand against empirical elementarism and inductionism.« Jürgen Habermas, »Uloga filozofije u marksizmu«, *Praxis* no. 5/6: »Gradjanski svijet i socijalizam« (1973): 606 (Translation: »Role of Philosophy in Marxism«, *Le Monde Bourgeois et le Socialisme*).

39   Jürgen Habermas, *Theory and Practice*, 263.

40   Ibid., 264.

41   See: Adrian Forty, »Dead or Alive-Describing the Social«, *Words and Buildings. A Vocabulary of Modern Architecture* (London: Thames & Hudson Ltd, 2000), 107.

42   Habermas, »Modern and Postmodern Architecture«, 425.

43   Ibid., 413.

44   Hays, *Architecture Theory Since 1968*, 413.

45   Habermas, *Theory and Practice*, 264.

46   Jürgen Habermas, *Der philosophische Diskurs der Moderne: Zwölf Vorlesungen* (Frankfurt am Main: Suhrkamp Verlag, 1985), English translation: *The Philosophical Discourse of Modernity. Twelve Lectures* (Cambridge Massachusetts, The MIT Press, 1990) 316, 317. Here, Habermas named the theory of communicative action as »just another version of praxis philosophy« from the origins of Marx's social praxis and Western Marxism.

47   Jürgen Habermas, *Theorie des kommunikativen Handelns, Band 2: Zur Kritik der funktionalistischen Vernunft* (Frankfurt am Main: Suhrkamp Verlag, 1981), English translation: *The Theory of Communicative Action 2. The Critique of Functionalist Reason* (Cambridge: Polity Press, 1987), 126.

48   Habermas, *Twelve Lectures*, 298.

49   Habermas, *The Theory of Communicative Action* 2, 126, 127.

50   Ibid., 138.

51   Ibid., 139, 136.

52   Habermas, *The Theory of Communicative Action* 2, 137; Habermas, *Twelve Lectures*, 299.

53   Letter from IMS Engineer Miloš Banić to secretary of the Institute, Belgrade, 28 December 1966; Letter from the Embajada de Cuba to Branko Žeželj, 30 March 1967. Both IMS Archive.

54   Svetozar Pejanović, IMS Principal. *Svetozar Pejanović to the Secretariat for Foreign Affair*, Belgrade, 5 October 1967. IMS Archive. The members of the group were: Amor Serjo, technologist Adolfo Gonzales, engineer Leonardo Ruiz and architect Basilo Piesecki.

55   *Work Program for Training*, IMS Archive. Practice included work on prestressing, production of concrete, work on construction site (3), assembly of elements (4) and the final testing process (5) of material samples. The participants were Carlos Garcia Campos (student), Pedro Silveira (student), Domingo Amechazurra, Luis Chade, Melquiades Sanches and José A. Cordero. Period of specialization: 20 October 1967–17 January 1968, from Branimir Grujić, Letter to the Institute for Technical Assistance (Zavod za tehničku pomoć) on the list of Cuban participants in training at the IMS Belgrade, 5 January 1968. IMS Archive.

56   Such as two-day course in the brick department, ten-day course in the metal department, 40-day course in the concrete department, 60-day course on the housing construction site in New Belgrade. Svetozar Pejanović, IMS Principal. Svetozar Pejanović to the Cuban Ministry of Construction, Belgrade, 9 January 1968. IMS Archive.

57   Miloš Banić. Letter from Miloš Banić, Employee of the IMS, to the Housing Institute upon his arrival from his stay in Cuba, December 1967 or January 1968. IMS Archive.

58   Ministry of Construction of the Republic of Cuba. Letter from the Ministry of Construction to the Principal of the IMS, Svetozar Pejanović, 7 November 1967. IMS Archive.

59   Contract between The Institute for Materials Testing FRS Belgrade and Institute for Housing of the Cuban Ministry of Construction, 15 November 1967, Havana. IMS Archive.

60   IMS Department V: Metals. *Report on the testing of steel samples from Cuba*, 22 September 1967. Scientific study. IMS Archive.

61   Branimir Grujić. Letter from Branimir Grujić from the IMS to the Cuban Embassy Belgrade, 25 February 1968. IMS Archive.

62   Grujić, »The Further Development of the IMS system in Cuba«, 41.

63   Letter from the IMS engineer to Branimir Grujić at the IMS on the state of works on the Experimental Building in Havana, 21 December 1969. IMS Archive. The letter is signed only with the name »Mika«.

64   Interview with Grujić, spring 2019.

65   V. Krstanović, »Flats for Cubans according to the Belgrade recipe«, *Borba*, 9 December 1968, 4

(Translated from: »Stanovi za Kubance po beogradskom receptu«).

66 Nelson N. Campos, José C. Temes, »Application and Development of the IMS-Žeželj System in Cuba«, *Bilten IMS* no. 1 (Belgrade: February 1975): 3–7.

67 José A. Cordero, José A. Cordero to engineer Stipanović at the IMS on the state of works on the Experimental Building in Havana, 9 January 1968. IMS Archive.

68 Nelson N. Campos, José C. Temes, »Application and Development of the IMS-Žeželj System in Cuba«.

69 Branimir Grujić, »Dalji razvoj sistema IMS na Kubi«, *Bilten IMS*, no. 4 (Belgrade 1974), 41. For a recent study of the characteristics of modern block in the context of CIAM 4, Functionalist City, see: Gregor Harbusch, Muriel Pérez, Kees Somer, Daniel Weiss, Evelin van ES, *Atlas of the Functional City: CIAM 4 and Comparative Urban Analysis* (Zurich: gta Verlag, 2014); Also: Le Corbusier, *Charte d'Athènes* (Paris: Plon, 1943).

70 *Microdistrito Plaza de la Revolucion* (Havana: November, 1975): 1.

71 Reinaldo Escobar, *La Grieta* (Madrid: Editorial Verbum, 2018), 115.

72 Ibid. 116.

73 From the correspondence of Reinaldo Escobar with Andjelka Badnjar Gojnić, November 2021.

74 Reinaldo Escobar, *La Grieta* (Madrid: Editorial Verbum, 2018), 116–120. The excerpt from the novel has been loaned by courtesy of Reinaldo Escobar.

75 Alber Sierra Madero interview with Reinaldo Escobar, »Mi norma personal es ajustarme a la verdad«, *Hypermedia Magazine*, 2 October 2020. URL: https://www.hypermediamagazine.com/columnistas/fiebre-de-archivo/reinaldo-escobar-mi-norma-personal-es-ajustarme-a-la-verdad/ (last accessed: 20 November 2021); »El periodista Reinaldo Escobar gana el premio Verbum de Novela 2018«, 14ymedio, 27 August 2018. URL: https://www.14ymedio.com/cultura/periodista-Reinaldo-Escobar-Verbum-novela_0_2499350044.html (last accessed: 20 November 2021).

76 Habermas, *The Theory of Communicative Action* 2, 121, 123.

77 Reinaldo Escobar, »The Odyssey«, 5 November 2020, Havana, https://www.14ymedio.com/blogs/desde_aqui/Odisea_7_2873182654.html (last accessed: 29 November 2021).

78 https://isoj.org/yoani-sanchez-will-explain-how-and-why-she-created-14ymedio-cubas-first-independent-news-platform-2/ (last accessed: 29 November 2021).

79 Nelson Navarro Campos, »The Implementation and Development of IMS Building Technology in Cuba«, in *Research, Projects and Realizations in Construction*, edited by Zoran Popović, Goran Petrović (Belgrade: Institute for Materials Testing, 2010), 217. Also, Nelson N. Campos, José C. Temes, »The Application and Development of the IMS-Žeželj System in Cuba«, *Bilten IMS*, 1 (Belgrade: February 1975): 3–7. Grujić interview.
       Grujić, »The Further Development of the IMS system in Cuba«, 41.

80 Habermas, *The Theory of Communicative Action* 2, 119, 120.

81 Armando Galguera, Armando Galguera as principal of the Institute of Housing, Cuban Ministry of Construction, to Svetozar Pejanović, Principal of the IMS, 20 June 1968. IMS Archive.

82 »El Sistema ofrece a los arquitectos un sinúmero de posibilidades, tanto en el proyecto de una vivienda o edificio, como para la solución urbanística de los desarrollos de vivienda.« Call for lecture. *Conferencias. Branimir Grujić*, 10 September 1968, Havana. Archive of the IMS.

83 Armando Galguera, Armando Galguera as principal of the Institute of Housing, Cuban Ministry of Construction, to Branko Žeželj, IMS, 15 October 1968. Archive of the IMS. Original: »Igualmente, en las actividades de montaje y presfuerzo, ambos mostraron una preocupación constante en la buena marcha y correccion del trabajo y el mejor aprovechamiento por nuestros técnicos de todos los niveles de las experiencias que sistemáticamente nos trasmitían. Por todo lo cual le repetimos, hemos quedado plenamente satisfechos de la labor por ellos realizada.«

84 Cuban Embassy, Pro-Memoria signed on 17 May 1971 between Arch. Osmundo Machado Ventura on behalf of the Nacional Housing Group, DESA and Svetozar Pejanović, representing the IMS, IMS Archive;
       Letter from the IMS to the Yugoslavian Bank for International Commerce (*spoljnu trgovinu*), Export of IMS Plants to Cuba, 13 May 1971. IMS Archive; *General contract between the National Housing Group of the Cuban Construction Sector and the Institute for Testing Materials*, Havana, 1970, IMS Archive.

85 Program of the Cuban delegation visiting the Institute for Materials Testing, September–December 1971, IMS Archive. The program included regular visits to the New Belgrade construction site.

86 »Visita nuestro país el profesor Branko Zezelj, inventor del sistema constructivo IMS«, Granma, Havana, 3 April 1976, 6.

87 Roy Darke, »Housing and Spatial Policies in the Socialist Third-World«, *Netherlands Journal of Housing and Environmental Research*, Vol. 4, no. 1 (1989): 55.

88 »Edifican en Cienfuegos una fábrica con capacidad para 1500 viviendas al año«, *JR Juventuo Rebelde*, 19 December 1976, front page of newspaper (1).

89 »Terminarán próximamente primera etapa de la planta de viviendas del Sistema IMS, en Camagüey«, La Habana, 13 January 1977, page not available.

90 See: *Alamar, The New Town Travel Guide*, 10, 15, 21, 49.

91 Marta Jimenez Almira, »La Vivienda en Cuba«, *Granma*, 1976, page and date not available.

92 Tomás Ernesto Pérez, »Microbrigadas«, 4 January 2016, URL: https://periodismodebarrio.org/2016/01/microbrigadas/ (last accessed: 4 May 2021).

93 Dania Gónzalez Couret, *Economía y calidad en la vivienda. Un enfoque cubano* (Havana: Editorial Científico -Técnica, 1997); See also: Dania González Couret, »Half a Century of Social Housing in Cuba«, *Revista INVI* no. 67 (November, 2009): 69–92. http://dx.doi.org/10.4067/S0718-83582009000300003.

94 Hugo Wainshtek, Hugo Wainshtek, Dean of the Faculty of Technology, University of Havana, to the Director of the Institute for Materials Testing, 14 January 1970. IMS Archive.

95 Protocol on talks in Havana (1–13 April 1976) between the IMS and DESA, 3, IMS Archive.

96 Anna Kats, »In Socialist Yugoslavia Mass Housing Wasn't Just Ugly Tower Blocks«, 8 November 2021, URL: https://www.jacobinmag.com/2021/08/yugoslavia-architecture-socialism-angola-soviet-housing (last accessed: 10 May 2021).

97 Interview with Grujić, spring 2019.

98 Interview with Grujić, spring 2019.

99 Adrian Forty, »Dead or Alive—Describing the Social, *Words and Buildings: A Vocabulary of Modern Architecture* (London: Thames & Hudson, 2004), 102–117.

100 Functionalist theory as a tool is necessary to Habermas because his vision of the cultural reproduction of the lifeworld rests on continuity. Newly arising situations are connected with existing conditions. This secures the continuity of tradition and the coherence of knowledge needed for daily practice. It secures for succeeding generations generalized competences for action and »sees that individual histories are in harmony with collective forms of life«. If the action was a self-repetitive process leading into the unknown, it would not be possible either to preserve knowledge or to have continuity into emancipation. Habermas, *The Theory of Communicative Action* 2, 141.

101 See: Hans Joas, »The Unhappy Marriage of Hermeneutics and Functionalism«, *Praxis International 1* (1988): 34–51, reprinted in Hans Joas, *Pragmatism and Social Theory* (Chicago: The University of Chicago Press, 1993), 127.

On Habermas's attempt to overcome isolation of the concepts of action and social order through social interaction based on the normative agreement of actors seeking interest, Joas replies that this implies theoretical assumptions about the nature of social order rather than actors' intuitive knowledge, as Habermas terms it. For Joas, it is not the deductive definition of microsocial phenomena on the basis of macrosocial function that guides us. Conversely, the theory of action as metatheoretical cannot be constructed but, rather, only assimilate the results of systems theory in solving the problem of social order as superior to it. System rationality does not require a rationality of action that is structurally analogous to it and subsystems cannot be characterized by reference to the type of action dominant in them.

102 *Praxis International* was the journal that succeeded *Praxis* and was published between 1981 and 1994. The new journal saw its role to »examine contemporary revolutionary experiences and to develop a theory of social transformation of economy, worker's self-government, participatory democracy, the nature of socialist enlightenment and a new socialist culture«. See: Editorial board, *Praxis International*, no. 1 (April 1981): 4.

103 The Inter-University Postgraduate Centre was founded by member universities and academic institutions from all over the world. On the initiative of Gajo Petrović, who was a leading member of the *Praxis* circle in Yugoslavia, the course »Philosophy and Social Science« started. Petrović asked Habermas to co-direct the course. See: Richard Bernstein, *Habermas and Modernity* (Cambridge MA: MIT Press, 1985), 32.

104 Bernstein, *Habermas and Modernity*, 32.

105 Editorial board, »Why Praxis International?«, *Praxis International*, no. 1 (April 1981): 1–2.

106 Editorial board, *Praxis International*, no. 1 (April 1981): 4–5.

107 Interview with Grujić, spring 2019.

108 Tess McNamara, »Urban Farm-Fed Cities: Lessons from Cuba's Organopónicos«, 23 November 2018, URL: http://www.sagemagazine.org/urban-farm-fed-cities-lessons-from-cubas-organoponicos/ (last accessed: 10 May 2021).

109 *Alamar, The New Town Travel Guide*, 96.

110 Tess McNamara, ibid.

111 Tess McNamara, »Urban Farm-Fed Cities«; *Latin American Herald Tribune*, »Cuba has more than 33,000 Urban Farms«, 22 May 2012, URL: http://www.laht.com/article.asp?ArticleId=508483&CategoryId=14510 (last accessed: 10 May 2021); Christopher D. Cook, »Cuba's Harvest of Surprises«, Winter 2015, URL: https://craftsmanship.net/cubas-harvest-surprises/ (last accessed: 10 May 2021).

112 Habermas, »Modern and Postmodern Architecture«, 423.

113 Kathleen James-Chakraborty, »Beyond Postcolonialism: New Directions for the History of Non-Western Architecture«, *Frontiers of Architectural Research* no. 3 (2014): 1–9.

114 Leonardo Padura, *The Man Who Loved Dogs* (New York: Farrar, Straus and Giroux, 2014), 488. Spanish original: Leonardo Padura, *El hombre que amaba a los perros* (Barcelona: Tusquets Editores, 2009).

115 Habermas, *Twelve Lectures*, 321.

116 Ibid.

CONCLUSION: PRAXIS AND THEORY

1   Jürgen Habermas, »Uloga filozofije u mark-
     sizmu«, *Praxis* no. 5-6 (1973): 601–607.
2   Roland Barthes, »The Structuralist Activity«,
     (1963) in *Critical Essays*, trans. Richard Howard
     (Evanston: Northwestern University Press, 1972),
     214, 215. Originally published as Roland Barthes,
     Essais critiques (Paris: Editions du Seuil, 1964).
3   Farhan Karim, »Introduction: Architecture and
     Social Engagement«, in *The Routledge Companion
     to Architecture and Social Engagement*, ed. Farhan
     Karim (New York and London: Routledge, 2018),
     xxxvi.

LITERATURE REVIEW

1   See Introduction.

Bibliography

Alamar, The New Town Travel Guide. Rotterdam: International New Town Institute in collaboration with TU Delft, 2017.

Alfirević, Djordje and Sanja Simonović-Alfirević. »Salon Apartment in Serbia Between the Two World Wars. Reassessing the Rationale Behind the Term.« *Arhitektura i urbanizam* no. 44 (2017): 7–13.

Andrić, Ivo. *Na Drini ćuprija*. Belgrade: Prosveta, 1945.

Andrić, Ivo. *Travnička hronika*. Belgrade: Prosveta, 1945.

Arrinda Pinero, Alberto. The Cuban Vice-Minister of Housing of the Cuban Ministry of Construction, Alberto Arrinda Pinero, to the Cuban Ambassador to Yugoslavia, José Luis Pérez, 9 June 1966, Habana, Cuba. IMS Archive.

Banić, Miloš. Miloš Banić, Employee of the IMS, to the Housing Institute upon his arrival from the stay in Cuba, December 1967 or January 1968. IMS Archive.

Banić, Miloš. Miloš Banić, Employee of the IMS, to the Secretary of the Institute, Belgrade, 28 December 1966.

Barthes, Roland. »The Structuralist Activity.« In *Critical Essays*, trans. Richard Howard, 213–221. Evanston: Northwestern University Press, 1972. Originally published as: Barthes, Roland. *Essais critiques*. Paris: Editions du Seuil, 1964.

Baudin, Katia, Tihomir Milovac, ed. *EXAT 51: Synthesis of the Arts in Post-War Yugoslavia*. Krefeld: Kunstmuseen Krefeld, 2017.

Bernstein, Richard J., ed. *Habermas and Modernity*. Cambridge, Massachusetts: The MIT Press, 1985.

Bernstein, Richard J. *Praxis and Action*. Philadelphia: University of Pennsylvania Press, 1971.

Biography of Branko Žeželj, IMS Archive.

Blagojević, Ljiljana. *Modernism in Serbia: The Elusive Margins of Belgrade Architecture*. Cambridge and London: MIT Press, 2003.

Blagojević, Ljiljana. *Novi Beograd: Osporeni modernizam*. Belgrade: Zavod za udžbenike, 2007.

Bloch, Ernst. »Causality and Finality as Active, Objectifying Categories (Categories of Transmission).« *Telos* no. 21 (Fall 1974): 96–107. The article in *Telos* journal was part of Bloch's later published book *Experimentum Mundi. Frage, Kategorien des Herausbringens, Praxis*. Frankfurt am Main: Suhrkamp Verlag, 1975.

Bloch, Ernst. »Die Bebauung des Hohlraums.« In *Das Prinzip Hoffnung*. Frankfurt am Main: Suhrkamp, 1959. Trans. Bloch, Ernst. »Building in Empty Spaces.« In *The Utopian Function of Art and Literature*, trans. Jack Zipes and Frank Mecklenburg, 186–200. Cambridge, Massachusetts, London, England: The MIT Press, 1988.

Bloch, Ernst. »Die bewusste und die gewusste Tätigkeit im Noch-Nicht-Bewussten, utopische Funktion.« *Das Prinzip Hoffnung*. Frankfurt am Main: Suhrkamp, 1959.

Bloch, Ernst. »Die bürgerliche Welt und der Sozialismus«. *Praxis*, no. 1/2: »Bourgeois World and Socialism«, (1974): 17.

Bloch, Ernst. »Eröffnung der Korčula Sommerschule.« *Praxis*, no. 1/2: »Marx and Revolution« (1969): 6.

Bloch, Ernst. »Geschichtliche Vermittlung und das Novum bei Hegel.« *Praxis* no. 1/2: »Hegel und die Gegenwart. Leninismus—die Neue Linke« (1971): 13–27.

Bloch, Ernst. »Jugoslawien nagelt die Flagge an den Mast.« SPIEGEL interview with Ernst Bloch about the blow to the *Praxis* circle.« *Der Spiegel*, no. 6, 1975.

Bloch, Ernst. »Marx als Denker der Revolution.« *Praxis* no. 1/2: »Marx and Revolution« (1969): 17.

Bloch, Ernst. »Marxismus und Dichtung.« *Literarische Aufsätze*. Frankfurt am Main: Suhrkamp, 1935. In English: Bloch, Ernst. »Marxism and Poetry.« *The Utopian Function of Art and Literature*. Cambridge Massachusetts, London England: The MIT Press, 1988.

In English: Bloch, Ernst. »The Conscious and Known Activity within the Not-Yet-Conscious, the Utopian Function.« *The Utopian Function of Art and Literature*. Cambridge Massachusetts, London England: The MIT Press, 1988.

Bloch, Ernst. »Why and For What Purpose A Large Majority of Philosophers Are Not Yet Materialists.« *Praxis* no. 3/4: »Marksizam i društvena svijest«, 1972: 483.

Bogdanić, Luka. »Čemu *praxis*? Ili o historijskom porijeklu i mjestu Praxisa.« In *Aspekti praxisa. Refleksije uz 50. obljetnicu*, edited by Borislav Mikulić, Mislav Žitko, 25–45. Zagreb: Filozofski fakultet Sveučilišta u Zagrebu, 2015.

Bošnjak, Branko. »Betrachtungen über die Praxis.« *Praxis*, no. 1: »A quoi bon Praxis?« (1965): 17. Available at: https://www.marxists.org/subject/praxis/praxis-international/Praxis%2C%20international%20edition%2C%201965%2C%20no.%201.pdf (last accessed: 24 February 2021).

Brown, Richard D. »Microhistory and Postmodernism.« *Journal of the Early Republic* Vol. 23, No. 1 (Spring, 2003): 1–20.

Call for lecture. *Conferencias. Branimir Grujić, 10 September 1968, La Habana*. IMS Archive.

Campos, Nelson Navarro and Temes, José C. »Application and Development of the IMS-Žeželj System in Cuba.« *Bilten IMS* no. 1 (Belgrade: February 1975): 3–7.

Campos, Nelson Navarro. »The Implementation and Development of IMS Building Technology in Cuba.« In *Research, Projects and Realizations in Construction*, edited by Zoran Popović, Goran Petrović, 215–221. Belgrade: Institute for Materials Testing, 2010.

Castoriadis, Cornelius. An Introductory Interview: »The Only Way to Find Out If You Can Swim Is to Get into the Water.« In *The Castoriadis Reader*, ed. David Ames Curtis, 1–34. Oxford UK, Malden USA: Blackwell Publishers, 1997.

Castoriadis, Cornelius, in dialogue with Robert Legros. »Breaking the Closure.« In *Postscript on Insignificance. Dialogues with Cornelius Castoriadis*, ed. Rockhill, Gabriel, 93–107. London, New York: Continuum, 2011.

Castoriadis, Cornelius. »Le projet de l'autonomie n'est pas une utopie.« Interview with Jocelyn Wolff and Benjamin Quénelle, *Propos*, 10 (March 1993): 34–40. In English published as Castoriadis, Cornelius. »The Project of Autonomy is Not Utopia.« In *A Society Adrift. Interviews and Debates 1974–1997*, ed. Enrique Escobar, Myrto Gondicas, and Pascal Vernay, 3–11. New York: Fordham University Press, 2010.

Castoriadis, Cornelius. *L'institution imaginaire de la société*. Paris: Editions du Seuil, 1975. Trans. Castoriadis, Cornelius. *The Imaginary Institution of Society*. Cambridge, Malden: Polity Press, 1987.

Castoriadis, Cornelius. »Marxisme et théorie révolutionnaire.« *Socialisme ou Barbarie* no. 36–40 (April 1964–June 1965) and reprinted in *The Imaginary Institution of Society*.

Castoriadis, Cornelius. »*Nomos/Phusis* Opposition.« *Bedeutung Magazine* no. 1: Nature&Culture (2008): 14–20.

Castoriadis, Cornelius. »On the Content of Socialism 1.« In *Political and Social Writings* Vol. 1 1946–1955, 290–309. Minneapolis: University of Minnesota Press, 1988. The article was originally published under the pseudonym Pierre Chaulieu, »Sur le contenu du socialisme«, *Socialisme ou Barbarie*, no. 17 (July 1955): 1–25.

Castoriadis, Corenelius. »Radical Imagination and the Social Instituting Imaginary.« In *Rethinking Imagination: Culture and Creativity*, ed. Gillian Robinson and John Rundell, 136–155. London and New York: Routledge, 1994.

Castoriadis, Cornelius. »The Yugoslavian Bureaucracy.« *Political and Social Writings Vol. 1, 1946–1955*, 179–198. Minneapolis: University of Minnesota Press, 1988.

First published as: Chaulieu, Pierre & Dupont, Georges. »La bureaucratie yougoslave.« *Socialisme ou Barbarie* no. 5–6 (March, April 1950): 1–76.

»Catalogue of international working brigades on the construction of The Brotherhood and Unity Highway.« Manuscript document. Fonds: Savez socijalističke omladine Jugoslavije. Međunarodna saradnja 1948–1969. Folder 229. Archives of Yugoslavia, Belgrade.

Center for Housing, *Model vrednovanja stanova i stambenih zgrada CS'80—1. Kvalitet stana*, Branka Gavrilović, Ivan Petrović, Ksenija Petovar, Mihailo Čanak, Miladin Životić. Belgrade: Institute Materials Testing, 1979.

Center for Housing, *Model vrednovanja stanova i stambenih zgrada CS'80—2. Kvalitet stambene zgrade*. Beograd: Institute for Materials Testing, 1980.

Chomski, Noam. »The Repression at Belgrade University.« *The New York Review of Books*, 7 February 1974. Url: http://www.chomsky.info/articles/19740207.htm (last accessed: 18 December 2021).

Clubs de Relations Internationales et groupements analogues brochure. UNESCO Publications, 1949. Fonds: Savez socijalističke omladine Jugoslavije. Međunarodna saradnja 1948–1969. Folder 229. Archives of Yugoslavia, Belgrade.

Collins, Peter. *Concrete. The Vision of a New Architecture*. London: Faber and Faber, 1959.

Contract between The Institute for Materials Testing FRS Belgrade and Institute for Housing from Ministry of Construction Cuba, 15 November 1967, Havana. IMS Archive.

Cook, Christopher D. »Cuba's Harvest of Surprises«, Winter 2015, https://craftsmanship.net/cubas-harvest-surprises/ (last accessed: 10 May 2021).

Cordero, José A. José A. Cordero to engineer Stipanović from the IMS on the state of works on the Experimental Building in Havana, 9 January 1968. IMS Archive.

Curtis, David Ames, ed. *The Castoriadis Reader*. Oxford UK, Malden USA: Blackwell Publishers, 1977.

Darke, Roy. »Housing and Spatial Policies in the Socialist Third-World.« *Netherlands Journal of Housing and Environmental Research*, Vol. 4, no. 1 (1989): 51–66.

Decision on registration of institution of the Institute for Materials Testing FR Serbia, People's Committee Topčidersko brdo, no. 499, 6 Sep 1955; chapter from the *Official Gazette* FR Serbia, no. 89, 15. 11. 1955, p. 900. (Rešenje o registraciji ustanove sa samostalnim finansiranjem Instituta za ispitivanje materijala NRS u Beogradu, Bul. Vojvode Mišića 43, Narodni odbor opštine Topčidersko brdo, no. 499, 6. IX 1955; Izvod iz *Službenog glasnika* NRS no. 89 od 15. XI 1955, p. 900.), IMS Archive.

Decree on transaction of property from Direction for Construction of Machines to the Serbian Academy of Sciences, Aug 7, 1951. (Rešenje o prenosu imovine generalne direkcije na Srpsku akademiju nauka, Sreski sud za grad Beograd, 7 August 1951), IMS Archive.

Delitz, Heike. »Architectural Modes of Collective Existence. Architectural Sociology as a Comparative Social Theory.« *Cultural Sociology* 12 (2018): 37–57. https://doi.org/10.1177/1749975517718435.

Department II: Concrete. »Study on the Testing of Prefabricated Floor Slabs.« Belgrade: Institute for Materials Testing FRS, 1960, IMS Archive.

Djurić, Dubravka, Miško Šuvaković, ed. *Impossible Histories. Historical Avant-gardes, Neo-avant-gardes, and Post-avant-gardes in Yugoslavia, 1918–1991*. Cambridge and London: MIT Press, 2006.

»Dnevni raspored života i rada u studentskim brigadama.« Fonds 114: Savez socijalističke omladine

Jugoslavije. Radne akcije 1948–1950. Folder 152. Archives of Yugoslavia, Belgrade.

Dosse, François. *Castoriadis une vie*. Paris: La Découverte, 2014.

»Edifican en Cienfuegos una fábrica con capacidad para 1500 viviendas al año«, *JR Juventuo Rebelde*, 19 December 1976.

Editorial board. »Why Praxis International?«, *Praxis International* no. 1 (April 1981): 1–5.

Embajada de Cuba, Embajada de Cuba to Branko Žeželj, 30 March 1967. IMS Archive.

Embajada de Cuba, Pro-Memoria signed on 17 May 1971 between Arch. Osmundo Machado Ventura on behalf of the Nacional Grupo por Viviendas, DESA and Svetozar Pejanović, representing the IMS, IMS Archive.

Enkciklopedija samoupravljanja (Belgrade: Savremena administracija, 1979).

Erb, Sebastian. »Gegen alle Blockaden«, Taz Magazine, 21 May 2015. URL: https://taz.de/Unabhaengiges-Onlinemagazin-aus-Kuba/!5200459/ (last accessed: 23 October 2022).

Escobar, Reinaldo. Correspondence with Andjelka Badnjar Gojnić, November 2021, Havana.

Escobar, Reinaldo. *La Grieta*. Madrid: Editorial Verbum, 2018.

Escobar, Reinaldo. »Mi norma personal es ajustarme a la verdad.« Interview by Abel Sierra Madero, 2 October 2020. https://www.hypermediamagazine.com/columnistas/fiebre-de-archivo/reinaldo-escobar-mi-norma-personal-es-ajustarme-a-la-verdad/ (last accessed: 20 November 2021).

Escobar, Reinaldo. »The Odyssey«, 5 November 2020, Havana. https://www.14ymedio.com/blogs/desde_aqui/Odisea_7_2873182654.html (last accessed: 29 November 2021).

Forty, Adrian. »Dead or Alive—Describing the Social.« *Words and Buildings. A Vocabulary of Modern Architecture*, 102–117. London: Thames&Hudson, 2000.

Fritzhand, Marek. »Marx's Ideal of Man.« *Socialist Humanism*, edited by Erich Fromm, 172–182. New York: Doubleday & Co., Anchor Books, 1965.

Fromm, Erich. »The Application of Humanist Psychoanalysis to Marx's Theory.« *Socialist Humanism*, edited by Erich Fromm, 228–246. New York: Doubleday & Co., Anchor Books, 1965.

Galguera, Armando. Armando Galguera as principal of the Housing Institute, Cuban Ministry of Construction, to Branko Žeželj at the IMS, 15 October 1968. IMS Archive.

Galguera, Armando. Armando Galguera as principal of the Housing Institute, Cuban Ministry of Construction, to Svetozar Pejanović, Principal of the IMS, 20 June 1968. IMS Archive.

General contract between the Nacional Housing Group of the Cuban Construction Sector and the Institute for Materials Testing, La Habana, 1970. IMS Archive.

Geras, Norman. *Marx and Human Nature: Refutation of a Legend*. London, New York: Verso, 1983. Kindle.

Gillette, Arthur. *One Million Volunteers. The Story of Volunteer Youth Service*. Harmondsworth, Ringwood: Penguin Books, 1968.

Ginzburg, Carlo. »Microhistory and world history.« *The Cambridge World History* Vol. VI, edited by Jerry H. Bentley, Sanjay Subrahmanyam and Merry E. Wiesner-Hanks, 446–473. Cambridge University Press: 2015.

Golubović, Jovan, ed. *Beograd grad akcijaša*. Belgrade: Gradska konferencija SSO Beograda Omladinska radna akcija »Beograd«, 1985. Also available at: https://sites.google.com/site/orabeograd/ (last accessed: 14 October 2021).

González Couret, Dania. *Economía y calidad en la vivienda. Un enfoque cubano*. Havana: Editorial Científico-Técnica, 1997.

González Couret, Dania. »Half a Century of Social Housing in Cuba.« *Revista INVI* no. 67 (November, 2009): 69–92. http://dx.doi.org/10.4067/S0718-83582009000300003.

Goode, Patrick. »Cooperative Association.« In *A Dictionary of Marxist Thought*, ed. Tom Bottomore, Laurence Harris, V.G. Kiernan and Ralph Miliband, 111–112. Malden, Oxford, Carlton: Blackwell Publishing, 1983.

Grujić, Branimir. Branimir Grujić to the Cuban Embassy Belgrade, 25 February 1968. IMS Archive.

Grujić, Branimir. Branimir Grujić to the Institute for Technical Assistance (*Zavod za tehničku pomoć*) about the list of Cuban participants in training at the IMS Belgrade, 5 January 1968. IMS Archive.

Grujić, Branimir. Interview with Andjelka Badnjar Gojnić, 28 April–5 May 2019, Belgrade.

Grujić, Branimir. »Use of the IMS System in Cuba.« *Izgradnja*, no. 4 (Belgrade 1970): 179–188.

Grujić, Branimir. »The Further Development of the IMS System in Cuba.« *Bilten IMS*, no. 4 (Belgrade 1974): 41–42.

Gély, Raphaël. »Imaginaire, affectivité et rationalité. Pour une relecture du débat entre Habermas et Castoriadis.« *Cahiers Castoriadis* no. 4 (2008): 139–182.

Habermas, Jürgen. »Bedingungen für eine Revolutionierung spätkapitalistischer Gesellschaftssysteme. *Praxis* no. 1/2: »Marx and Revolution« (1969): 199–212. https://www.marxists.org/subject/praxis/praxis-international/Praxis%2C%20international%20edition%2C%201969%2C%20no.%201-2.pdf (last accessed: 7 January 2021).

Habermas, Jürgen. *Der philosophische Diskurs der Moderne: Zwölf Vorlesungen*. Frankfurt am Main: Suhrkamp Verlag, 1985. Trans. Habermas, Jürgen. *The Philosophical Discourse of Modernity. Twelve Lectures*. Cambridge, Massachusetts: The MIT Press, 1987.

Habermas, Jürgen. *Erkenntnis und Interesse*. Berlin: Suhrkamp Verlag, 1968. English translation: Habermas, Jürgen. *Knowledge and Human Interests*. Boston: Beacon Press, 1972.

Habermas, Jürgen. »Modern and Postmodern Architecture.« In *Architecture Theory since 1968*, edited by Hays, K. Michael, 412–428. Cambridge Massachusetts, London England: The MIT Press, 2000.

Habermas, Jürgen. »Technischer Fortschritt und soziale Lebenswelt.« *Praxis* no. 1/2: »Qu'est que l'histoire«, 1966.

Habermas, Jürgen. »Tehnički napredak i svijet društvenog života«, *Praxis* no. 6: »Što je povijest?« (1965): 846–865.

Habermas, Jürgen. *Theorie des kommunikativen Handelns, Band 2: Zur Kritik der funktionalistischen Vernunft.* Frankfurt: Suhrkamp Verlag, 1981. Trans. Habermas, Jürgen. *The Theory of Communicative Action 2. The Critique of Functionalist Reason.* Cambridge: Polity Press, 1987.

Habermas, Jürgen. *Theorie und Praxis.* Paris: Hermann, 1963. English translation: Habermas, Jürgen. *Theory and Practice.* Boston: Beacon Press, 1973.

Habermas, Jürgen. »Uloga filozofije u marksizmu.« *Praxis* 5/6: »Gradjanski svijet i socijalizam« (1973): 601–609.

Harbusch, Gregor, Muriel Pérez, Kees Somer, Daniel Weiss, Evelin van Es. *Atlas of the Functional City: CIAM 4 and Comparative Urban Analysis.* Zurich: gta Verlag, 2014.

Hays, K. Michael. *Architecture Theory since 1968.* Cambridge Massachusetts, London England: The MIT Press, 2000.

Hobsbawm, Eric. *The Age of Extremes 1914–1991.* London: Abacus, 1995.

Hofman, Ivan. »Susret drugačijih svetova: Strani državljani na omladinskim radnim akcijama u Jugoslaviji 1946–1951. Godine.« *Godišnjak za društvenu istoriju* 1 (2012): 35–56.

Horvastvi, Joža. »Franscuska brigada posjetila Beograd.« *Bratstvo-Jedinstvo,* 20 August 1949.

Horvat, Branko. *The Political Economy of Socialism.* New York: M. E. Sharpe, Inc., Armonk, 1982. (Yugoslavian edition: Horvat, Brando. *Politička ekonomija socijalizma.* Zagreb: Globus, 1983.)

Ilić, Ljubo. »Uz izgradnju Novog Beograda.« *Arhitektura* no. 8–10 (1948): 9.

IMS Department V: Metals. *Report on the Testing of Steel Samples from Cuba,* 22 September 1967. Scientific study. IMS Archive.

IMS engineer's letter to Branimir Grujić at the IMS on the state of works on the Experimental Building in Havana, 21 December 1969. IMS Archive. The letter is signed only by the nickname Mika.

IMS. IMS to the Yugoslavian Bank for International Commerce. Export of IMS Plants to Cuba, 13 May 1971. IMS Archive.

Institute for Materials Testing booklet, Activities section. Belgrade: Radnička štampa, 1968.

Institute for Materials Testing. DVD. Directed by Aleksandar Ilić. Belgrade: Institute for Materials Testing FR Serbia.

James-Chakraborty, Kathleen. »Beyond Postcolonialism: New Directions for the History of Non-Western Architecture.« *Frontiers of Architectural Research* no. 3 (2014): 1–9.

Jarić, Miloš. »Organizacioni i tržišni uslovi za industrijalizaciju stambene izgradnje.« In *Savetovanje o industrijalizaciji stambene izgradnje,* IV–1–IV–12. Belgrade: Savezna gradjevinska komora, 1960.

Jarić, Miloš. »Specijalizacija, kooperacija i udruživanje u gradjevinarstvu.« In *Almanah 1961,* ed. Milutin Maksimović, Radmio Živković, Pravoslav Trajković, 98–107. Belgrade: Savez gradjevinskih inžinjera i tehničara Jugoslavije.

Jimenez Almira, Marta. »La Vivienda en Cuba«, *Granma,* 29 September 1971, page unknown.

Joas, Hans. »Institutionalization as a Creative Process: The Sociological Importance of Cornelius Castoriadis's Political Philosophy.« In *Pragmatism and Social Theory,* 154–172. Chicago, London: The University of Chicago Press, 1993.

Joas, Hans. »The Unhappy Marriage of Hermeneutics and Functionalism.« *Praxis International,* no.1 (1988): 34–51, reprinted in Joas, Hans. *Pragmatism and Social Theory,* 125–154. Chicago: The University of Chicago Press, 1993.

Jovanović, Jelica. »From Yugoslavia to Angola: Housing as Postcolonial Technical Assistance City Building through IMS Žeželj Housing Technology.« *Architektúra & Urbanizmus* 3–4 (2019): 170–181.

Joyner, Charles. *Shared Traditions. Southern History and Folk Culture.* Chicago: University of Illinois Press, 1999.

Kardelj, Edvard. *Samoupravljanje u Jugoslaviji 1950–1976.* Belgrade: Privredni Pregled, 1977.

Kats, Anna. »In Socialist Yugoslavia Mass Housing Wasn't Just Ugly Tower Blocks«, 8 November 2021. URL: https://www.jacobinmag.com/2021/08/ yugoslavia-architecture-socialism-angola-soviet-housing (last accessed: 10 May 2021).

Kirn, Gal. *Partisan Ruptures. Self-Management, Market Reform and the Spectre of Socialist Yugoslavia.* London: Pluto Press, 2019.

Krstanović, V. »Stanovi za Kubance po beogradskom receptu.« *Borba,* 9 December 1968, 4.

Kulić, Vladimir and Bojana Videkanić, ed. *Histories of Postwar Architecture* no. 6, »Thick descriptions: Socialist Yugoslavia in Construction« (October 2020). https://doi.org/10.6092/issn.2611-0075/v3-n6-2020.

Kulić, Vladimir. *Building Babylon,* Volume 2, *Non-Aligned Modernisms.* Belgrade: Museum of Contemporary Art, 2014–2017.

Kulić, Vladimir, Maroje Mrduljaš and Wolfgang Thaler, ed. *Modernism In-between. The mediatory Architectures of Socialist Yugoslavia.* Berlin: Jovis, 2012.

Kušić, Aleksandar V. »Change of Urban and Architectural Paradigm Exemplified by Belgrade Housing Estates: The Period of Yugoslav Late Socialism (1965–1991).« PhD diss., University of Belgrade, 2014.

Laclau, Ernesto, Chantal Mouffe. *Hegemony and Socialist Strategy: Towards a Radical Democratic Politics.* London: Verso, 1985.

Latin American Herald Tribune. »Cuba has more than 33,000 Urban Farms«, 22 May 2012. URL: http://

www.laht.com/article.asp?ArticleId=508483&-CategoryId=14510 (last accessed: 10 May 2021).

Lavin, Sylvia ed., *Architecture Itself and Other Postmodernization Effects*. Montreal: Canadian Centre for Architecture, 2020.

Lebowitz, Michael A. »Seven Difficult Questions.« In *Build It Now: Socialism for the Twenty-First Century*, 73–84. New York: NYU Press, 2006.

Le Corbusier. *Charte d'Athènes*. Paris: Plon, 1943.

Lefebvre, Henri. »Le socialisme en vacances.« *France Observateur*, no. 746, 20. August 1964, 20.

Lefebvre, Henri. *Métaphilosophie*. Paris: Éditions de Minuit, 1965. English translation: *Metaphilosophy*. London, New York: Verso, 2016. Kindle.

Lefebvre, Henri. »Socijalizam za vrijeme ljetnjeg odmora.« *Praxis* no. 1: »Suvremeni problemi socijalizma« (1965): 164–167.

Lefebvre, Henri. *Sociologie de Marx*. Paris: Presses Universitaires de France, 1966.

Lefebvre, Henri. »Sur quelques critères du développement social et du socialisme.« *Praxis* no. 2/3:»Sinn und Perspektiven des Sozialismus« (1965): 151–156.

Letter from chairman Fritz Walter Brichacek to the Central Council of the People's Youth, Vienna, 12 February 1948. Fonds: Savez socijalističke omladine Jugoslavije. Medunarodna saradnja 1948–1969. Folder 229. Archives of Yugoslavia.

Levi, Giovanni. »On Microhistory.« In *New Perspectives of Historical Writing*, edited by Peter Burke, 93–113. Cambridge: Polity Press, 1991.

Lešaja, Ante. *Praxis Orientation, Journal Praxis and The Korčula Summer School*. Belgrade: Rosa Luxemburg Stiftung, 2014.

»Macht zersetzen.« *Der Spiegel* no. 36, 1.9.1968. https://www.spiegel.de/kultur/macht-zersetzen-a-de7da828-0002-0001-0000-000045950125?context=issue (last accessed: 6 May 2021).

Madero, Alber Sierra. Interview with Reinaldo Escobar, »Mi norma personal es ajustarme a la verdad«, *Hypermedia Magazine*, 2 October 2020. URL: https://www.hypermediamagazine.com/columnistas/fiebre-de-archivo/reinaldo-escobar-mi-norma-personal-es-ajustarme-a-la-verdad/ (last accessed: 20 November 2021).

Malcovati, Silvia. »Das alte Frankfurt: Urban Neighborhood versus Housing Estate, the Rebirth of Urban Architecture.« *Urban Planning* vol. 4, no. 3, edited by Luca Ortelli, Chiara Monterumisi and Alessandro Porotto (2019): 117–133. URL: https://www.cogitatiopress.com/urbanplanning/issue/viewIssue/134/PDF134 (last accessed: 23 July 2022).

Marcuse, Herbert. *Beiträge zu einer Phänomenologie des Historischen Materialismus*. Berlin: Verlag der Philosophischen Hefte, 1928.

Marcuse, Herbert. *Uber die philosophischen Grundlagen des wirtschafts wissenschaftlichen Arbeitsbegriffs*. Tübingen: Verlag J.C.B. Mohr (Paul Siebeck), 1933.

Marin, Maggie. »Edificios Altos.« *Bohemia económica*, no. unknown (Havana 1974): 16–21.

Marković, Predrag. *Beograd izmedju istoka i zapada 1948–1965*. Belgrade: Službeni list Beograd, 1996.

Marx, Karl & Frederick Engels. *Collected Works Vol. 3, 1843–1844*. London: Lawrence & Wishart, 1975.

Marx, Karl. »Theses on Feuerbach.« *Writings of the Young Marx on Philosophy and Society*, edited by Loyd D. Easton and Kurt H. Guddat, 400–402. New York: Doubleday & Co., Anchor Books, 1967.

Marx, Karl. *Ökonomisch-philosophische Manuskripte aus dem Jahre 1844*. Berlin: Zenodot Verlagsgesellscha, 2017. Originally published in Karl Marx, Friedrich Engels. *Werke*, Band 40. Berlin: Dietz-Verlag, 1968. Available at: http://www.mlwerke.de/me/me40/me40_465.htm (last accessed: 21 January 2021).

Mathéy, Kosta. »Microbrigadas in Cuba: A Collective Form of Self-Help Housing«, *The Netherlands Journal of Housing and Environmental Research* vol. 4, no. 1, Special issue »Housing in the Third World: Self-Help and Governmental Programs« (1989): 67–83.

Matošević, Andrea. »Više od zbroja infrastrukturnih postignuća: omladinske radne akcije i fenomenologija moralne ekonomije dara.« *Narodna umjetnost* no. 53/2 (2016): 61–77.

Matvejević, Predrag. »Requiem za jednu ljevicu.«In *Praxis: Kritika i humanistički socijalizam*, ed. Dragomir Olujić, Krunoslav Stojaković, 7–8. Korčula: Rosa Luxemburg Stiftung Souteast Europe, 2011.

McNamara, Tess. »Urban Farm-Fed Cities: Lessons from Cuba's Organopónicos«, 23 November 2018. URL: http://www.sagemagazine.org/urban-farm-fed-cities-lessons-from-cubas-organoponics/ (last accessed: 10 May 2021).

Medosch, Armin. *New Tendencies. Art at the Threshold of the Information Revolution 1961–1978*. Cambridge and London: The MIT Press, 2016.

Microdistrito Plaza de la Revolucion. Havana: November, 1975.

Mihailović, Srećko. »Ciljevi ORA i njihovo ostvarenje.« In *ORA—Mladost naše zemlje 1942–1982*, edited by Toma Dragosavac, 70–116. Belgrade: Poslovna politika i Mladost, 1983.

Mihailović, Srećko. »Karakteristike omladinskih radnih akcija.« *Omladinske radne akcije—mladost naše zemlje 1942–1982*, edited by Toma Dragosavac, 56–69. Belgrade: Poslovna Politika i Mladost, 1983.

Ministry of Construction of the Republic of Cuba. Ministry of Construction to the Principal of the IMS, Svetozar Pejanović, 7 November 1967. IMS Archive.

Mioli, Teresa. »Yoani Sánchez will explain how and why she created 14ymedio, Cuba's first independent news platform«, 2 March 2016. URL: https://isoj.org/yoani-sanchez-will-explain-how-and-why-she-created-14ymedio-cubas-first-independent-news-platform-2/.

Moravánszky, Ákos, Torsten Lange, Judith Hopfengärther and Karl R. Kegler, ed. *East West Central. Re-Building Europe 1950–1990*. Basel: Birkhäuser, 2017.

Mrduljaš, Maroje and Vladimir Kulić, ed. *Unfinished Modernisations—Between Utopia and Pragmatism*. Zagreb: Udruženje hrvatskih arhitekata, 2012.

Mumford, Eric. *The CIAM Discourse on Urbanism 1928–1960*. Cambridge MA: MIT Press, 2000.

Mumford, Lewis. *The City in History: Its Origins, Its Transformations, and Its Prospects*. New York: Harcourt, Brace & World, 1961.

Márkus, György. »A Society of Culture: The Constitution of Modernity.« In *Rethinking Imagination. Culture and Creativity*, edited by Gillian Robinson and John Rundell, 15–29. New York: Routledge, 1994.

Nešić, Dragoljub. »Ideja asocijacije proizvođača kod socijaliste-utopiste Charlesa Fouriera.« *Pogledi* no. 2 (December 1952): 66–78.

»Novi Beograd-ponos petoletke.« *Duga* no. 218–219, October 1949.

»Novi Beograd. Svedočanstvo socijalističke izgradnje u novoj Jugoslaviji.« *Yugoslavia* no. 14–16 (1948): 180–184.

Obradović, Mirjana. Interview with Andjelka Badnjar Gojnić, 11 December 2020, Belgrade.

»Odluka o programu, planovima i uputstvima u radu CK NOJ.« Decision sent by the Central Youth Committee of Yugoslavia to the Main Head-quarters of Work Brigades on the construction of Belgrade. 8 March 1949. Fonds 114: Savez socijalističke omladine Jugoslavije. Radne akcije 1948–1950. Folder: 152. Archives of Yugoslavia, Belgrade.

Olujić, Dragomir and Krunoslav Stojaković, ed., *Praxis, Kritika i humanistički socijalizam*. Belgrade: Rosa Luxemburg Stiftung, 2012.

»Omladina Jugoslavije je juče počela svoje veliko delo—izgradnju Novog Beograda.« *Politika*, 12 April 1948.

Padura, Leonardo. *The Man Who Loved Dogs*. New York: Farrar, Straus and Giroux, 2014. Spanish original: Leonardo Padura. *El hombre que amaba a los perros*. Barcelona: Tusquets Editores, 2009.

Pajević, Milan. Interview with Andjelka Badnjar Gojnić, 6 November 2018, Belgrade, followed by the talk in summer 2018 in Sveti Stefan, Montenegro.

Palmer Thompson, Edward. »An Open Letter to Leszek Kołakowski.« *The Socialist Register* (1973): 1–100. Available at: https://www.marxists.org/archive/thompson-ep/1973/kolakowski.htm (last accessed: 12 September 2022).

Palmer Thompson, Edward, ed. *The Railway: An Adventure in Construction*. London: The British Yugoslav Association, 1948.

Panić, Ana, Jovo Bakić, Srđan Cvetković, Ivana Dobrivojević, Hrvoje Klasić, Petrović Vladimir. *Yugoslavia 1918–1991*. Belgrade: Museum of Yugoslavia, 2014. Published following the exhibition *Jugoslavija: od početka do kraja* at the Museum of Yugoslavia, Belgrade, 1 December 2012–17 March 2013.

Pejanović, Svetozar. »Development of the Institute.« In *20 godina rada 1948–1968*, ed. Milutin Mak-simović, 35–43. Belgrade: Institut za ispitivanje materijala SR Srbije, 1968.

Pejanović, Svetozar. IMS Principal. Report on negotiations on the application of the IMS system in Cuba to The Federal Institute for International Technical Cooperation, 28 September 1966. IMS Archive.

Pejanović, Svetozar. IMS Principal. Svetozar Pejanović to the Cuban Ministry of Construction, Belgrade, 9 January 1968. IMS Archive.

Pejanović, Svetozar. IMS Principal. Svetozar Pejanović to the Secretariat for Foreign Affairs Belgrade, 5 October 1967. IMS Archive.

People's Youth of Yugoslavia Open Call via the World Federation of Democratic Youth. Fonds: Savez socijalističke omladine Jugoslavije. Međunarodna saradnja 1948–1969. Folder 229. Archives of Yugoslavia, Belgrade.

Petovar, Ksenija. Interview with Andjelka Badnjar Gojnić, 19 May 2017, Belgrade.

Petranović, Branko. *Istorija Jugoslavije*, knjiga III *Socijalistička Jugoslavija 1955–1988*. Belgrade: Nolit, 1988.

Petričić, Branko. »Izgradjeni stambeni blokovi 1 i 2 u Novom Beogradu. Eksperimentalni rejon.« *Urbanizam Beograda* no. 2 (1969): 14–19. http://urbel.com/uploads/Urbanizam_Beograda/UB2.pdf) (last accessed: 12 April 2021).

Petričić, Branko. »Prve urbanističke realizacije. Novi Beograd 1955–1975.« *Godišnjak grada Beograda XXII* (Belgrade: Belgrade City Museum, 1975), 219–233. http://www.mgb.org.rs/images/godisnjaci/GodisnjakXXII/219-234GodisnjakXXII.pdf (last accessed: 18 April 2021).

Petrović, Boško. »Evolution of Prestressed Concrete Structures.« In *20 godina rada 1948–1968*, 207–227. Belgrade: Institute for Testing Materials FR Serbia, 1968.

Petrović, Gajo. »A quoi bon Praxis?« *Praxis* no. 1 (1965): 3–7. https://www.marxists.org/subject/praxis/praxis-international/Praxis%2C%20international%20edition%2C%201965%2C%20no.%201.pdf (last accessed: 10 August 2022).

Petrović, Gajo. »Ein Gewisser Ernst Bloch.« TÜTE special edition: *Zum hundertsten Geburtstag von Ernst Bloch*, June/July 1985.

Petrović, Gajo. »Filozofija u SSSR-u od Oktobarske revolucije do 1938.« *Pogledi* no. 2 (December 1952): 79–86.

Petrović, Gajo. *Marx in the Mid-Twentieth Century*. New York: Anchor DoubleDay, 1967.

Petrović, Gajo. »Praxis.« *A Dictionary of Marxist Thought*, edited by Tom Bottomore, Laurence Harris, V. G. Kiernan, Ralph Miliband, 435–440. Malden, Oxford, Carlton: Blackwell Publishing, 1983.

Petrović, Ivan. »Idejni projekat eksperimentalne zgrade u IMS sistemu u Luandi.« *Bilten IMS* no. 1 (January 1979): 3–27.

Petrović, Ivan. »Mogućnosti primene IMS sistema u individualnoj stambenoj izgradnji na područji-ma sa tropskom i sub-tropskom klimom.« *Bilten IMS* no. 1–2 (December 1980): 3–6.

Petrović Todosijević, Sanja. *Za bezimene: Delatnost UNICEF-a u Federativnoj Narodnoj Republici Jugoslaviji 1947–1954*. Belgrade: Institut za noviju istoriju Srbije, 2008.

Piškur, Bojana, ed. *Southern Constellations. The Poetics of Non-Aligned*. Ljubljana: Moderna galerija, 2019.

Piškur, Bojana. »Southern Constellations: Other Histories, Other Modernities.« In the exhibition catalogue *Southern Constellations. The Poetics of Non-Aligned*, curated by Bojana Piškur, 9–25. Ljubljana: Moderna galerija, 2019.

»Plan izdavačke delatnosti uredništva za inostrana izdanja pri izdavačkom preduzeću *Novo pokoljenje* za 1949. godinu« and »Plan izdavačke delatnosti uredništva za inostrana izdanja pri izdavačkom preduzeću *Novo pokoljenje* za 1950. godinu.« Fonds: Savez socijalističke omladine Jugoslavije. Međunarodna saradnja 1948–1969. Folder 223. Archives of Yugoslavia, Belgrade.

»Pravilnik izdavaštva za inostrana izdanja pri izdavačkom preduzeću *Novo pokoljenje*.« Fonds: Savez socijalističke omladine Jugoslavije. Međunarodna saradnja 1948–1969. Folder 223. Archives of Yugoslavia, Belgrade.

Prashad, Vijay. *The Darker Nations*. New York, London: The New Press, 2007.

Praxis no. 1/2: »Créativité et réification« (1968).

Praxis no. 3: »Misao Lukacs-a i Bloch-a« (1966).

Programme of the Cuban delegation visiting the Institute for Materials Testing from September until December 1971. IMS Archive.

Protocol on talks in Havana between the IMS and DESA, 3, 1–13 April 1976. IMS Archive.

Pérez, Tomás Ernesto. *Microbrigadas*, 4 January 2016. URL: https://periodismodebarrio.org/2016/01/microbrigadas/.

Radojković, Ljubica. »Omladinske radne brigade na izgradnji Beograda 1947–1950 godine.« *Godišnjak grada Beograda* V (1958): 363–420.

»Rad omladinskih radnih brigade na izgradnji Novog Beograda 1949.« Fonds 114: Savez socijalističke omladine Jugoslavije. Radne akcije 1948–1950. Folder: 152. Archives of Yugoslavia, Belgrade.

»Razvijajmo što bolji propagandno-agitacioni rad u brigadama.« *Novi Beograd*, 3 April 1949, front cover.

Record of the meeting of the board and department principals of the Institute for Materials Testing, 26 June 1961, 1–3, from *Zapisnici sa uprave 1959–1961*. Institute for Materials Testing, Belgrade, IMS Archive.

Record of the meeting of the board and department principals of the Institute for Materials Testing, 10 August 1961, 1–6, from *Zapisnici sa uprave 1959–1961*. Institute Materials Testing, Belgrade, IMS Archive.

Records of meetings of the Scientific Council, book 2, 1967–1968, *Naučno veće. Zapisnici sa sednica*, Institute Materials Testing, Belgrade, IMS Archive.

»Report on The Fourth Conference of International Non-Governmental Organizations at Geneva.« United Nations document, June 1950. Fonds: Savez socijalističke omladine Jugoslavije. Međunarodna saradnja 1948–1969. Folder 229. Archives of Yugoslavia, Belgrade.

Risselada, Max, Dirk van den Heuvel, ed. *Team 10: In Search of a Utopia of the Present*. Rotterdam: NAI Publishers, 2006.

Ristanović, Slobodan V. *Novi Beograd, Graditeljski poduhvat veka*. Belgrade: IA KSE-NA, 2009.

Roš, Mirko. ETH Archive Zurich. Erinnerungsalbum, Hs 359:2.

Roš, Mirko. Letter to the presidency of Government of Serbia, July 3 1952, IMS Archive (Pismo predsedništvu Vlade NR Srbije od upravnika instituta Mirka Roša na potraživaju opereme, 3. VII 1952), IMS Archive.

Roš, Mirko. Report of work on founding the institute IM-SAN to the Serbian Academy of Sciences, 11–20 January 1952 (»Izveštaj o radu na osnivanju instituta IM-SAN Srpskoj akademiji nauka«, 11–20 January 1952), IMS Archive.

Roš, Mirko. Report of work on founding the institute IM-SAN to the Serbian Academy of Sciences, July 1952, IMS Archive.

Rubinstein, Alvin. *Yugoslavia and Nonaligned World*. Princeton: Princeton University Press, 1970.

Rulebook on the procedure of the Council of the Institute for Testing Materials Serbia (*Poslovnik o radu Saveta Instituta za ispitivanje materijala SR Srbija*), Belgrade: Institute for Testing Materials, 1965. IMS Archive.

Rundell, John. »Introduction.« In *Rethinking Imagination. Culture and Creativity*, edited by Gillian Robinson and John Rundell, 1–11. New York: Routledge, 1994.

Samoupravljanje u radnim organizacijama. *Pravni leksikon*, 814–815. Belgrade: Savremena administracija, 1964.

»Savezna akcija Novi Beograd. Učešće omladine 1948.« Fonds 114: Savez socijalističke omladine Jugoslavije. Radne akcije 1948–1950. Folder 152. Archives of Yugoslavia, Belgrade.

»Savjet za nauku i kulturu Vlade FNRJ dostavlja brošuru *To Combine Our Efforts* svim savjetima za prosvetu, nauku i kulturu.« 4 October 1951. Fonds: Savez socijalističke omladine Jugoslavije. Međunarodna saradnja 1948–1969. Folder 229. Archives of Yugoslavia, Belgrade.

Sekulić, Dubravka. *Constructing Non-Alignment: The Case of Energoprojekt*, Volume 3 of *Non-aligned Modernisms*. Belgrade: Museum of Contemporary Art, 2014–2017.

Sloterdijk, Peter. *Critique of Cynical Reason*. Minnesota: University of Minnesota Press, 1987. Originally published as: Sloterdijk, Peter. *Kritik der zynischen Vernunft*. Frankfurt am Main: Suhrkamp Verlag, 1983.

Socialisme ou Barbarie. »Entretien avec un ouvrier yougoslave.« *Socialisme ou Barbarie* no. 26 (November

December 1958): 141–144.

Somborski, Miloš. »Problemi urbanističkog planiranja Beograda.« *Beograd. Generalni urbanistički plan 1950*, edited by Oliver Minić, 5–11. Belgrade: Izdanje IONO Beograda, 1951.

»Spisak društvenih organizacija, listova i rukovodstava Saveza omladine Jugoslavije kojima treba slati Tanjugov bilten *Omladina u svetu*.« Fonds: Savez socijalističke omladine Jugoslavije. Međunarodna saradnja 1948–1969. Folder 223. Archives of Yugoslavia, Belgrade.

Stanek, Łukasz. *Architecture in Global Socialism: Eastern Europe, West Africa, and the Middle East in the Cold War*. Princeton: Princeton University Press, 2020.

Stanek, Łukasz, ed. *Team 10 East: Revisionist Architecture in Real Existing Modernism*. Warsaw: Museum of Modern Art Warsaw, 2013/2014.

Stierli, Martino and Vladimir Kulić, ed. *Toward a Concrete Utopia: Architecture in Yugoslavia 1948–1980*. New York: The Museum of Modern Art, 2018.

Stojanović, Bratislav. »Istorija Novog Beograda I.« *Godišnjak grada Beograda* no. XXI (1974): 211–236.

Stojanović, Bratislav. »Istorija Novog Beograda II.« *Godišnjak grada Beograda* XXII (1975): 199–217.

Stojanović, Bratislav. »Posleratna beogradska arhitektonska izgradnja.« *Godišnjak grada Beograda* XVII (1970): 201–234.

Supek, Rudi. »Bratstvo i drugarstvo omladine na Autoputu.« *Naše teme*, no. 6 (1958): 719.

Supek, Rudi. »Henri Lefebvre: Sociologie de Marx.« *Praxis* no. 3: »Aktuelnost Marksove misli« (1967): 421–423.

Supek, Rudi. *Omladina na putu bratstva. Psihologija radne akcije*. Belgrade: Mladost, 1963.

Supek, Rudi. »Some Contradictions and Insufficiencies of Yugoslav Self-Managing Socialism.« *Praxis* no. 3/4: »Un moment du socialisme Yougoslave« (1971): 375–399.

Supek, Rudi. »The Sociology of Workers' Self-Management.« *Self-Governing Socialism. Volume 2. A Reader,* edited by Branko Horvat, Mihailo Marković, Rudi Supek, 3–14. New York: Routledge, 2015. The first edition was published by M. E. Sharpe, New York in 1975.

Szacka, Léa-Catherine and Véronique Patteeuw. »Critical Regionalism For Our Time.« *The Architectural Review* 1466 (November 2019).

»Terminarán próximamente primera etapa de la planta de viviendas del Sistema IMS, en Camagüey«, La Habana, 13 January 1977, page not available.

Till, Jeremy. »Foreword.« In *The Routledge Companion to Architecture of Social Engagement*, edited by Farhan Karim. New York: Routledge, 2018.

Turin, Branko. *Novi Beograd*, Belgrade City Museum, 24 x 18 cm, Urban Planning and Architecture Collection (Ur_12170, Ur_12180), 1962.

Ujedinjene nacije brochure. Beograd: Radio služba odjeljenja za informacije pri Ujedinjenim nacijama New York, October 1951. Fonds: Savez socijalističke omladine Jugoslavije. Međunarodna

saradnja 1948–1969. Folder 229. Archives of Yugoslavia, Belgrade.

United Nations. *European Housing Situation*. Geneva: January 1956.

»United Nations Youth Welfare Seminar India«, 1–21 November 1951. Fonds: Savez socijalističke omladine Jugoslavije. Međunarodna saradnja 1948–1969. Folder 229. Archives of Yugoslavia, Belgrade.

Valentinčić, Jože. »Jugoslovensko gradjevinarstvo u period 1945–1960.« In *Almanah 1961*, edited by Milutin Maksimović, Radmio Živković, Prvoslav Trajković, Ratko Jovčić, 26–36. Belgrade: Savez građevinskih inženjera i tehničara Jugoslavije, 1961.

Vesić, Jelena, Rachel O'Reilly and Vladimir Jerić Vlidi. *On Neutrality*, Volume 6 in the series *Non-aligned Modernisms*. Belgrade: Museum of Contemporary Art, 2016.

Videkanić, Bojana. *Nonaligned Modernism: Socialist Postcolonial Aesthetics in Yugoslavia*. McGill-Queen's University Press, 2020.

»Visita nuestro país el profesor Branko Zezelj, inventor del sistema constructivo IMS«, *Granma*, Havana, 3 April 1976, 6.

Vojinović, Branislav. »Mirko Roš (1879–1962).« In *Lives and Work of the Serbian Scientists*, book 14. Belgrade: Serbian Academy of Sciences and Arts, 2014.

Vrtačič, Ludvik. »Marxist-Leninist literature in Jugoslavia (1945–1959).« *Studies in East European Thought* 1 (1961): 111–119.

Wainshtek, Hugo. Hugo Wainshtek, Dean of the Faculty of Technology, University of Havana, to the Director of the Institute for Materials Testing, 14 January 1970. IMS Archive.

Williams, Raymond. *Keywords. A Vocabulary of Culture and Society*. New York: Oxford University Press, 1976.

Zeyfang, Florian, Lisa Schmidt-Colinet, Alexander Schmoeger. *Microbrigades-Variations of a Story* (2013) HD 31 min.

Čanak, Mihailo. »Architectonic Activities.« In *20 godina rada 1948–1968* ed. Milutin Maksimović, 295–307. Belgrade: Institut za ispitivanje materijala SR Srbije, 1968.

Čanak, Mihailo. »Dinamika stambenih funkcija i njen uticaj na formiranje stambenog prostora«, *Bilten. Centar za stanovanje* no. 29/30 (Belgrade, 1981): 24–35.

Čanak, Mihailo. »Funkcionalni aspekti stambenih zgrada u sistemu IMS.« *Izgradnja* no. 4 (April 1970): 8–16.

Čanak, Mihailo. Scientific work »Ljudske potrebe i stambene funkcije«, 1973 Center for Housing IMS. Summary published in *Informativni bilten. Centar za stanovanje* no. 15 (Belgrade, 1974), 10.

Žeželj, Branko. Introduction. In *20 godina rada 1948–1968*, ed. Milutin Maksimović, 3–11. Belgrade: Institut za ispitivanje materijala SR Srbije, 1968.

Žeželj, Branko. Letter to The Executive Council FRS dated 10 March 1953 on the occasion of the authorization to use the whole building (Pismo Branka Žeželja u svojstvu zamenika upravnika Izvršnom veću NRS povodom prava na korišćenje čitave zgrade, 10. III 1953), IMS Archive.

Žeželj, Branko. »Role of the Institute in the Development of Science and Industry.« In *20 godina rada 1948–1968*, ed. Milutin Maksimović, 11–23. Belgrade: Institut za ispitivanje materijala SR Srbije, 1968.

Žeželj, Branko. »Uslovi i izgledi za punomontažno gradjenje stanova u Jugoslaviji.« In *Savetovanje o industrijalizaciji stambene izgradnje*, 1–10. Belgrade: Savezna gradjevinska komora, 1960.

14ymedio, »El periodista Reinaldo Escobar gana el premio Verbum de Novela 2018«, 27 August 2018. URL: https://www.14ymedio.com/cultura/periodista-Reinaldo-Escobar-Verbum-novela_0_2499350044.html (last accessed: 20 November 2021).

Acknowledgements

During this research, I crossed paths with many people whose contributions became an integral part of it. The starting point was in the Department of Architecture Theory at RWTH Aachen, a place where I would continue to return to present, discuss and reflect further. Therefore, my thanks go in the first instance to Professor Axel Sowa, who accompanied me as a mentor throughout the process, for his efforts to understand a rather distant history of construction in Yugoslavia and his skill in recognizing and reinforcing the key points. The decision to focus on the process of making as the main theme of my argument was certainly made on his advice. The same applies to the keen interest in expanding views towards philosophy and the plurality of different sources. In addition, I would like to thank our group of doctoral students at the department, with whom I discussed topics over and over again: Adria Daraban, Kasia Osiecka, Frédéric Schnee, Ayça Sancar, Gregor Schmitt, Medine Altiok, Hootan Ahranjani and Zhen Zhang. The variety of their positions and backgrounds, explicit in their comments, influenced my attempts to simplify the writing in order, hopefully, to reach a broader understanding. The wealth of their own research, generously shared in regular colloquiums, helped me to test my methods and the credibility of the argument. In this respect, other members of the department also contributed with their perspectives and interests, and my appreciation goes to Andrea Dutto, Frederike Lausch and Duy Mac. As regards the faculty, I would also like to thank RWTH Aachen Faculty of Architecture for providing me with a scholarship to conduct the research.

 A significant part of my studies took the form of archive work and conversations with the people involved. The experience revealed to me the beautiful world of people working in archives filled with serenity and the willingness to invest time and help. Specific conversations, different spaces otherwise hard to access, and the impression of frozen time that I spent with them and with the material marked my days in the research bubble. In this respect, I would like to thank Miloš Milović, Goran Petrović and Dejan Dramlić, who uncovered the rich, forgotten archive of the Institute for Materials Testing (IMS). There, I found thousands of valuable documents telling the story of the establishment of a prefabricated system in Yugoslavia, and its transfer to Cuba. I was also lucky enough to come into contact with Mirjana Obradović, with whom I established a long-term correspondence about the fonds of the Historical Archives of Belgrade. With her patience and huge responsiveness, she shared with me not only possible sources and large amounts of material about the initial construction of New Belgrade, but also her personal familial history of being some of its first inhabitants. In Belgrade City Museum, I was warmly welcomed by curator Angelina Banković, whom I thank for sharing thoughts, documents and photographs with me. Talks that I had with Ivan Hofman at the Archives of Yugoslavia were very helpful to understanding the reality of youth work actions without idealising them. In addition, I would also like to thank him for sharing his own research and photographs, and for directing me to precise, relevant historical sources about the post-war period in Yugoslavia. Ana Graovac from the Urban Planning Department of Belgrade offered me her extensive knowledge of the history of planning of New Belgrade during our talks in her inspiring office, full of storyboard research and good energy. I am grateful to her for telling me a simplified planning history that accompanied the core of my research, and for putting me in touch with original city planning drawings that helped me to understand the architects' vision of modern living. People from libraries such as Belgrade City Library and the National Library of Serbia helped me to gain insight into newspapers and magazines where I could study the other side of the modern imaginary.

As well as archives and libraries, a series of interviews with protagonists of the process were very valuable for the range of actors they included. The engineer Branimir Grujić from the Institute for Materials Testing was of enormous help in explaining the process of construction, the performance of the prefabricated system and the role of builders. His life-long experience with exporting Yugoslavian technology abroad, together with its social vision, provided me with a large amount of data with which I could interpret the story. My thanks also go to sociologist Ksenija Petovar, with whom I spent pleasant Belgrade mornings listening to her evocation of the atmosphere at IMS, where she worked in the Centre for Housing. Her bold, lucid critique of politics and housing policies from the perspective of residents allowed me to discern the value of the Institute's mediation in an attempt to increase participation in many aspects of housing construction. Talking to UN member Milan Pajević showed me another side of the Institute's story, dealing with its relations with the UN and its support in the development of housing in the Middle and Far East. Another key figure at the Institute, engineer Branimir Vojnović, helped me to understand its constitution and the transfer of technology and knowledge about concrete from Switzerland. IMS architect Živojin Kara-Pešić explained issues regarding housing design and the flexibility of the system. In my exploration of different viewpoints, I had the help of librarians; Milica Ševkušić, from the Institute of Technical Sciences in Belgrade, provided me with journals and kept me supplied with relevant material, and Ljilja Dmitrović at the IMS went to great lengths to find rare books for me.

Curators Ivan Manojlović and Radovan Cukić at the Museum of Yugoslavia enabled me to obtain appropriate photographs and knowledge about the economy and consumer culture in Yugoslavia. Miloš Jurišić at the Museum of Science and Technology, a lifelong collector of old photographs, constantly sent me images documenting everyday life at New Belgrade sites. I am more than grateful for his kindness, co-operation and manners, characteristic of times past. Snežana Toševa at the same institution introduced me to the museum's library, where I studied a well-documented construction journal, *Izgradnja*, and several early planning proposals for New Belgrade. Kind people at the Yugoslav Film Archive, Aleksandar Erdeljanović and Božidar Marjanović, provided me with access to a series of early documentaries recording the building process, the experiences of the first residents and their response to the idea of modernity (directed by Miloš Bukumirović, 1960–1963). During archival work, I came into contact with researchers such as the historians Saša Ilić and Goran Antonić, and the architects Mila Pucar, Vanja Panić, Djordje Alfirević and Bartislav Ilić, who shared advice, sources and contacts, and to whom I am also grateful.

In my study of the philosophy of praxis, which went hand in hand with research into the history of construction, I relied primarily on the rich *Praxis* journal archive, with online access. People at the local Ivan Vidali Library on Korčula helped me to gain access to films documenting the summer schools of philosophy, which were helpful for learning about the general mood. As well as to them, I would like to express my gratitude to Ante Lešaja for the inspiring conversation in his house next to the sea. As a devoted chronicler and connoisseur of *Praxis* history, he thought through the lectures and articles by philosophers that are relevant to my topic. My correspondence with *Praxis* philosopher Božidar Jakšić cast new light on the internal dynamics and the ups and downs of the group. My talk with established theorist Miško Šuvaković influenced my critique of this history, including philosophical practice, but also convinced me to look for positive aspects in the attempted participation in politics, economy, philosophy and construction. I am also especially grateful for the contributions of my doctoral advisors, Petar Bojanić and Pep Avilés. The philosopher Petar Bojanić, with his interest in architecture, helped save me time by suggesting the right references and contacts. The possibility of sharing my research with his group at the Institute for Philosophy and Social Theory in Belgrade opened up my research to new questions suggested by the local environment, and also strengthened my construction of a historically consistent argument. Pep Avilés, an inspiring person in my education during the courses he organized and taught at the Barcelona Institute of Architecture, approached me with valid criteria for researching the connection between architecture history and theory. Talks that I have given at conferences and seminars at various international universities, and the range of questions from the audiences have helped to make a rather peripheral history recognisable in a universal sense.

While approaching the final phase of my research, I was more than grateful to come into contact with Cuban journalists and dissidents Yoani Sánchez and Reinaldo Escobar, one of the people who constructed housing in Cuba using the Yugoslav system. Escobar's inspiring struggle for freedom of speech, also manifest in his involvement in construction, opened a door for me to thousands of oral histories he witnessed and represented during the Cuban revolution. I am deeply grateful to him for sharing with me his novel on the construction of a Yugoslavian building on the Plaza de la Revolución in Havana, which he wrote after years spent on the construction site.

The common interests that I share with my dear friend, researcher and artist Irena Lagator Pejović made the content of this research a frequent topic in our conversations when I examined it from the viewpoint of contemporary political theories.

Although they were not directly involved in this research, I have to express my gratitude to my very first teachers of architecture in Belgrade, Professor Branislav Mitrović, Marija Milinković and Ljiljana Blagojević who helped lay the bases of my interest in architecture and society.

The text itself has been devotedly proofread and corrected by Elaine Fradley, Jessica Glanz and Theresa Hartherz, to whom I owe my enormous thanks for going through it and improving the clarity of its expression. In addition, I would like to express gratitude to Felix Holler and Stefan Rolle for their effort in making the book visually appealing.

Finally, work on this research would not have been possible without the support and inspiration of Vuk, Dunja and Matija, with whom I once again discovered the value of play; Tijana, with whom I have shared my thoughts since our childhood, and the rest of my family and dearest friends.

I dedicate this text to my parents, Sonja and Luka Badnjar, who have been building the world, a fragment of which I have attempted to capture.

The Author

Andjelka Badnjar Gojnić is an architect and theorist trained at the faculties of architecture in Belgrade and Barcelona. She is a PhD candidate in the Architekturtheorie department of RWTH Aachen. Her research interests are focused on histories of construction sites as a source for studying collective practices of making and on links between social theories and the collective production of architecture.

Imprint

Dissertation at the RWTH Aachen (Rheinisch-Westfälische Technische Hochschule Aachen), Faculty of Architecture, Teaching and Research Area Architectural Theory: »Praxis of Collective Building: Narratives on Philosophy and Construction«
Mentor: Univ.-Prof. Axel Sowa
Advisors: Prof. Dr. Petar Bojanić, University of Belgrade, and Asst. Prof. Pep Avilés, The Pennsylvania State University

Cover image: The first participants in youth work action at the New Belgrade construction site, 1947, detail © Historical Archives of Belgrade, Nemanja Budisavljević personal fonds

Design and setting: Felix Holler, Stoffers Graphik-Design, Leipzig
Lithography: Stefan Rolle, Stoffers Graphik-Design, Leipzig
Printed in the European Union

Bibliographic information published by the Deutsche Nationalbibliothek:
The Deutsche Nationalbibliothek lists this publication in the Deutsche Nationalbibliografie; detailed bibliographic data are available on the Internet at http://dnb.d-nb.de

jovis Verlag GmbH
Lützowstraße 33
10785 Berlin

www.jovis.de

jovis books are available worldwide in select bookstores. Please contact your nearest bookseller or visit www.jovis.de for information concerning your local distribution.

ISBN 978-3-86859-772-1 (Softcover)
ISBN 978-3-86859-788-2 (PDF)